NOTORIOUS LADIES OF THE FRONTIER

NOTORIOUS LADIES

OF THE FRONTIER

HARRY SINCLAIR DRAGO

ILLUSTRATED WITH PHOTOGRAPHS

DODD, MEAD & COMPANY

NEW YORK

Library of Congress Catalog Card Number: 78-80710

*Printed in the United States of America
by The Cornwall Press, Inc., Cornwall, N. Y.*

Preface

It is one of the enduring myths of American history that prostitution made a significant contribution to the settling of the West, based on the charitable and widely held opinion that countless numbers of the so-called "frails" broke away from their old profession, married and became good wives and mothers. Some did. But the number becomes insignificant when one is confronted by the fact that no less—and very likely more—than 50,000 bawds plied their trade in the western United States, that is, between Kansas City, Missouri, and the Pacific Coast, in the years when in every cow town, mining camp and railroad junction point some form of legalized prostitution flourished.

Like the pioneers who were lured westward, the painted Jezebels kept pace with the advancing frontier. They were in California a year after gold was discovered in John Sutter's millrace. When San Francisco, always jealous of its reputation as the wickedest city in the world, had in excess of 10,000 strumpets on its streets and in the parlor houses, cribs and cowyards, it would have been difficult to find one who was a native Californian. They came from the East, Europe, especially France, Mexico and China —women of all colors.

Wherever commercialized vice flourished unchecked, so did crimes of violence, robbery, murder and various forms of mayhem. That was as true in the deep-water ports of the Pacific Northwest and such inland cities as Butte and Denver, as it was in San Francisco's notorious Barbary Coast. The fraudulent argument of corrupt politicians and the saloon interests, that prostitution could be controlled by confining it to a recognized red-light district, was as dishonest as the men who profited by advancing it. The only way that open, licensed prostitution could be controlled was by abolishing it. Eventually that was done.

Then, as now, prostitution operated on many levels—social as well as economic. The aging, hard-working streetwalker was at the bottom of the heap, scorned by the women of the cribs, to whom she was a constant reminder of what the future held for them. The young and attractive parlor house girls rated themselves superior to other members of the profession. The parlor houses themselves ran the scale from shoddy luxury to the elegance of the bordellos of Mattie Silks and Jennie Rogers in Denver. But even in the most expensive and popular, depravity, drunkenness, drug addiction and suicide were a commonplace.

The reader will quickly discover that this narrative is not a history of prostitution; that many of the women who are considered in some detail were not prostitutes. Far from it. Some were adventuresses, professional gamblers, women whose morals were a departure from the norm but whose impact on their time and environment was noteworthy. Several of them, including the much-publicized Belle Starr and Martha Jane (Calamity) Cannary, are controversial figures even today, while Eilley Orrum (Mrs. Sandy Bowers), a paragon of wifely virtue who waged unremitting war on the scarlet fraternity, is almost unknown.

A careful sifting of the evidence reveals beyond doubt that the two most revolting crimes in the annals of the West were the lynching of Elizabeth Taylor in Clay County, Nebraska, and Ella Watson on the Sweetwater in Wyoming. Mrs. Taylor was accused of trading her charms for the work the young Texans performed on her ranch; Ella Watson was an admitted brushwood tart, allegedly selling her body for the maverick cattle that cowboys brought to her pasture. In neither case were the women hanged for their immorality; that was an afterthought, a smoke screen used to blacken the reputation of the victims and win some measure of justification for the perpetrators.

Harry Sinclair Drago

Contents

Illustrations

ix

NOTORIOUS LADIES OF THE FRONTIER

The Barbary Coast

IT WAS NOT UNTIL 1855 that San Franciscans began referring to the old Sydney-Town red-light district at the foot of Telegraph Hill as the Barbary Coast. As far back as 1849, however, when the first great rush to the California gold fields began, the criminal scum from Australia, Tasmania and New Zealand—the notorious Sydney Ducks—had settled there after driving out a colony of Chilenos (Mexicans), many of whom they had butchered. Not one man in a hundred had ever heard of the Barbary pirates, so the phrase had no historical significance to them, but it had a savage sound and, once applied, it quickly became popular.

Pacific Street was the heart of the district which began at the waterfront and, running east to west, crossed Montgomery, Kearney, Dupont (Grant Avenue) and Stockton Street. From north to south it spread out over Broadway, Pacific, Jackson and Washington streets. In addition there were a dozen unimportant "side streets" and "places." The underworld population gathered in those approximately twelve city blocks totaled an estimated 20,000 in 1870, according to the San Francisco *Call*. Of that number, over 3,000 were listed as prostitutes. The others, presumably, were criminals, brothelkeepers, saloonkeepers and the operators of various kinds of dives. In his *Lights and Shadows in San Francisco*, published in 1876, Benjamin E. Lloyd says:

"The Barbary Coast is the haunt of the low and the vile of every kind. The petty thief, the house burglar, the tramp, the whoremonger, lewd women, cutthroats, murderers, all are found here. Dance halls and concert-saloons, where blear-eyed men and faded women drink vile liquor, smoke offensive tobacco, engage in vulgar conduct, sing obscene songs and say and do everything to heap upon themselves more degradation, are numerous. Low gambling houses, thronged with riot-loving rowdies, in all stages of intoxication, are there. Opium dens, where heathen Chinese and God-forsaken men and women are sprawled in miscellaneous confusion, disgustingly drowsy or completely overcome, are there. Licentiousness, debauchery, pollution, loathsome disease, insanity from dissipation, misery, poverty, wealth, profanity, blasphemy, and death, are there. And Hell, yawning to receive the putrid mass, is there also."

Lloyd's indignation may have been heightened by the fact that he was a crusader for civic and moral decency, but others were attacking the cesspool of vice in even stronger terms, especially the fighting, militant *Call*. Time after time it leveled its guns on the district.

"The Barbary Coast!" it screamed. "That sink of moral pollution, whose reefs are strewn with moral wrecks, and into whose vortex is constantly drifting barks of moral life, while swiftly down the whirlpool of death go the sinking hulks of the murdered and the suicide! The Barbary Coast! . . . The coast on which no gentle breezes blow, but where rages one wild sirocco of sin!"

With ill-concealed glee the *Call* reported the findings of a board of supervisors' investigation into the prevalence of venereal disease in San Francisco. A member of the Board of Health and other physicians had testified that they knew of no city in the world that harbored as many diseased children, the fathers of whom had contracted some form of venereal disease in the brothels of the Barbary Coast.

The *Call* received a rebuff from an unexpected corner when it proposed that a municipal clinic be opened for diseased bawds and that they be compelled to report to it until they received a medical discharge. To the *Call's* surprise, the Protestant clergy of the town, instead of supporting the proposal, bitterly opposed it, protesting that fear of contamination kept hundreds of men from visiting the vice dens of the Barbary Coast; that to give the abandoned women of the district a clean bill of health would only increase the trafficking in sex. However well-intentioned, it was a foolish argument. But for years the clergy successfully fought off any attempt to establish a clinic for public women, and a quarter of a century passed before common sense finally prevailed.

If the succeeding political machines that controlled San Francisco decade after decade had wanted to curtail or abolish the crime and debauchery of the Barbary Coast, they could have done it by reducing the number of liquor licenses that were granted annually. But that would have been striking at the heart of the political spoils system, and any leader rash enough to suggest anything of the sort could not have survived the storm it would have aroused. A license to sell beer, whisky and other intoxicating beverages was a valuable commodity to be sold to the highest bidder. And all such licenses had to be renewed annually, which made them a never-failing source of revenue for those who had the power to dispense them.

It can be taken for granted that the overlords of graft and corruption were well aware that alcohol was the handmaiden of vice; that without the excitement of intoxication the Barbary Coast would be as drab by night as it was by day. But instead of decreasing, the traffic in liquor licenses continued to flourish. In 1875, over two thousand licenses were dispensed, 304 for premises located in a twelve-block area of the Coast. This did not include the scores of blind pigs and deadfalls where liquor was sold illegally. There was not a dance hall, low variety theater presenting some form of obscene entertainment, or parlor house in the district in which alcoholic beverages were not sold. In one block on Pacific Street, there were ten saloons, door to door.

The Bella Union, at Kearney and Washington streets, variously a gambling house, variety theater and finally a penny arcade and waxworks museum, was the longest-lived and most popular resort on the Barbary Coast. In the years of its greatest popularity it was the self-proclaimed "Wickedest Place in the West," a distinction it did not merit. Its shows were bawdy and obscene but never as lewd as the performances put on by several of its competitors. In its heyday half a dozen or more unknown young actors who were to become famous trod its boards, among them Ned Harrigan, James A. Hearne, Eddie Foy and Lotta Crabtree.[1]

The original Bella Union, an ornate gambling casino, had opened its doors in 1849. It had been destroyed by fire in 1851, and the building that replaced it shared a similar fate. The second Bella Union was razed in 1868 and replaced by a two-story brick and stone theater that was to last until the great holocaust of 1906. In the days when no man believed he had seen San Francisco until he had visited the Bella Union, only males were admitted, it being a provable fact that it was men who spent money, not women. And spending money was something the management encouraged, hiring twenty-five to thirty young lovelies to work the upper and lower tiers of curtained boxes that circled the auditorium between their brief appearance on the stage.

When a girl entered a box, she wantonly perched herself on the occupant's lap and induced him to buy drinks. If he demurred at purchasing champagne, she settled for something less expensive. Usually by some display of her charms she aroused the customer's desire for entertainment of a more personal nature. Drawing the curtains, she was pleased to supply it at a price, afterwards splitting her earnings for the night with the management.

In the same category as the Bella Union but offering less luxury and less attractive girls were the Olympic, the Pacific and Gilbert's Melodeon, where the drinks were cheaper, sometimes drugged, and robbery often occurred. Melodeon was a popular word on the Coast and at one time or another there were as many as ten "melodeons," which was a euphemism for the low vaudeville saloon where obscenity and lewdness passed for entertainment. Strangely enough the Barbary Coast's entrepreneurs of salaciousness were slow to recognize the belly dancer as a profitable attraction. In fact it was not until several years after the Chicago World's Fair of 1893, where the original Little Egypt had wiggled her way to fame, that San Francisco saw its first bump-and-grind muscle dancers.

Remarkably, it was not the Barbary Coast that did the pioneering, but a Market Street emporium known as the Midway Plaisance that led the way. It was a low, vicious dive, admission only ten cents. The nearly nude dancers writhed and contorted their bodies in time with the shrill screaming of an Egyptian flute. Crude as it was, the exhibition was an instant success. In a matter of days every so-called melodeon on the Barbary Coast was presenting its own version of alleged "harem" dancers.

After the passing of such early-day organizations as the Regulators, the criminal element of the Barbary Coast did not coalesce into anything comparable to today's gangs of hoods. Instead, there were at least a score of rival groups, each headed by some well-known Coast leader, usually the proprieter of one of its most prosperous dives. The life of no man was safe if he entered one of their establishments, especially if he appeared to be, in the jargon of the district, "well-heeled." Customarily after his drinks were loaded with knockout drops, he was rolled into the alley and robbed. If he was able to resist, he was either shot or bludgeoned to death. It happened too frequently for the police to do much about it. In fact, it appears that they were not inclined to over-exert themselves.

Of all Barbary Coast characters, none was more widely known than Ned—Bull Run—Allen, so named because he claimed to have participated in both battles of that name. He was a huge, coarse, flamboyant thug who operated the notorious Hell's Kitchen, rated by the police as the toughest place in San Francisco. Allen, who was a fashion plate in his frock coat, cream-colored breeches, tile hat and ruffled silk shirt ornamented with a cluster of diamonds, spent his days drinking in the establishments of his competitors.

For all his sartorial splendor, he was an ugly-looking character, with a flaming red, cancerous nose that had become dilated to twice its natural size. His special vanity was his handlebar mustache, the ends of which were so long that they could be tied together while he was being shaved.

His emporium of vice at Pacific Street and Sullivan Alley was housed in a three-story building, with a dance hall and bar in the cellar, a similar arrangement on the street floor, with the floors above divided into cubicles (cribs) for the amorous use of what he called his "pretty waiter girls"—mostly French and Spanish, a concession to the popular myth that they were more passionate than their American sisters. In addition to the girls who sold drinks and lined up customers for an interlude upstairs, he had a score of females who took part in the stage performances, either as singers or dancers, usually both. It was Allen's boast that he never employed fewer than forty girls, some of them as young as fourteen. All were for sale to any man who fancied them.

The "show" at Hell's Kitchen began early in the evening and ran until dawn. It had frequent breaks, which gave the girls time to attend to their real business on the upper floors. To expedite matters, Allen outfitted them in a costume that was calculated to be a timesaver, consisting of a short red jacket, black stockings, ruffled silk garters, red slippers—and nothing else. On the theory that an intoxicated strumpet added to the hilarity of the evening, Allen gave the women attached to his resort hard liquor to drink, rather than the colored water or ginger ale they were served in other places. When one of his female staff became unconscious from drink, she was carried upstairs, laid on a bed and the right to violate her as she lay helpless sold for a dollar or less—not to one man, but to as many as craved the privilege. The San Francisco *Call* took dead aim on Bull Run Allen's resort time after time, calling it "the abiding place of the worst criminals in town."

"The women . . . are of the lowest class," said the *Call*. "These females air themselves with offensive publicity and boldness. . . . The wonder is that such exhibitions should have so long escaped the notice of those who ought to be able to suppress them, and have the authority to do so, but who do nothing."

Although it was a long time coming, Bull Run Allen's pugnacity finally led to his downfall under circumstances that were almost identical with those that sent Happy Jack Harrington, his chief rival for the title of King of the Barbary Coast, into oblivion.

In one of his drunken sorties Allen stormed into the Clover Club, an undistinguished Pacific Street dive, and was wrecking the place when he encountered Bart Freel, a well-known pimp and habitual criminal. Freel was armed only with a clasp-knife, but he used it with such dexterity that Allen sank to the floor mortally wounded. Regretfully, the law sent Freel away for ten years, it being the general consensus that he had done the city a favor.

Happy Jack Harrington's resort, the Opera Comique, at the corner of Jackson and Kearney streets, was a somewhat smaller version of Hell's Kitchen, but equally vicious. As soon as it was demonstrated that belly dancers were a profitable attraction, he presented a line of them, clad in strings of beads for a skirt. There wasn't anything exotic about their dancing, but they moved everything they had but their feet and the audience clamored for more. Another of the novelties he introduced was his topless waiter girls, which was to have some shock value many years later for a generation of San Franciscans then unborn.

Like Bull Run Allen, whom he detested, Happy Jack lavished money on his own personal adornment. In the years when he was coining a fortune, he was a gay, strutting figure as he moved about the Coast, but he ended up broke. One night when he was feeling his liquor, he walked into Danny O'Brien's saloon, across the street from the Opera Comique, and got into a quarrel with a Virginia City, Nevada, boxer by the name of Billy Dwyer, in the course of which he plunged a knife into Dwyer's stomach and killed him. He was charged with murder. Eventually he succeeded in getting the charge reduced to manslaughter and was sent away to San Quentin. The story goes that it cost him $35,000 to save his neck.

The Well Runs Dry

THROUGHOUT THE COAST'S LONG YEARS of iniquity, the fate of the men and women who most successfully pandered to vice and depravity seemed to follow a pattern—a brief period of reckless prosperity suddenly vanishing and leaving them the castaways of their folly. It was the landlords, the property owners like the infamous Mammy Pleasant, and the politicians who siphoned off the profits.

There is always an exception to any rule, and for years it appeared that Jerome Bassity (his honest name was Jeremy McGlane) was to be that exception and never relinquish his title of boss of San Francisco's underworld. He had one thing going for him that neither Bull Run Allen nor Happy Jack Harrington nor anyone else ever had: that was the all-out support of Abe Ruef, the corrupt political boss of San Francisco, and of his henchman Eugene Schmitz, three times mayor of the city, and after Schmitz, his successor, Mayor P. H. McCarthy.

That Abe Ruef was Bassity's silent partner and shared in the profits of his vast underworld operations was exposed in the grand jury investigation into the corruptness of Ruef's political machine. According to sworn testimony, his share of the spoils seldom fell below $4,000 a week.

Bassity operated more houses of prostitution than any other red-light character in the city, and shared in the earnings of more than two hundred prostitutes. He was no Barbary Coast dude; he was as hard as nails, and men who got in his way had a habit of mysteriously disappearing.

By its own reckoning, prostitution on the Barbary Coast was conducted on four levels. At the top was the parlor house, where prices were highest and operations were conducted with what was deemed an air of gentility. The inmates—never more than eight or ten—were supposed to be younger and more attractive than could be found in the cheaper dives. Next to the parlor houses were the cowyards, some of which housed as many as a hundred abandoned women of all races and colors. A step lower were the dance-hall bawds. The scorned streetwalker was relegated to the bottom rung of the social ladder.

Bassity did business on all four levels. He either owned or controlled three cheap hotels for the convenience of the streetwalkers and their customers. He owned a "piece" of the Nymphia in Pacific Street, the Marsicania in Dupont Street at the edge of Chinatown, and the infamous Municipal Crib in Jackson Street, the three largest and most profitable cowyards on the Coast.[1] At least half a dozen so-called "melodeons" or dance halls paid him tribute, in return for which they received his "protection." He had a financial interest in several of the better-class parlor houses, and when he had demonstrated that his connections at City Hall were powerful enough to free a house from police harassment, the madams of other establishments found it advisable to cut him in on their profits.

As befitted a man of his stature in the sporting world, he had a Market Street saloon, which he used as his headquarters. Bassity's greatest accomplishment was in opening the Uptown Tenderloin, centering on Mason, Powell and O'Farrell streets, as a higher-priced adjunct to the Barbary Coast—something which others had tried to do but failed. He had the assistance of such noted madams as Johanna Schriffin and Bertha Kahn, and a newcomer to San Francisco, Tessie Wall. Where she hailed from remained her secret, but it is generally believed to have been Chicago. She was an experienced, well-padded, truculent two-hundred-and-thirty-pound

blonde who tolerated no nonsense, either from her girls or gentlemen callers. Prominently displayed in the parlor was a sign reading:

No vulgarity permitted in this house.

She dressed her girls in expensive evening gowns and presented
them against a background of tawdry elegance. Her place was
popular, but it was only the Barbary Coast with flourishes, from
which her strumpets were transplants, doing what they had been
doing for years at cheaper prices. It is pleasant to report, however,
that the flamboyant Tessie saved her money and retired from the
profession with a comfortable fortune. She, not Jerome Bassity,
was the exception that proved the rule.

Bassity's political power was drastically reduced with the over-
throwing and criminal prosecution of the Ruef-Schmitz machine.
When a new regime took office, pledged to clean up the Barbary
Coast, William Randolph Hearst's *Examiner* joined forces with
the *Bulletin* and the *Call* in demanding that the California Supreme
Court rule favorably on the constitutionality of the recently passed
Red-Light Abatement Act. Bassity could read the handwriting on
the wall. He knew the end of open prostitution or, as the newspapers labeled it, "commercialized vice," was near. He refused to
believe, as some of his competitors did, that the Barbary Coast
could exist as a great amusement area, attracting thousands of
tourists, without its hordes of degraded women to give it spice.

The great fire of 1906 leveled the Coast. It rose from its ashes
phoenixlike. But it was not the same; something was gone. Savants
shook their heads nostalgically and said that what the Barbary
Coast had lost was its old-time, tarnished glamor. In a vain attempt
to regain its lost popularity, it publicized its obscenity and depravity as it had never done in the past. Barkers were employed
to harangue the passers-by from a platform in front of the melodeons, and the Salome or harem dancers were brought out to give
brief free exhibitions. Prices were cut. For two-bits (twenty-five
cents) spectators at peep shows could watch a pair of Lesbians in
a homosexual orgy.

But the ballyhooing and free entertainment failed to bring back the jostling crowds that had once jammed Pacific, Morton and Kearney streets. When the Red-Light Abatement Act became law and the City Police Commission was given the authority to enforce it, the Barbary Coast was soon as dead as a mackerel that had been out of water too long. Jerome Bassity was not one of the mourners. He had sold out in time and gone to Tia Juana, Mexico, to engage in a long and losing struggle with the celebrated Jim Coffroth for control of the Tia Juana race track. When he died in San Diego in 1929, less than ten thousand dollars remained of the fortune he had amassed as the King of the Barbary Coast.

For years horse-drawn sightseeing buses had brought thousands of tourists to the old red-light district to ogle the whores for an hour and be shocked by their depravity. Invariably parties of slummers were greeted with a barrage of obscene profanity. But they had licensed guides to protect them against physical violence. It was to the guide's interest to see that the party he was conducting got its money's worth. If a tour threatened to pass without an incident occurring, he could always stage one.

Guiding was a lucrative business. Needless to say, it was a political plum that was handed out to the "right" people. At first the tour of the Barbary Coast included a visit to the opium dens and brothels of Chinatown. An enterprising Irishman named Charlie Blaney is generally credited with the idea that two distinct tours would be better than one, and that the slums and dens of Chinatown rated special attention of their own. This innovation was immediately successful. The strange sights, sounds and smells of Chinatown soon proved to have a greater attraction for sightseers than the Coast. In fact, long after the red-light district had lost its appeal, slummers were trooping up old Dupont Street to peer into the fan-tan dens and the warrens in which the slave girls of Chinatown sat placidly waiting for customers.

By the time the Chinese Exclusion Act went into effect, barring the entrance into the United States of all Orientals, at least twelve thousand Chinese were huddled together in Chinatown. They lived by the rules of the Five Companies, the tongs, rather than by American law. Murders were frequent and, if possible, not reported to the police. For the wretched Chinese prostitute, suicide was a favorite means of escape from her cell-like cubicle that was both her home and place of business. As a whole the Chinese girls were younger than their white sisters of the profession. The hard life they were forced to lead soon wore them out, and when they began to lose their looks, they were of no further value to their owner, who had either imported them from China or bought them after their arrival in San Francisco. Instead of pensioning them off, he resold them to some Chinese farmer for a hundred dollars or less.

There were a few bordellos in Chinatown to which white men were not admitted; they were for the exclusive pleasure of Chinese businessmen who did not possess concubines of their own. In the high-priced opium parlors, only Chinese could gain entrance. In the cheaper parlors, whites and Chinese mingled, as did the sexes. It was observed that the majority of the female addicts were white.

Of all the several thousand daughters of the Flowery Kingdom who were brought across the sea to take their place in the foul brothels of Chinatown, only three or four are mentioned in the extensive literature of the city that sits beside the Golden Gate. In the words of one lyrical historian, "the most famous of all was almond-eyed, golden courtesan, Ah Toy."

Ah Toy arrived in San Francisco in the summer of 1850, when the Gold Rush frenzy was at its height. She was young and lovely, evidently having escaped the hardening life of a prostitute in Canton or one of the other seaboard cities of China. Unlike the great majority of the slave girls of Chinatown, who never were able to speak more than half a dozen words of the white man's language, Ah Toy soon acquired a working knowledge of pidgin English. She is credited, perhaps apocryphally, with having originated the singsong sales chant of the Chinatown cribs: "Two bittee lookee, flo bittee feelee, six bittee doee."

In those early days when men who had had nothing suddenly found themselves wealthy, several, in response to the satisfaction she had given them, clubbed together and gave her the money to buy her freedom. She put it to good use and opened her own crib in China Alley, a dingy defile off Jackson Street. By 1870, she was operating three such establishments in San Francisco, another in Sacramento and one in the flourishing mining camp of Columbia. Soon thereafter she began importing girls from China and selling them to the trade. By the time she was fifty, she was recognized as one of the most prosperous dealers in Chinese prostitutes in California. Her success was possible only because she had the protection of the Hip Sings, one of the most powerful tongs, to whom she paid tribute.

Every Oriental in California, no matter how lowly his station, lived secure in the knowledge that when death overtook him, the tong to which he belonged would return his body to the Celestial Kingdom for burial. It was an obligation that was never defaulted, even in unusual circumstances such as the explosion that shattered the big Sacramento River steamer *Yosemite* as she was heading downriver from Rio Vista on the evening of October 2, 1865. There were twenty-nine Chinese aboard, and in keeping with the rules of the river at that time, they were herded together below decks in the forward hold. The twenty-nine, all Hip Sings, were killed and buried temporarily at Rio Vista. Ah Toy opened her purse strings and donated half of the money needed to remove the dead Hip Sings to their homeland. In the early 1890's, she disposed of her various businesses and returned to China, presumably to live in comfort for the rest of her days.

It is difficult to discover a human being, no matter how deep he or she may have sunk into depravity, who has not shown at one time or another, even if briefly, some redeeming trace of decency. Such a charitable axiom, however, does not appear to be warranted in the case of Mary Hastings, who must be regarded as the most infamous woman in the history of the Barbary Coast. To say that she had the conscience of a vulture would be to defame the vulture.

She was born in Brussels and served her apprenticeship in the brothels of that city before moving on to Paris. She was undeniably French, "Mary Hastings" being only an alias. Though her career in the underworld was long, she never disclosed her true name. She was only twenty-five or thereabouts when she arrived in San Francisco, and by that time a veteran whore. Her "solid man," pimp, that is, was Tom Gaynor. But he had no money other than what he got from her. He could not have set her up in business. Someone backed her, however, very likely Jerome Bassity, and she made her entrance on the Coast as the madam of a tough parlor house on Kearney Street.

She staffed her house with ten women, all of them from Chicago. She saw to it that the district was informed that every one of her harlots had been tossed out of what she called "decent houses." "Any girl who is good enough for a high-class house is too good for my joint," she told anyone who was interested.

She took down the curtains from the front windows and posted several girls there to solicit the male passers-by. Kearney Street was one of the leading streets of the town, running from the commercial district to the residential area. As a result it was a busy thoroughfare. In addition to the bawds exposing themselves at the windows in scanty attire, others solicited from the steps. The police frowned on that type of hustling and finally forced her to desist.

But Madame Hastings had made a splash. She followed it up by boasting that no man could suggest any act of perversion that her whores could not and would not perform. She revived the old, so-called "circus" that had not been seen in San Francisco since the days of the Sydney Ducks, a sexual exhibition in which a woman and a small Shetland pony participated. These soirees were held twice a month, with admission twenty-five dollars. Early in 1887, a year after she had burst on the Barbary Coast, she was sent to prison for six months for "abnormal practices" that shocked even a corrupt mayor and his political machine.

Six months behind bars failed to convince her that her days on the Coast were over. Purchasing a young girl from a procurer who had lured her away from her Oregon home, she put on a performance showing how a virgin was "broke into the business." For the occasion two strapping Negroes were hired to do the breaking in. This time it wasn't the law that was outraged; the blast that she had overstayed herself in California came from six-foot, two-fisted Maggie Kelly, the terror of Pacific Street, who owned the Cowboy's Rest, a saloon and assignation house in the heart of the district.

Cowboy Mag, as she was familiarly known, was her own bouncer and wielded a club with such efficiency that she had been arrested scores of times for breaking the peace. She was from Texas and such a rabid white racist that no Negro was allowed to enter her premises. It was Madame Hastings' employment of Negroes in the entertainment she had offered that infuriated Cowboy Mag, not its degeneracy. To her myopic eyes the woman had shamed the Coast, and she sent word ringing up and down Pacific Street that she was going to do something about it. Arming herself with a pistol, she threatened to kill Mary Hastings on sight.

Madame Hastings must have believed that Cowboy Maggie meant it, for she left San Francisco for Chicago in a hurry, instructing her solid man to dispose of her properties and meet her in the Windy City, where she opened a bordello at 144 Custom House Place. With the World's Fair at hand and Chicago running wide-open, she prospered fantastically and soon had three brothels and a saloon going full blast in what was described as the "toughest block this side of hell." But in 1897 she ran into serious trouble with the Chicago Crime Commission. Three young girls who were being kept prisoner on the third floor at 144 Custom House Place escaped by sliding down a rope of knotted bed sheets and ran to the Harrison Street police station. Their story resulted in two indictments being returned against Mary Hastings, who was released on bail of a $1,000, provided by her man, Tom Gaynor. She fled to Canada, forfeiting her bail, only to return and to have the case against her set for trial. This performance was repeated until the witnesses against her had disappeared and the state dropped the case.

In the course of the legal maneuvering she had assigned all her properties to Gaynor. When she tried to reclaim them, he cast her out with a pittance of several hundred dollars. She is known to have gone to Toledo, where she lived briefly on the charity of beautiful Belle Stevens, the town's most prosperous madam. But it was the end of the trail, proving again the old adage that the wages of sin are poor wages.

Although the sleeping public conscience of San Francisco permitted the overlords of vice to justify its claim to the title of being the wickedest city in the world, there was seldom a time when one or more bands of dedicated citizens were not battling for public decency and reform. Perhaps the most successful crusader was Father Terence Caraher, pastor of the Roman Catholic Church of St. Francis. For fifteen years he waged incessant warfare on the Barbary Coast, his favorite tactic being to blockade a dive with volunteer pickets while he mounted a figurative soapbox and delivered an impassioned harangue against the real owners of the property. Time after time he hailed the operators of the bordellos into court and denounced them. If he accomplished nothing else, he made an expensive nuisance of himself.

Without city or federal help, the little group of women led by Donaldina Cameron, who established and maintained the Chinatown missions, accomplished the greatest good. Despite the language barrier, Miss Cameron, a maiden lady of remarkable tenacity who devoted most of her adult life to the project, succeeded in gaining the support of some Chinese businessmen in her crusade to free the slave girls of the cribs. Due to her, the conditions in which they lived and the treatment they received were vastly improved. Final victory was a long time in coming, but in 1916, two years after the Red-Light Abatement Act became law, largely because of the campaign she had waged, slavery disappeared from Chinatown.

It has been said, often with little justification, that the prostitute played an important role in the settling of the American West. Certainly the early ones shared the dangers and privations of the rowdy cow towns and crude mining camps, where for a time they were the only women. When epidemics of smallpox or outbreaks of cholera occurred, they nursed the sick and the dying. They were bold, tough-fibered, as they had need to be, but although they were strumpets, they should not be equated with their sisters of the profession who wallowed in the infamy of the Barbary Coast or the red-light districts of Denver and Seattle.

With gentlemanly tolerance, frontier newspapers referred to them as Fair Cyprians and used no harsher designation. This may have been out of deference to the fact that it was not unheard-of for a town tart to marry a good man and become a faithful wife.

However, it was not until February 14, 1967, Saint Valentine's Day, that the first plaque ever dedicated to the scarlet sisters was installed in concrete in Jackson, California, the seat of Amador County in the Mother Lode country. In gold rush days Jackson was a lively camp. On the main street, three large, decaying frame houses, rich in history but poor in upkeep, once were the home of the town's shady ladies. It seemed fitting to the sponsors of the plaque that it should be embedded in the sidewalk within sight of those still existing mementos of the past.

Undoubtedly thousands of tourists will stop to read the long inscription on this mockingly heart-shaped plaque, which begins— "World's oldest profession flourished here for many years—"

Mammy Pleasant—Woman of Mystery

CENTERING ON PACIFIC STREET and spreading out over a dozen city blocks, the Barbary Coast was to flourish for almost seventy years without a serious setback. Whenever a reform element threatened its existence, corrupt politicians were always waiting to blunt and turn the attacks aside. Many of them owned property in the district, from which they were collecting fantastic rents, and therefore had a vested interest in its running wide-open. Then, too, while San Franciscans publicly deplored its wickedness, they secretly enjoyed its bawdy reputation. If the growth of the city had followed the traditional pattern, the development of its underworld would have, as Herbert Asbury, its most widely read historian, has said, "been indistinguishable from any other large American city." That, of course, had become impossible with the discovery of gold in John Sutter's millrace on the south fork of the American River in 1848, for with the thousands of frenzied gold seekers had come an army of gamblers, thieves, harlots, venal politicians and parasites.

But paradoxically San Francisco's underworld district, its depravity unmatched even in New York's Five Points or London's St. Giles, had an air of glamor. This was in spite of its nightly robberies and murders, which went almost unnoticed, and its deadfalls and cribs where thousands of prostitutes of all nations—as many as six thousand at one period—plied their trade. Over it hung the cacophonous blaring of its hundreds of mechanical musical devices and the squealing fiddles from the dance saloons.

All of the usual characters of such extravaganzas of vice and corruption were present—politicians, saloonkeepers, gamblers, procurers, pimps and females of all colors; but there were others who were obeyed although they never appeared on the scene. Such a one was Mary Ellen Pleasant, the woman familiar to San Franciscans as Mammy Pleasant. Contrary to much that has been written about her, she was never a prostitute, nor in the usual use of the word a madam, although she often supplied the gentlemen guests of her several fashionable "boarding houses" with obliging young women.

Mammy Pleasant had arrived in San Francisco in 1852, preceded by her reputation as a famous New Orleans cook. By her own efforts, many of them mysterious and criminal, including the blackmailing of prominent men, she had made herself a very wealthy woman. If she was never seen in the red-light district, her agents were. A considerable portion of her wealth came from the properties she had purchased in what was to become the heart of the Barbary Coast, where even a cellar could be rented for immoral purposes for $1,000 a month, cash in advance. Ruthless in a way that the underworld understood, she was hated and feared.

Attired in an expensive black silk dress, a knitted shawl of the same color draped over her shoulders, and a snug-fitting black Quaker bonnet that framed her rather patrician face, she had become a familiar figure in the financial and business district. Any prominent man who suddenly found himself in need of immediate cash could get it from her on a short-term note at usurious interest. When Duncan and Company, the Montgomery Street auctioneers, put Lola Montez's jewels up for sale, Mammy Pleasant was the principal purchaser.

In a city where anything was possible, Mammy Pleasant was unique. To understand her rise to power, it is necessary to go back to the April day in 1852; when, according to the widely accepted story, she came down the gangplank of the steamer *Oregon*, just arrived from Panama, to find half a dozen wealthy San Francisco tycoons waiting on the wharf to bid for her services as a famous New Orleans cook.

The scene at the wharf has been told so many times, in one way or another, that to cast doubt on its ever having occurred is a thankless undertaking. But although it has been explained how and why the reception committee knew in advance that she was due to arrive, and on what steamer, no substantial evidence has been presented to warrant its acceptance. According to the familiar tale, Mammy Pleasant, living in Louisiana under the name of Mrs. Mary Ellen Smith, had left New Orleans on the sailing vessel *Bolivia* for the long voyage around the Horn to Panama, where she transferred to the *Oregon*. Someone who knew she had left, by sailing himself via the shorter Panama route, preceded her to San Francisco by five weeks and spread word of her coming.

This ignores the fact that Mary Ellen Smith was at the time, and had been for several years, an active agent in the Underground that was successfully helping Negroes to escape from slavery; that the authorities who were hunting her were closing in, with death the penalty if she was captured; that she slipped aboard the *Bolivia* disguised as a steerage passenger.

Nor is there any evidence to warrant identifying her as "a famous New Orleans cook." She was better than the average plantation cook and her culinary skill won her some acclaim from the visiting gentry who dined at the Bayou St. John plantation where she was employed. Although her reputation did not extend to the city, it was sufficient to draw attention to her, the last thing she wanted. Realizing that she had inadvertently betrayed herself, she fled to California.

In San Francisco in the early 1850's, no one wanted to do menial work. The Chileno women did the washing and did it in such an unsatisfactory manner that men who had already become wealthy were sending their soiled linen to the Orient and waiting three months for it to be returned. House servants were not obtainable and the recurring complaint was made that there were not half a dozen good cooks in the city. Twenty years were to pass before Californians discovered that the pig-tailed Chinese made dependable domestics, whether in the kitchen or the laundry.

Accepting Mammy Pleasant's storied arrival as factual does not exclude the fact that Charles Case and Charles Heiser, the wealthy Sansome Street commission merchants, very likely had other business at Long Wharf that morning than acquiring a cook. Case, who did the talking for himself and his partner, reportedly ended the bidding by offering her $500 a month as cook and housekeeper of their Washington Street bachelor establishment, which they maintained for themselves and their office staff.

Some of the dialogue on that memorable occasion has been preserved. Before accepting Case's offer, Mammy Pleasant made some stipulations.

"There's to be no washing," she told him.

"No washing," he agreed.

"Not even dishwashing."

Down through the years these have become the unanimously accepted terms on which the bargain was sealed. No such unanimity exists in describing and characterizing Mary Ellen—the future Mammy Pleasant. The usually authentic Herbert Asbury calls her "a gigantic Negress from New Orleans, black as the inside of a coalpit, but with no Negroid features whatever, whose culinary exploits were famous." Equally absurd is the statement of one of her leading biographers that "she had decided that she must pass herself off as a white woman. She was already used to assuming disguises and she was artful in duplicity . . . she could 'pass,' for her eyes, although large, were long, her nose perfectly straight, and her lips well shaped in a strong archer's bow."

It is difficult to believe that a woman as astute as she had not settled on the course she was to pursue long before she reached California. Certainly she could not have doubted her ability to pass for white, if that was what she wanted to do, which in the light of later events seems unlikely. In her role with the Underground she had been a passer for years, not only in New England but in Pennsylvania, West Virginia and Ohio. It was as a white woman that she had married James W. Smith, a wealthy contractor and flour merchant, in Boston in 1842. Smith was an ardent Abolitionist, and his tobacco plantation near Charles Town, West Virginia, was manned by Negroes whose freedom he had purchased and who worked for wages.

When Smith died two years after marrying Mary Ellen, he placed his fortune in her hands, making her promise to spend it in the fight against slavery. For the following six years she risked capture and death in the Deep South, moving from one plantation to another, running off slaves and starting them up the Underground to freedom in the North. On these repeated forays she had more difficulty in being taken for a Negro than she ever had in passing for a white. Her skin was so light that she had to darken it with walnut stain.

Slavery was not the burning question in California that it was in the East. But the Legislature had recently enacted a sort of fugitive slave law of its own that threatened the freedom of every runaway slave in the state. This law is said to have been responsible for Mary Ellen's alleged decision to pass herself off as white. If that had been her intention, she did not pursue it. Instead of cutting herself off from what she regarded as her own people, she surrounded herself with Negroes, found employment for them, and began her amazing rise to leadership and the undisputed control of their lives, exploiting them to her own enrichment. Claiming to have the occult powers of a queen of voodoo, she led her followers in the performance of the orgiastic rites of that savage religion.

This narrative is not concerned with the abolitionist activities of Mary Ellen Smith and her close connection with the fanatical John Brown who, years later, was hanged following his failure to capture the U.S. arsenal at Harpers Ferry, which was only a few miles from the Smith plantation at Charles Town. But who was this woman who was to become the sinister Mammy Pleasant? She was the daughter of a white man and born of a Haitian quadroon mother on a plantation near Augusta, Georgia. As an attractive, well-mannered child of ten, Mary Ellen attracted the attention of Americus Price, of Price's Landing, Missouri, who bought her for $650, delivery to be made to him in New Orleans in sixty days. When she arrived, he provided her with suitable clothing and, moved by a generous impulse, took her to the convent of the

Ursulines, registering her as white, and arranging with the sisters to begin her education. On his return a year later, he found the nuns so enthusiastic about the progress the child had made that he arranged with friends, a family named Williams, living in Cincinnati, to take her in and give her the advantages of being brought up in a Christian home and of attending an endowed school.

All went well until Americus Price died. When the money he had been sending stopped arriving, Williams shipped Mary Ellen off to a relative on Nantucket Island as a bond servant. She lived here long after she had worked out her period of bondage, subsisting on the pittance she received for clerking in the general store of the old woman to whom she had been indentured.

The principal business of Nantucket was its trade with the whalers and sea captains of New Bedford, Boston and other New England ports. Almost without exception they were Abolitionists of one degree or another. It cannot be doubted that the opinions they expressed implanted in Mary Ellen the decision to take part in the battle against slavery.

She was twenty-four when she left Nantucket to find work in Boston and become part of the Abolitionist movement. Some of its leaders and backers patronized the Merrimac Street tailor shop in which she found employment. They were happy to welcome to their ranks this attractive young woman who had an excellent figure and a seductive smile, suggesting that the plight of the slaves was not their only concern. Although he was twice her age, Marry Ellen set her trap for James Smith, the wealthy widower, and several months later she maneuvered him into marrying her.

Smith took her to his tobacco plantation at Charles Town, West Virginia, for their honeymoon. It was to have consequences far more important to her than her marriage to Smith, for when John James Plaissance, the new overseer, faced her, a dark and savage impulse to possess him overcame her. Plaissance was several years younger than she, a tall, lean, handsome man with a golden skin almost as light as hers. He called himself a Cuban but proudly claimed to be related to Henri Christophe, the late black king of Haiti. That relationship, whether true or fancied, was unimportant; he knew it would not save him from the penalty he would suffer if he were discovered having an affair with Mary Ellen Smith, the supposedly white wife of his employer. But his lust for her was uncontrollable as her passion for him.

A summerhouse overlooking the Shenandoah River became their trysting place. When Mary Ellen was sure that her husband was asleep for the night, she would slip a light robe over her nightdress and hurry down to the summerhouse, where Plaissance would be waiting. Smith's unexpected death not only put an end to their dalliance but produced a new, ruthless, domineering Mary Ellen. It marked the beginning of the character changes in her that eventually reached full flower in the dark and devious woman of mystery, Mammy Pleasant.

After warning Plaissance that she would hold him to the same strict accountability she would demand from any other man, she placed him in charge of the plantation and left for Boston. When her pregnancy could no longer be concealed, she hid herself in the home of a friend. Here she gave birth to a daughter, the unwanted issue of her illicit relations with John Plaissance. With a callousness that her years of work in the Underground could not excuse, she deserted the child after arranging to pay for her keep.

As the years passed, she visited Plaissance at various intervals both as her manager and lover. But her activities as an agent of the Underground railroad became so well-known that she was no longer safe below the Mason-Dixon line. When she dared to visit Charles Town, where the authorities were waiting to arrest her, she sold the plantation and ordered Plaissance to come to her at New Bedford, Massachusetts, an Underground stronghold. Fearing that they were marked for destruction, she gathered up what money was still due her from the Smith estate. To break their trail, they sailed for Nantucket, and there they embarked for New Orleans and were married at sea.

If fleeing to New Orleans was akin to entering the enemy's stronghold, it was also true that it was the last place anyone would look for her. To Mary Ellen it was only a temporary refuge. She ordered her pliable husband, who at her insistence had changed his name to John Pleasants, to sail as a steward on a ship bound for California, promising to join him in San Francisco as soon as she could. Calling herself Mrs. Ellen Smith, she arrived there on April 7, 1852.

Months had passed since she had last seen Plaissance (or Pleasants). In the meantime he had found employment on the steamship *Orizaba,* plying between the Isthmus and San Francisco. When he arrived in port some weeks after her coming, he had no difficulty in locating her, but aside from satisfying her sexual urges, he was no longer important to her. A few weeks after she took charge of Case and Heiser's bachelor establishment, Tom Mosler, a forty-niner who had made his fortune and was often a guest there, became her new lover. Doubtless there were others, for she was never known for her fidelity to any man, unless it was to Thomas Bell, who if he was not her lover was the "front man" for her many financial speculations.

She had met Bell on her way to California. He had come aboard the *Bolivia* at Valparaiso and transferred with her to the steamer *Oregon* at Panama. He was an affable Scotsman and had been employed in the banking and investment business in various parts of the world. Through the years Mary Ellen alternately badgered and cajoled him. In the process, largely due to her superior judgment, both became wealthy. Although she had received some formal education, her intelligence and native shrewdness, unhampered by moral inhibitions, served her better than the knowledge she might have acquired in a dozen classrooms.

On his deathbed Smith had extracted from her the promise to expend the tidy fortune he was leaving her in furthering the abolition of slavery. She spent much of it in that cause, but she could not have had much less than $20,000 when she arrived in San Francisco. The inflated wages she received for managing Case and Heiser's establishment enabled her to add to her nest egg. Subsequently she was employed in a similar capacity by the Woodworth brothers, Fred and Selim, who had made a fortune buying and selling waterfront property.

It should be explained that the term "boarding house," as used in the San Francisco of that day, was applied to what were expensive dinner and supper clubs catering to men of means. The food they served was far superior to the best the hotels offered.

From conducting such operations for others, Mary Ellen launched her own, first in rented premises, then in property she had purchased. To her first venture on Washington Street she added two others. All were immensely profitable. She staffed them with colored help and ruled over them with a stern hand.

Her success led to other ventures. She bought a Sansome Street saloon and placed two of her adherents in charge. She next acquired a livery stable and followed that by embarking in the laundry business. Before long she had three such establishments. As more and more Negroes began arriving in San Francisco, she found employment for them as servants in the homes of the well-to-do. Her efforts on behalf of the penniless members of her race have been highly commended by many, but her seeming charity had an ulterior motive. Providing them with jobs was part of her diabolic scheme to make herself their master. They were ordered to bring her the secret scandals of the households in which they worked so that she could turn them to her advantage. But she had a far greater hold over her subjects than the purely economic one of keeping them employed: she made them fear her by establishing herself a queen of voodoo, as her mother had been before her. She made them believe she had the power of life and death; that she could cast spells, read the future and restore the ailing to health.

However incredible this mumbo-jumbo may appear today, factual evidence exists that during her years in San Francisco she conducted secret voodoo rites at night in a wooded glen several miles from town. She and her followers stripped down to loincloths as they writhed and contorted themselves around a bonfire in sensuous dances, bowing and praying to the boxed snake in the center of the circle of sweating, lusting bodies, their stamping feet keeping time to the throbbing beat of a drum. The climactic moment came when the participants tore off their loincloths and each man seized a female, the couple running off into the darkness to satisfy their lust.

The participants were ignorant ex-slaves. That such savage orgies could appeal to what passed for educated, cultured white men puts a further strain on the reader's credulity, but documentation exists that in the late 1870's, following the crash of the supposedly impregnable Bank of California, Mammy Pleasant used her country home, Geneva Cottage, as a suburban assignation house for a few carefully chosen gentlemen of wealth, presenting for their entertainment a divertissement that was in fact an obscene voodoo dance, performed by ten comely young and almost nude Negro girls who danced to the savage rhythm of a jungle drum. When exhausted, they fled to the bedrooms and the guests rushed in after them to satisfy their aroused erotic appetites.

Along with the mountain of trash that has been written about Mammy Pleasant, several serious attempts have been made to untangle the snarled threads of her bewildering career. Diaries, newspaper files and court records were examined, but the published findings were as incredible as the woman herself, including the misinformation that long before she set foot in California, a little girl on a Missouri plantation had called her Mammy Pleasant, which ignores the fact that in those ante-bellum days *mammy* was a term of endearment given exclusively to elderly female slaves.[1] At the time, Mary Ellen was in her early thirties and successfully passing herself off as white.

Unquestionably it was in a San Francisco newspaper that the name Mammy Pleasant first appeared in print. Despite the secrecy with which she shrouded her activities, they were becoming known, and they were of a nature that made her a safe target for the slings and arrows of the press. Stories about "the woman of mystery whose deeds are evil," who was said to be the wealthiest woman in San Francisco, were eagerly read by thousands. These attacks were not racist in nature; it was the Mexicans and Chinese who suffered the injustice of white racism.

In the original gold rush, generally recognized as extending from 1849 to 1855, more than three hundred thousand people, not all of them Americans—arrived in California. Following the conclusion of the War Between the States, a second rush of emigration occurred. It reached its peak when thousands of Chinese laborers were brought in to build the western end of the first great transcontinental railroad. With the laborers came Chinese merchants, gamblers, criminals, and slave dealers with their female chattels. They settled on what is now upper Grant Avenue but was then

Dupont Street. In short order San Francisco had the second largest Chinatown in the United States. If the whole city experienced a phenomenal growth, so did the Barbary Coast. The unbroken block of saloons, dives and cribs on Pacific Street between Kearney and Montgomery, where the lights were brightest and the noise loudest, remained the heart of the district, but it had spilled out over a nine-block area in which every house displayed a welcoming red light and where every alley and cul-de-sac harbored a bordello.

When the Barbary Coast had been confined to Pacific Street and the value of property several blocks away depreciated because of its proximity to the red-light district, Mammy Pleasant had picked up different pieces at her own price, gambling that as the city grew, the Coast would grow. The expected had happened and she was collecting a fabulous return on her investments. Anything on Montgomery and Kearney streets between Washington and Broadway that had a roof over it could be rented for almost any price the owner demanded.

In her unrelenting drive for power and wealth she moved a madam and her bawds out of a ramshackle house she owned on Kearney Street and without appearing on the scene personally, rebuilt it and spent $15,000 furnishing it as a luxurious parlor house. As far as the public knew, the proprietor of this flossy establishment was the woman who ran it, a professional madam known as French Em or Madame Em. This was not Mammy Pleasant's first venture in commercialized vice. In addition to the buildings she owned on Pacific Street, which were being used for immoral purposes, two of her other properties were being operated as houses of assignation. That she could keep her many enterprises flourishing was possible only because her network of spies and talebearers kept her informed about what the men and women whom she had placed in charge were doing. It enabled her to sit at home at 920 Washington Street and keep her finger on her expanding business.

Being unscrupulous herself, it followed that she did not trust anyone completely, whether black or white, with the possible exception of William Willmore, her black handyman, who was also her most dependable agent. He served her in many ways. No one knew her better than he, for he was often a party to the crimes she committed or those committed on her orders. And he never talked until she was in her grave. At least on four occasions she took girls out of houses of prostitution, tranformed them into young ladies with a veneer of culture, and married them off to rich men. The next step was to blackmail them by threatening to reveal what she knew. If a man refused to marry one of her "protégées" after having had sexual relations with her, Mammy could rely on Willmore to produce a baby, bought or stolen, with which she could confront the alleged father and bring him to terms. She even resorted to that kind of trickery with Thomas Frederick Bell, her banker and business partner.

It would be impossible to concoct a melodrama more outrageously unbelievable than the story of Mammy Pleasant. Credulity falters as one outrageous incident follows another. Casting aside all that is unprovable or cannot be documented to some degree, what remains is a chain of progressively sinister and criminal incidents. Her life in California seems to divide into two periods—the first from her arrival in San Francisco in 1852 and extending to 1865, when Thomas Bell became an important factor, and the second running to her death at eighty-eight in 1904.

1661 Octavia Street—the House of Evil

THOMAS BELL, the young Scotsman whom Mammy had met on the voyage to San Francisco in 1852, had returned to Valparaiso to remain there some years and prosper. He was back in California by 1863, buying and selling mining shares and speculating on the stock exchange. Mammy watched him closely. The success he was enjoying convinced her that he was the right man to take hold of her money and multiply it into a great fortune. Not that she thought his judgment, or any man's, better than her own, but he could do things for her that she could not do for herself. From being an infrequent guest at her fashionable Washington Street boarding house, he began dining there almost nightly and then remaining to spend the evening in her parlor or possibly in her bedroom. Although she was past fifty, she had lost none of her sexual attractiveness. It cannot be said positively that at first she envisioned more than a business arrangement with him, but certainly that came to pass.

As her agent and partner, Bell soon found himself being forced to defer to her judgment rather than relying on his own. His cautiousness and her boldness resulted in their steering a middle course that brought them success. The frenzied speculation in silver shares was the principal business of the exchange. A man could be a millionaire today and a pauper tomorrow. Over the wires of the California Telegraph Company a daily message was received from Virginia City giving the news of mining operations on the Comstock Lode. It was posted on the board and set the tone of the day's trading. The daily messages were often weighted with deceit and treachery. They could send a stock tumbling or raise it a hundred points in an hour.

Mammy knew nothing about mines or their prospects. But she knew men, which was more important and dependable. Many of the big speculators in the Comstock issues often dined at 920 Washington Street. Judging them by her own ruthless standards, she picked out several whose maneuvering, she was convinced, would be profitable for Bell and her to follow. It brought them no noticeable measure of success until, through Milton S. Latham, the head of the San Francisco and London Bank, they became involved with Big Ben Holladay, the steamship magnate and former stagecoach king. He had dumped his stage lines on Wells Fargo for two and a half million dollars in cash and stock in the express company, as a result of the latter's miscalculation that the railroad connecting East and West would not be completed for another five to six years—the costliest mistake Wells Fargo ever made. Holladay was now engaged in making a second fortune from his speculations in Comstock silver stocks.

Whether Mammy realized that in Ben Holladay there was an unscrupulousness that matched her own, no one can say. In any event she appears to have been ready enough to engage in his stock-rigging scheme. It was well-known that he was a heavy investor in the rich Ophir mine. No issue being traded on the San Francisco Exchange was more highly regarded. Because stockholders were receiving big dividends, very few shares were available and they could be had only at a fantastic price. Holladay's scheme was not new. What he proposed to do was to begin selling off a few shares a day, which would cause some concern, and then circulate the rumor that the main ore body in Ophir was pinching out. The price would plummet and the timid would throw their stock on the market, which would further depress it.

What he wanted Bell and Mammy to do was to begin buying the stock when he passed the word to them. When the price began to rebound, he would drive it up beyond its old level and they could sell or hold onto what they had bought.

The manipulation was carried out successfully. Mammy remained in the background but Bell was lifted into prominence and hailed as a financial wizard. With better than a quarter of a million dollars to add to their original bankroll, Mammy and he no longer could regard themselves as small operators. Other opportunities offered. The two hundred thousand dollars they invested in the bonds of the California Steam Navigation Company enabled the company to complete its monopoly of river steamboating, and returned a handsome profit.

Success changed Thomas Bell from a colorless individual to one of the best-dressed men in the city. Although Mammy Pleasant distrusted what she called "the bank crowd"—D. Ogden Mills, William Sharon and William Ralston—Bell craved their recognition as a financial equal. To help his cause, he opened offices in the Bank of California Building. In keeping with his improved social standing, he built a mansion for himself on Bush Street, the first of several.

California's only railroad was the little Sacramento Valley Railroad, which ran from Sacramento to Folsom, a distance of twenty-one miles. But in the fall of 1868, when it became apparent that the rails of the Union Pacific–Central Pacific would meet in a few months and the great transcontinental railroad would be an accomplished fact, railroad fever swept the West Coast. In San Francisco and Portland promoters fastened their eyes on government land grands—millions of acres of rich farm and timber land— that would be won by the first road to lay its rails from Portland to the California line. Thomas Bell, his friend Milton S. Latham, head of the San Francisco and London Bank, and several others chartered the California and Oregon Railroad Company and began surveying a route up the Sacramento Valley from Marysville to Jacksonville, a roaring mining town in southern Oregon, where it was expected the California line would meet the Oregon Central that would be building down from Portland.

A bitter fight was developing between two groups of Portlanders to determine which would build the Oregon railroad, but Bell and the others entertained no doubt about the outcome. Latham had informed them that Ben Holladay was in Portland,

had grabbed control of the so-called "East Siders" and was prepared to throw his entire fortune into the battle with the "West
Siders."

Bell was so confident of success that he invested his own money
in the paper California and Oregon Railroad and did not consult
his silent partner. It resulted in their first angry confrontation.
Mammy did not break with him, but neither did she forget the
incident. Eventually both of them, and Holladay as well, were
to learn that a pioneer railroad was a monster that could devour
money faster than it could be poured into its rapacious mouth.[1]

Bell and his San Francisco group lost every dollar they put
into the California and Oregon Railroad—which must have given
Mammy some satisfaction. But two years later, when Holladay,
by brazen political skulduggery, had made himself the acknowledged master of the situation in Oregon, she compelled a reluctant
Bell to invest $200,000 of their joint funds in the bonds of the
Oregon and California Railroad, a new corporate name for the
original Oregon Central.

The financial panic that swept the country in 1874 forced her
to appeal to Bell to extricate them from disaster. It gave him an
ascendancy over her which he was never to lose. Holladay was
in desperate trouble; not only was the company treasury bare and
several hundred miles of track yet to be built but the deadline for
qualifying for the land grant was getting ever nearer. To save
the day, Bell induced Milton Latham to risk his honorable reputation abroad in a campaign to dispose of five million dollars' worth
of the company's worthless bonds to his English and German correspondent banks at sixty cents on the dollar.

It gave Holladay the money he so urgently needed. But it provided only temporary relief. When the Oregon and California
defaulted on its bonds, the roof fell in. Mammy had many things
going for her, all of which were immensely profitable, but the
thousands she lost in Oregon appeared to have been her last big
venture. Bell, on the other hand, became an increasingly prominent
financier. Being as devious as she was, she very likely believed that
in some way he and his friend Latham had defrauded her.

Important as Thomas Bell was to Mammy, it was around Teresa

Marie Percy that her life revolved from the time they first met in the summer of 1868 until Mammy's death in 1904, alone and impoverished, in a run-down house on Webster Street that she had once owned but from which she was about to be ejected. In 1868 Teresa Percy was a beautiful young blonde in her early twenties. She had an intelligent face with a strange but appealing look of bewilderment in the depth of her violet blue eyes. While still in her teens she had fled from her home in Auburn, New York, to escape the consequences of an affair with a man named James Percy Hoey.[2] She had recently arrived in San Francisco from New York where she had briefly been an inmate in a Division Street bordello. At the moment she was one of the attractions in a Barbary Coast parlor house.

Mammy was convinced at once that Teresa Percy was ideal material on which to work one of her Pygmalion-like transformations, to the end that some wealthy man could be entrapped into marrying the girl or blackmailed for his dalliance with her.

Mammy took Teresa in with her at 920 Washington Street and established her in her own apartment. Despite the wardrobe with which Mammy supplied her and the tutors and music teachers that were brought in to "improve" her, Teresa became a virtual prisoner. She was not permitted to leave the house unless accompanied by Mammy, and on those rare occasions it was by carriage.

In her various enterprises Mammy employed over half a hundred men and women, all black. Over them she exercised a despotic control. They did their work well, not out of loyalty so much as fear, for they knew that if she turned them adrift they were not likely to find comparable employment elsewhere. When things were running smoothly, she did not hesitate to leave the city for weeks at a time and conduct her business from her country establishment at Geneva Cottage. She took Teresa with her on these long absences. Geneva Cottage had an attraction for Mammy that could not be concealed from Teresa. George Gammons, her current lover, was living there. He was a companionable spendthrift who had run through a tidy fortune and was living on Mammy's bounty. In the account book of Geneva Cottage he was carried as the manager.

It seems obvious that Mammy Pleasant's reluctance to push Teresa into the arms of any wealthy man, and a number were available, was because she had selected the man she wanted for her. That man was Thomas Frederick Bell. This does not necessarily refute the widely held belief that Mammy had been Bell's mistress. It does suggest that the intimacy had ended. She proved she was content to bide her time with Teresa by bringing her sister out from the East to be with her for a year, and then by providing the money for them to return across the country for an extended stay.

Aside from her successful preying on the weaknesses of man, there is nothing in the provable record to warrant identifying Mary Ellen–Mammy Pleasant as a shrewd financial genius. Money came easy to her, and if one venture failed, her fertile mind could always invent another equally promising and venal. Her reckless extravagance reached its peak when she squandered $100,000 on the ornate thirty-room, three-storied house she built on half a block of land on Octavia Street between Bush and Sutter. This, with its mansard roof and iron railings, was the infamous House of Mystery which was to become a landmark of evil until it was destroyed in the great fire of 1906.

A year was required to build it and half again as long to complete the furnishings. With its crystal chandeliers, imposing spiral staircase, marble floors and frescoes it had a garish elegance that could not be matched in San Francisco. In the rear was a detached carriage house and stable. When the grounds had been lavishly landscaped and the circular driveways surfaced, 1661 Octavia Street would have satisfied a millionaire's idea of grandeur.[3] When it became tarnished with succeeding scandals and its evil reputation was darkened by rumors of the crimes and orgies that took place behind its bronze doors, few people doubted the stories about the secret passages in its walls and the hidden panels that could be opened with the pressure of a finger.

Mammy moved into her luxurious second-floor suite long before the rest of the house was finished. When Teresa returned from the East, her third-floor apartment on the Bush Street corner was waiting for her. Across the hall at the head of the stairway, three rooms—parlor, study, and bedroom with bath—outfitted with costly antique furniture, Tiffany lamps and assorted objects of art, were reserved for the "master," who was not in residence and showed no inclination to become a member of the household at 1661 Octavia Street. Every day one of Mammy's colored maids was instructed to give what she called "Mr. Bell's apartment" a thorough dusting and airing and to place fresh flowers from the garden in the parlor and study.

But the expected guest did not arrive; Thomas Bell was living in his bachelor home at 1107 Bush Street and appeared to be content to stay there. The quicksilver mines, in which he was a heavy investor, had made him a millionaire. When Mammy had to confer with the so-called Quicksilver King, she went to him; he did not go to her. And it must have been often, for years later when the settling of the Bell estate was dragging through the courts, it was revealed that during the time she had been spending money with such a reckless hand that she had borrowed great sums from him, giving the Octavia Street house as security. Sometime before his death those borrowings had reached a point that made him the legal owner of the property.

The mind reels as it confronts the known crimes that were committed in the House of Mystery. Babies born to unwed mothers were suffocated at birth; others were brought there to grow up in its depraved atmosphere. At least five men who were part of the household were murdered under its roof or followed when they left and were killed elsewhere. Sydney Smith, one of her collectors who had been caught cheating her, disappeared under strange circumstances and was never heard of again. Three of the others were Negro servants; the fourth was Thomas Frederick Bell. In each instance the murderer was Mary Ellen Pleasant. There were three other related killings that occurred at Geneva Cottage and in Bell's Bush Street house.

Killing three of her servants had no purpose other than to still their tongues. In the case of Sam Whittenton, her head butler, Leroy Jackson, and Eugene Paillet, a gardener, her motive was even more sordid. Whittenton, a popular waiter at the Palace Hotel, had received a legacy of several thousand dollars. With the market tips he received from the brokers who dined at his tables, he had built up a comfortable nest egg and bought a piece of waterfront acreage across the Bay at Berkeley, which Mammy figured was worth $20,000. But his wife was suing him for divorce which, if granted, would give her half of his estate as community property. Mammy assured him that she could prevent that happening if he put the matter in her hands. He quit his job at the hotel and went to work for her. After she had him under her thumb for several days, she told him that all he had to do was to put the Berkeley property in her name temporarily; she would give him a proper receipt, and as soon as his domestic troubles were over she would return it to him. He agreed, and the following afternoon they crossed the Bay to inspect Whittenton's land and the unoccupied house that stood on it.

A week later Sam Whittenton's bloated body was discovered in a patch of tules at the water's edge. He had been shot to death. Needless to say, the receipt Mammy had given him was missing. Leroy Jackson just disappeared and no trace of him was ever found. Eugene Paillet was found lying dead in a ditch several blocks from 1661 Octavia Street, from which his lifeless body had been dragged. The police wrote it off as an accidental death, though Paillet's life savings could not be located. He had loaned them to Mammy Pleasant on her offer to pay him ten per cent a month for three months. Once the money was in her possession, she had conducted him on a tour of the house, and from the roof had pitched him over the low railing that surrounded the slanting mansard to his death on the flagging sixty feet below. Another man, known simply as French John, was found beaten to death in a Sutter Street alley.

John James Pleasant was in San Francisco and slowly drinking himself to death. Mammy supplied him with money on the understanding that he was to keep his distance from her. When he died of diabetes, she had him buried in her plot at Laurel Hill.

To keep in perspective an accounting of the crimes and immoralities that occurred in or were related to the House of Mystery, it must be remembered that they were spread out over a quarter of a century. In all that time, however, there appears to have been few protracted periods in which Mammy Pleasant was not engaged in furthering some plot for her enrichment. She had long since disposed of her laundries, livery stable and saloons. The handsome income she received from Barbary Coast properties came in almost automatically and left her time for her nefarious schemes, the most important of which was to make Teresa Percy Mrs. Thomas Frederick Bell.

No investigator has been able to explain how she succeeded in getting the eccentric Bell to leave his bachelor establishment and move into the Octavia Street house. When that occurred, Mammy knew the battle was better than half won, for it put Bell in unavoidable contact with the beautiful Teresa. He often had a glass of wine too many after dinner and had to be helped up the stairs to his apartment. Usually it was Mammy who looked after him, at times Teresa.

One morning Bell awakened to find the latter in bed with him. He couldn't recall what had occurred during the night, but he assumed that their relations had been intimate—which she did not deny. After that it was she who brought him the hot toddy Mammy prepared and spent the night with him.

Bell was deaf to Mammy's suggestion that he should marry Teresa, but it made him realize how deeply he had got himself involved. To make amends, he agreed to pay the household expenses which, with a staff of ten, were not small. Mammy did not press the point; she knew she had Bell safely hooked and herself protected as she had pressured Teresa into giving her a power of attorney.

Mammy expected her "protégée" to become pregnant in a reasonable time. When that failed to happen, she packed Teresa off to the East for ten months in order to conceal the true state of affairs from Bell. To find a baby that could be palmed off on him as his offspring was not difficult. When a young woman named May Thompson found herself in "trouble," she appealed to Mammy for help, and the latter gave her shelter in one of her Sutter Street houses. There, on December 8, 1875, she gave birth to a baby, a boy. Mammy told the mother not to worry; she would adopt the child later on and May could continue to live where she was.

Before Teresa returned to San Francisco late in 1876, the unfortunate May Thompson was pregnant for the second time. This complicated the situation, but Mammy was equal to it. She instructed Teresa to resume her relations with Bell but not to inform him that in her absence she had borne him a son.

Bell left San Francisco in the spring of 1877 with one of his partners to inspect some mines in Mexico in which they were interested. When he returned three months later, Mammy explained Teresa's absence by informing him that she (Teresa) was in a "delicate condition" and had gone to Geneva Cottage to await the birth of her baby. He acknowledged his responsibility in the matter and told Mammy to take care of everything. He gave Mammy a sum of money (reportedly $10,000) for that purpose, none of which ever reached Teresa.

Over the years Mary Ellen had never doubted her ability to bend Bell to her will, but as she began urging him to marry Teresa, he adamantly refused, even though she informed him that he was already the father of a boy by her. Her opportuning finally drove him out of the house, and he returned to his bachelor home on Bush Street. It was only by giving him her repeated assurances that she would not mention the subject of marriage again that she induced him to return to Octavia Street. In the meantime she had taken May Thompson's two children to St. Paul's Roman Catholic Church and had them baptized as Thomas Frederick and Marie Teresa Bell, the children of Thomas Frederick Bell and Teresa Marie Percy.

When Marie was a year and a half old and her brother about three, Mammy brought them to Octavia Street and put them in charge of a nursemaid. Their presence in the house softened Bell and he acknowledged them as his children.

As the days passed, Mammy realized to her dismay that despite all her cunning and scheming, it was to Teresa rather than to herself that Bell was turning. She knew they were exchanging confidences from which she was excluded. A surprise was in store for her, however, for when she left the city to spend a weekend at Geneva Cottage with George Gammons, Teresa hastily invited a few of Bell's friends to an impromptu dinner party in his honor at Octavia Street. There was some drinking before dinner and an air of gaiety prevailed. Then by arrangement Teresa escorted a priest from St. Paul's into the drawing room. She beckoned to Bell and with unsteady step he joined her and the priest. With the guests looking on in amazement, the marriage ceremony was performed. No civil license had been obtained, but Father Breslin was convinced that he was righting an injustice to the children by marrying their parents. Bell and Teresa signed the marriage certificate, dated April 12, 1879.

When Mammy came rushing home in response to a telephone call from one of her spies and learned what had happened, she was aghast. What shocked and angered her most was the inescapable fact that the inexperienced Teresa, whom she had moved back and forth across her chessboard of intrigue, had accomplished what she, the master, had been unable to do. There would be a battle now to determine who would control the Bell estate. Teresa was Mrs. Thomas Frederick Bell, but the carefully guarded power of attorney Mammy held gave her the whiphand.

Bell left Octavia Street the morning after the marriage and was not seen in San Francisco for seven months. Teresa also disappeared. Mammy told the press that the Bells had left on a European honeymoon, which was accepted as the truth. Actually Bell was fighting for his financial life, for investors in mining stocks were facing a decade of boom and bust which ruined many. Bell escaped disaster but without any help from Mammy Pleasant. Although she was heavily in debt to him, when he demanded payment of some of the loans he had made her, she informed him that she was so hard-pressed herself that she could do nothing for him. In a huff Bell stopped paying the bills for the Octavia Street house.

In the hope of recouping the fortune she had squandered, Mammy sold some of her properties and used the money to prosecute Sarah Althea Hill's divorce action against William Sharon, the multimillionaire head of the Bank of California. After months of legal wrangling the Sharon-Hill marriage contract was declared a forgery. The Sharon-Hill case must have cost Mammy $100,000. Her little empire was crumbling and nothing could stay its decay but the death of Thomas Bell.

In 1892 he and Teresa were back at 1661 Octavia Street, as were the children. Fred had been sent home from a military academy in the East by the headmaster for drunkenness and dishonorable conduct. His sister Marie was growing into a sullen, insolent young woman who refused to recognize the authority of Mammy Pleasant or Teresa. It was what might have been expected of children raised in that atmosphere.

Mammy avoided an open break with Teresa, but the latter saw the implacable hatred that lurked in the older woman's veiled eyes. It warned her that she never would be free as long as the power of attorney she had signed could be used against her. Methodically she continued searching for it every time Mammy left the house. She found secret panels in the bedroom walls that contained valuable papers, but not the one she sought. But finally beneath the brocaded drapes that shaded the Bush Street windows her fingers touched an unseen spring and a tiny door flew open. Among other papers was the document she wanted. She took it to her bedroom and burned it at once. For the first time in over twenty years she was free of the shackles that had bound her to Mammy Pleasant.

Several weeks later, on the night of October 15, 1892, an event occurred which is proof enough that Mammy was not aware that the paper on which she was counting to give her control of the Bell estate had been removed from its hiding place. Bell was not feeling well and had retired early. Teresa was in the country and there were only three servants in the house. They were in the kitchen when Mammy walked in, the red blanket which she customarily wore on cool evenings draped over her shoulders. There was no central heating at 1661 Octavia Street. They watched as she poured a decanter of port into a saucepan, warmed it slightly and then poured the wine back into the container. After wrapping a towel around it so that it would not cool too quickly, she placed it in a champagne bucket. They understood that the wine was for Mr. Bell. After she left, they heard her going up the stairs. Peering out into the hall, they saw that she had left a single light burning in the cut-glass lamp that surmounted the newel post.

There were no witnesses to what followed. The decanter of

wine was found in Bell's bedroom, but whether it was carried in before or after the tragedy that occurred a few minutes later, no one can say. Likewise, it is impossible to say whether Bell wandered out into the gloom at the head of the stairs or was led out. In any event, he was pushed over the balustrade and sent plunging down the stairwell to the tiled floor below. Lashing out wildly to clutch anything that might break his fall, his fingers fastened on something. That something was Mammy's red blanket. It was found snagged by the fringe halfway down the stairwell.[4]

Bell's wild scream and the thudding of his body as it struck the floor brought the servants running from the kitchen. They saw Mammy Pleasant on her knees bending over the bleeding, stricken man. Doctors were hastily summoned, but there was nothing they could do. Shortly after 1 A.M. Thomas Frederick Bell was pronounced dead. Without an autopsy being performed, a coroner's jury found that the deceased had died as the result of an accidental fall.

The way was now open for the reading of Thomas Bell's will and the beginning of the ten-year legal battle to settle his estate. When the lawyers got through with it, there wasn't much left. They had been aided and abetted by the rapacity of two of the three executors Bell had named. The most bitterly disappointed person of all was Mary Ellen Pleasant; she got nothing. She had lived for years on his assurance that he had named her his executor, which had been true, but he had made a new will in which she was not even mentioned. She could take some satisfaction out of the position in which it placed Teresa. Although it made the latter the legal owner of the estate, she could not touch the principal. Bell had directed that his estate not be divided until his youngest child had reached its majority. In the meantime, as the children's guardian, Teresa was entitled only to the income it produced.

It would be wearisome to follow the legal maneuvering that ground on for years. But there came a day in 1898, when Teresa was on the stand in Judge Coffey's court testifying in a suit brought by young Fred Bell to have her removed as the legal guardian of himself and Marie, when a dénouement occurred that shook the legal rafters. Answering a direct question by opposing counsel, Teresa answered:

"Thomas Frederick Bell is not my son; Marie Teresa Bell is not my daughter. They were not born of my body."

Mammy Pleasant was called to the stand to affirm or deny the statement just made. Teresa held her breath, not knowing what her enemy would say. To her surprise Mammy said:

"The words uttered by Mrs. Bell, disclaiming Fred and Marie as her children, were words of truth. She is not their mother."

It created a sensation. Not only was Fred Bell's lawsuit dismissed, but the way was now open for a reappraisal of the will. Five months later Teresa was declared its sole beneficiary. Even though she still feared Mammy, she tried to effect a reconciliation with her. Any hope of that faded when she caught her trying to falsify title to a Sutter Street piece of property. The next step was inevitable: Mammy had to go.

April 19 was a day of bitter wrangling between them, but the following morning Mammy started packing and on April 21, preceded by two expressmen carrying her trunks and a servant bearing a canvas bag filled with her personal belongings, she left the house she had planned and built at 1661 Octavia Street for the last time.

As previously noted, she settled in the second-floor flat of a shabby building she owned on Webster Street and which was already attached for debt. From her windows at night she could see the glow of the lights of the Barbary Coast and catch its noisy bedlam. Several pieces of furniture that Teresa had permitted her to have were delivered, but they did not belong in the small rooms at her disposal.

In a futile attempt to win back the allegiance of her former black supporters, she went into police court and charged that a bus being operated by the California Transportation Company had refused to stop and pick her up because she was a Negro. Not only was the case thrown out of court but it had no effect on the black community she wanted to impress with her loyalty. She had fooled them too often.

Only a handful of people kept in touch with her. They reported that she was sick and ailing. Out of the past her old lover, Tom Mosler, appeared to see that she was cared for. She was eighty-eight. On January 11, 1904, her long life of crime, intrigue and immorality came to an end. San Francisco, the city where she once had been a power, scarcely noted her passing. The war with Spain was over and dozens of transports were discharging thousands of troops returning from the victorious Philippines campaign. Mammy Pleasant and her House of Mystery belonged to an era that was gone.

The Magnificent Lola

W<small>HEN LOLA MONTEZ ARRIVED</small> in San Francisco late in 1852, she gave California its first taste of European elegance and sophistication. Famous as the beautiful courtesan who had toppled King Ludwig (Louis 1) of Bavaria from his throne after he had enobled her with the twin titles of Baroness Rosenthal and Countess Landsfeld in 1848, she was still one of the most talked about women in the world.[1]

Although she had been born Eliza Gilbert, in Limerick, Ireland, of English parents, the stage name she gave herself of Lola Montez fitted her perfectly. She had the dark, sultry beauty and exquisitely moulded features of the highly-born women of Castile. Indeed from the time she made her first tour of Europe, in 1847, billed as "Lola Montez, the Premier Spanish Ballerina, Offering her Sensational Spider Dance" she liked it so well that she never again acknowledged any other, save on a brief appearance in a legal action in England. To further her purpose, she invented a line of Spanish ancestors and a girlhood spent in Seville.

Fanny and Therese Elssler were the great ballerinas of their day. If Lola scarcely rated comparison with them, she had something more than the artistry of her dancing to hold and excite audiences. She had fire and a graceful, lithesome body, which her costumes were designed to reveal rather than conceal. The Spider Dance, with which her name was to become inseparably connected throughout her career, was described as "suggestive, lewd and immoral" by her critics. It was danced to the fiery, heel-tapping rhythm of the *La Tarantella*. Rushing on stage, she whirled and pirouetted back and forth, flailing her arms in a desperate effort to free herself from the imaginery cobweb in which she had become enmeshed, the angry spiders scurrying up her bare arms and legs or trying to conceal themselves in her bosom. Once free of the web, she began searching for the spiders, casting them out one by one until the last was stamped to death beneath her feet, the extent and intensity of her searching depending on the acclaim of her audience. Exhausted in the end, she sank wearily to the stage.

If this sounds tame today, it was daring enough in the 1840's. A decade later, she could still invest it with enough fire and excitement to bring rowdy San Francisco audiences to their feet with cries of "Higher! Higher!" when she began searching beneath her skirts for the elusive spiders.

Lola Montez was largely unknown when her third tour of the German and Polish kingdoms and principalities was drawing to a close. Her final performance took place in Munich, where, by chance, the first link in the chain of events that was to lift her from obscurity to world wide prominence occurred.

That evening Franz Liszt, the romantic Hungarian composer, already world famous, occupied a stage box with several male companions. Smitten with Lola on sight, he presented himself at her dressing room and arranged a small supper party in her honor. Her readiness to accept him as a lover may have been sheer romance, but not without her realizing that, as yet, he was the biggest fish to swim into her net.

Liszt accompanied her to Munich and shared her bed. The following evening, to his dismay, brooding, intent King Ludwig occupied the royal box. Fearing in him, with his fat purse, a rival for Lola's affections, Liszt hastily persuaded her to let him take her to Paris.

Being introduced to the brilliant art, music and literary circles of Paris, which centered in the woman known to the world by her pseudonym of George Sand and included such notables as Victor Hugo; Alexandre Dumas; Ferdinand Delacroix, the painter;

Honoré de Balzac and Theophile Gautier was equivalent to opening the world to Lola. Under the sponsorship of the dissolute, extravagant *avant-garde* she soon had her choice of lucrative engagements. But she interrupted her rise to fame by falling desperately in love with Henri Dujarier, the penniless, self effacing literary editor of the Paris *La Presse*. Although their relations could not have been otherwise than intimate, he became involved in a duel in defense of her honor and was killed.

For the rest of her life she was to say that Dujarier was the only man she had ever truly loved. Whether true or not, his death seemed to set a pattern that brought most of her romantic affairs to an end. Desolate over his passing, she shut herself away from her friends and moved to the country. There, in her retreat at Fountainebleu, the agents of King Ludwig found her. They presented her with letters from the king and a casket of jewels, which in itself amounted to a royal summons to Munich and the Court of Bavaria.

As the world knows, her response was favorable. After acquiring an extensive wardrobe, she departed by coach for Munich, where she found a completely staffed castle awaiting her exclusive use. The king's infatuation became a public scandal, but to the day of her death, fifteen years later, Lola clung to the preposterous fiction that her relations with Ludwig were only those of friend and advisor.

In the end, after several weeks of rioting, with angry mobs marching up and down the Ludwigstrasse shouting: "Down with the whore!" Lola was fortunate enough to escape to Switzerland. Here she learned that the King had abdicated in favor of his son, Maximilian II.

She returned to Paris to receive reams of sensational newspaper publicity, favorable and unfavorable, all of which could be exploited at the box office. She proceeded to do so by having a play written for her entitled *Lola Montez in Bavaria*, in which she was to play the title role. Henri Roux, her new manager, persuaded her to cross the Channel for a long engagement in London. She had not been in England since her schooldays, when she had attended the Montrose Seminary at Bath. Not only was she apprehensive about how she would be received by English audiences, but her mother, from whom she had been bitterly estranged for years, was in London. Formerly a music hall performer she was now Lady Elizabeth Craigie, the widow of the late Sir Patrick Craigie, Adjutant General of her Majesty's forces in India. What Lola feared from her mother, of course, was that her true identity and early life, which she had gone to great lengths to conceal, might be exposed.

Although her acting and dancing won no acclaim from the critics, her London engagement and the tour of the provinces that followed was a tremendous success financially; what the English public wanted to see was the beautiful woman for love of whom a king had lost his throne.

The feared confrontation with her mother did not materialize. But Lola managed to get into serious trouble, and it was of her own making. It occurred when she foolishly married young George Trafford Heald, heir to great wealth. He was not yet twenty-one—a mere babe in her eyes. But he was handsome and he amused her. The marriage had no sooner taken place, however, than Susanna Heald, a maiden aunt and the executrix of the Heald estate, turned her guns on Lola, hoping to have the marriage annulled. Her solicitors were instructed to hire detectives and to spare no expense in gathering information about what she publicly labeled "this notorious harlot who has married my nephew to gain possession of his fortune."

Evidence was produced to the effect that in her twenties Lola, using her legal name of Eliza Gilbert, had married Captain Thomas James, 21st. Regiment of Bengal Native Foot in 1837, and had accompanied him to India, where five years later they had secured a legal separation but had never been divorced. Under English law she was now guilty of bigamy. To escape its consequences she and young Heald fled to France immediately, where she learned that her marriage to Heald had been annulled. Later the charge of bigamy was dropped, it having been discovered that Captain James had died of natural causes in India some years back.

Purchasing one of the most fashionable residences in the French capital, Lola established her own salon. The circle of sophisticates she attracted had no place for young Heald. He blamed her for the mess he had made of his life. They quarreled so violently that when she left Paris for a triumphal tour of the Continent, he remained behind. She was never to see him alive again, for after sulking and drinking heavily for several months, he took himself off to Spain and Portugal and was drowned in a boating accident in Lisbon harbor.

When newspapers the world over began devoting columns of space to the discovery of gold in California and printing fabulous tales of the fortunes that were being taken out of the streams and hillsides of the Mother Lode, a wave of speculation swept over the French capital. Thousands of shares of California mining stock were hawked on the Paris bourse. Some of the promoters were honorable men; the majority were unscrupulous rogues. The public had no way of distinguishing one from the other.

Lola was caught up in the frenzied speculation and purchased stock in the Eureka mine, about which she knew nothing, other than that it was located at an unheard-of California settlement named Grass Valley, with ore so rich that anyone who invested in its development was sure to be handsomely rewarded. Undoubtedly this was the first time she had ever given any thought to America.

Miraculously the Eureka began to pay dividends. Lola's financial position was such that if she had received no return on the few thousand francs she had invested it would not have been a matter of major concern. But it must be assumed that the checks she received quickened her interest in far-away California.

Always a woman controlled by her varying moods, she surprised her intimates when, following a successful professional tour of the Low Countries, she turned from the worldly life she had been leading to spiritualism, consulting mediums and attending seances. She was known to have expressed the conviction that the spirit of Henri Dujarier, the great love of her life, hovered near her. Doubtless it was with the hope of contacting him that she turned to spiritualism. The charlatans who took her money failed to make him materialize, but it was a recurring hallucination of Lola's that Dujarier was never far away. Later, in California, her

lonely vigils in the hills were undertaken for the express purpose
of trying to communicate with him.

Edward Willis, an enterprising and successful theatrical agent
and manager, arrived in Paris. He had crossed the Atlantic for
the express purpose of persuading Lola to make an extended tour
of the United States. The terms of the contract he offered were
so attractive that she could not say no. She disposed of her house
in Paris, and in November, 1851, accompanied by her maid and
Willis, sailed from Le Havre for New York.

Willis realized that he had a celebrity rather than a great performer to promote. He persuaded her to add Sheridan's *A School
for Scandal* and *The Maid of Saragossa* to her repertoire and he
surrounded her with competent actors who could carry a performance. With the ingenuity of a Barnum he kept her name in
the newspapers, whetting the public's appetite to see the famous
Lola Montez. Crowded houses greeted her in New York, Boston
and Philadelphia, but as her tour proceeded, the reception she
received in city after city had the reverse of a mellowing effect on
Lola. Tales of her terrible temper, of her horse-whipping critics
and fighting with hotel managers were usually publicity stunts
but now they became real enough. In St. Louis, during a rehearsal,
she struck Willis across the face with a whip, breaking his nose.
J. S. Henning, a competent showman who had ranged as wide as
New Orleans and California replaced him.

The tour was to end in New Orleans. The turn-away audiences
that greeted Lola convinced her that she must go on to California.
San Francisco was still a city of fewer than 50,000 inhabitants,
but it had three theaters and a sizable resident theatrical colony.
Some of the foremost actors on the American stage had appeared
in San Francisco and Sacramento, supported by local talent, and
had enjoyed great financial success. Henning proposed to do as
they had done. He would dismiss the supporting company in New
Orleans and recruit a new one on Lola's arrival in San Francisco.

He left a week in advance to arrange for her passage across the
Isthmus from Aspinwall to Panama City and to prepare San Francisco for her coming. Lola, accompanied by her new maid, a tall,
light-skinned, New Orleans mulatto with the improbable name of

Hyacinthe Fhlery (who, because her blue-green eyes seemed to change color without warning, like sea water, Lola renamed Periwinkle) followed in due course, and at Panama they boarded the *S.S. Northerner* for San Francisco.

The sea voyage was to sweep Lola headlong into another romantic affair that was to end in disillusionment and unhappiness. One of her fellow passengers was Patrick Purdy Hull, a tall, affable, witty San Franciscan, writer and part owner of the *Whig*, the newspaper with which he was associated. What their relations were aboard ship must be left to conjecture, but she married Pat Hull a few days after reaching San Francisco. Her marriage so surprised and incensed Henning that they quarreled. He did not care how many lovers she took—from his standpoint the more the better—but even in bawdy, free-spending San Francisco some sanctity was attached to marriage. Audiences that of necessity would be 95 per cent male were not likely to be attracted to a theater by innocence and virtue; what they wanted was the Lola Montez who had been the mistress of a king.

When she and Henning parted company, Pat Hull took over as her manager. The energy he displayed partly made up for his lack of experience. Her fears that the San Francisco engagement might be a failure were dispelled on opening night, when many of the town's leading civic and business leaders were in the audience. Pat Hull had taken a leaf of Willis' book and filled the newspapers with stories about Lola's past that were calculated to titillate the imagination of men whose contact with the opposite sex was largely limited to the Mexican and Central American prostitutes in the Chileno colony at the foot of Telegraph Hill.

Two of the great fires that were to ravage San Francisco periodically, culminating in the holocaust of 1906, had already swept away the original tent and tarpaper shack town, and it was taking on the appearance of a substantial brick and stone city. Portsmouth Square was still the hub from which it radiated. Day and night it was thronged with miners from the gold camps down for a fling, and waiting to relieve them of their pokes were a horde of thieves, thugs and gamblers. In every building on three sides of the square—hotels, saloons, "concert" saloons offering some form of musical entertainment and gambling casinos—all or part of the premises was devoted to gaming.

To reach the theater for the evening's performance, Lola had to pass along two sides of the square. The women-hungry dealers and players could not be certain when she would pass. To make sure they didn't miss her, it was common practice to station a man at the entrance to notify those within of her approach. When he called out "She's comin'!" there was an immediate rush to the door, where they stood in awed admiration as she passed on Pat Hull's arm. But their mute admiration turned to vociferous applause when they beheld her on the stage. Nightly, at the conclusion of the Spider Dance, she rewarded them by stripping a silken garter off one of her shapely legs and tossing it across the footlights into the audience. The winner of the scramble that ensued for its possession triumphantly waved the token aloft as an Apache Indian might have done with a freshly taken scalp.

When the twice extended San Francisco engagement ended, Lola next appeared at Sacramento, where another enthusiastic reception greeted her. Emboldened by success, Hull sought to induce her to undertake a tour of the mining towns on the Mother Lode—Placerville, Downieville, Dutchman's Flat, Nevada City, Grass Valley—a dozen or more in all—each of which had a town or miners' hall suitable for staging a performance. Several musicians and a singer could be engaged to round out an evening's entertainment. They would travel by carriage, which would make it unnecessary to wait on the arrival and departure of the coaches of the California Stage Company.

Admittedly the tour he was proposing would be comfortless, rugged and dangerous, for they would have to use the unimproved mountain roads where masked highwaymen often lay in wait for the stagecoaches and unwary travelers. But bringing entertainment to mining towns that had none could not fail to be immensely profitable.

Lola was won over, and late in May the little cavalcade of two carriages set out from Sacramento. Hull handled the reins on the first team and Lola was wedged in between him and the silk-hatted shotgun guard hired from the enterprising express firm of

Wells, Fargo. The "company" and Periwinkle trailed behind in the second carriage.

That a woman of fashion, long accustomed to the luxuries and conveniences of sophisticated living, could face the primitive accommodations and coarse food of the mining camps for weeks, without losing her expressed fondness for California, was hardly to be expected. But it did not have that effect on Lola. In the majestic peaks of the distant Sierra Nevada, the flashing mountain streams and forested foothills of that wild country, she found something that fascinated her.

Before the tour ended, she fulfilled an old resolve to visit the Eureka mine someday. But the Eureka had paid its last dividend and had been abandoned. All that remained were the hills of tailings and some rusting mining machinery. She could regard it as no more than a minor disappointment, for the few thousand francs she had invested in the mine had been returned to her several times over.

Grass Valley was the last stop. When Lola rode into the pleasant little town, with its gardens, substantial houses and tree-lined streets, she astounded Pat Hull by declaring that she was going to make Grass Valley her permanent home. Having become acquainted with her mercurial temperament, he did not take her seriously at first, but when she purchased a white clapboard cottage on Mill Road, which sat back some distance from the highway, amid stately sycamores and screening shrubbery, he was convinced that she was in earnest.

Hull did not intend to spend his days vegetating in a small hill-country town remote from San Francisco. He was normally a heavy drinker, and his tongue was sharpest when he was well-liquored. Lola told him that she had hired a contractor to remodel the house to her liking, at a cost of several thousand dollars. He rebuked her with ridicule. It precipitated a quarrel, and although they returned to San Francisco together, their relations were never to be the same again.

In due course wagonloads of the costly furnishings Lola had purchased, including a parlor suite in goldleaf and a zinc bathtub that had to be filled and emptied by hand, began arriving at Grass

Valley. "It is her intention," the *Alta California* observed, tongue in cheek, "to establish a *salon* where the visiting nabobs and literati of these flush times will be welcome."

When she returned to Grass Valley in the fall, the work on the house had been completed. Hull accompanied her, but only because he was now financially dependent on her. His gambling losses had got him into deep trouble and he had been compelled to turn to Lola to bail him out. As usually happens, having to turn to her for such a favor filled him with resentment rather than gratitude.

As Lola was getting settled, Dr. Karl Adler, a German geologist and sportsman who was using Grass Valley as his headquarters, presented her with a bear cub. She made a pet of the animal and kept it chained to a post at the side door, where there was grass and shade. One morning Hull found the cub lying in his path. As he raised his boot to kick it aside, the bear nipped him. Enraged, he rushed into the house, seized a gun and killed it.

Such a minor incident was all that was needed to bring them to the parting of the ways. When the southbound stage for Sacramento left Grass Valley the following morning, Pat Hull was a passenger. In San Francisco, before the year ended, Lola won an uncontested divorce from him.

Lawyers, judges and political leaders had to pass through Grass Valley on their way to Marysville and Oroville. They made it a practice to avail themselves of Lola's hospitality. There were others, men like redoubtable Sam Brannan, the apostate Mormon who had organized and led the first Vigilance Committee that hanged the leaders of the Sydney Ducks and rescued San Francisco from the reign of terror imposed on it by that notorious gang of thieves and cutthroats. The acclaim he had won enabled him to become one of the state's important merchants and promoters.

It may be that Sam Brannan's interest in Lola Montez went deeper than friendship, as her most devoted and often inaccurate biographer suggests, but it is to be doubted. There can be no doubt, however, about the romantic nature of Dr. Adler's dalliance with her. Although by his own choice Californians knew him only as Dr. Adler, he was the young, blond and personable Baron Adler.

By reputation Lola was no stranger to him. She had not forgotten the German she had learned in Bavaria. Her ability to converse with him in his native tongue undoubtedly helped to draw them together, nor could the costly, European-flavored elegance with which she had surrounded herself in her retreat have failed to inflame his desire for her.

But Lola, who had never given any thought to being discreet in her amours, realized that if she wanted to live in a town as small as Grass Valley, public opinion was a weapon she didn't want turned against her. The male population was pleased to have her as a neighbor. Understandably their enthusiasm was not shared by their womenfolk.

Very likely Dr. Adler became Lola's lover. But not for long. As with so many of the men in her life, tragedy overtook him and he was killed in a hunting accident. It was shortly after Adler's death that Lola began her lonely vigils in the hills. Men reported seeing her seated on a rocky crag, staring off into space for hours at a time. We have her word for it that on such occasions the spirit of the long dead Henri Dujarier appeared and she was able to communicate with him.

That anyone as worldly as she could accept with complete conviction such hallucinatory contacts with the spirit world may seem incredible, and yet it is one of the basic tenets of modern psychology that it is exactly such persons who are most apt to accept spiritual manifestations.

In the days when no newspaper or magazine was complete without several sensationally romantic so-called feature stories, reams of trash were published, most of it untrue. Lola, a bizarre figure with whom the names of famous men could be associated, was a favorite subject of many of the writers of this type of fictional history.[2]

One of the myths they almost perpetuated was that while she was living in Grass Valley she was in touch with the ex-king of Bavaria through his agents, who brought her such trinkets as a diamond necklace valued at $20,000 and pleaded with her to return to Ludwig, who was living in Rome, and be united to him in a morganatic marriage, which she refused to do. This tale of a fallen monarch and his mysterious secret agents skulking about the California countryside had possibilities for enlargement that were not exhausted by one telling. Consequently, versions of it were produced over the years by other writers, but in all its variations the diamond necklace was dangled before the reader's eyes until the day it supposedly was sold at auction in San Francisco.

Despite the unpredictable moods of its mistress, Lola's little establishment at Grass Valley functioned as more conventional households did; a Mexican woman named Maria came in by the day to do the cleaning and washing; Periwinkle attended to the cooking. On those occasions when more help was required, or when a dinner was to be served important guests that was beyond Periwinkle's skill to prepare, Mary Ann Crabtree, a cultured, educated Englishwoman who ran a boarding house a short distance down the road, was called in to take charge.

Mrs. Crabtree came as a friend rather than as a servant, for she and Lola had a more or less similar background. As a consequence she could regard the other's numerous escapades with tolerance if not approval, a charitableness that found no echo among the churchgoing, "good" women of Grass Valley.

Mary Ann Crabtree had a husband, but she had seen very little of him since arriving in California with her child, a girl of six, in 1853, for like so many others John Crabtree was a goldseeker who never found any gold. Although struggling to make ends meet, Mary Ann dreamed of finding gold, not in a rocky ledge or quartz outcropping, but in her red-haired, impish daughter, who had just passed her seventh birthday. That this unknown child, with her gift of being able to burlesque the eccentric characters of Grass Valley would one day be hailed as the greatest mimic and commedienne of her time, famous the world over and beloved by all Californians, could hardly have occurred to the celebrated Lola Montez, who taught her the rudiments of stage dancing and romped in the garden with her. But no less was to happen, for the child whose first impromptu stage was the top of a poker table in the mining camp of Rough and Ready was Lotta Crabtree, soon to be known as the "Incomparable Lotta." [3]

Lola and the Californians

ONCE, LATE IN LIFE when the eyes of the world were no longer focused on her, Lola is reputed to have said, "I was always notorious; never famous." This must be regarded more as a matter of semantics than a dispassionate appraisal of herself, for she never exhibited any capacity for self-criticism. And yet, as the winter snows went off and brown patches appeared on the mountain slopes that spring, she did not leave the house for days at a time. The few visitors from Sacramento, whose business required them to travel the muddy roads, found her strangely dejected.

Her moodiness was due, at least in part, to the fear that she had cut herself off too long from the world of the theater and might return only to find her popularity gone. She knew from reading the newspapers that San Francisco was maturing rapidly in the theatrical fare it was offering. New theaters were being built, old ones enlarged and modernized. Catherine Sinclair and Carolina Chapman had become reigning favorites.

But far more terrifying to Lola than having to compete with such established rivals was the unescapable truth that she was growing old; that in another seventeen months she would be forty. Harassed by the fear that she soon would be fading, she recklessly put herself in the arms of—and her career in the hands of—young Noel Follin, as unlikely a candidate for her favor as she could have found. Her excuse was that he reminded her of Dujarier.

Two young Frenchmen who were mining in the district, one

of whom is said to have been related to Victor Hugo, visited Lola occasionally. They arrived at the cottage one evening accompanied by Follin. He had a pleasing personality and was well-mannered, but there was nothing outstanding about him. In the three years he had been in California he had held a variety of jobs, but without improving his lot financially. Although Lola had not noticed him, he had been in charge of the box office when she was appearing at the American Theater, and had been similarly employed at other theaters in San Francisco. He appeared to be well-acquainted with the changing theatrical fare in the city.

In Lola he had an appreciative audience for his gossip and small talk about people connected with the stage. It may be assumed that it quickened her interest in him, hungry as she was for such news.

Whether or not he was in the employ of one of the express companies at nearby Nevada City is immaterial. Wherever he was located, it did not prevent him from visiting Lola at frequent intervals. In fact as the spring advanced he was seen at the cottage so much of the time that it could not be doubted that he was living there.

There is no reason to believe that Noel Follin, the son of a New Orleans Frenchman and the ex-mistress of a fashionable New York bordello, was a scoundrel, but he was a weakling and a fool. Since she first attracted public attention, Lola's romantic affairs had often ended unhappily. She had always been able, however, to disengage herself without getting hurt. With Follin, however, her good sense seemed to desert her and she provided him with money to manage her return to the stage.

The new Metropolitan, with its upholstered seats, rich hangings and gas footlights, was the best house in San Francisco. He leased it for six weeks, which required posting a guarantee acceptable to the owners. Lola's former director was not available. Another man had to be engaged to assemble a supporting cast and begin rehearsals. Word of the return to the stage of Lola Montez was not greeted by the newspapers with the excitement Follin had anticipated. When she came down from Sacramento on the *Yosemite*, only a handful of admirers were at the wharf to welcome her.

By the end of the second week of the projected long engagement it was obvious that San Francisco had lost interest in Lola. Due in part to Follin's bungling inexperience, her return to the stage was to be a costly failure. Somehow he persuaded her to undertake a tour of Australia to recoup her losses.

American singers and actors had made the long trip—thirty-seven days by clipper from San Francisco to Sydney—and met with singular success. Certainly money was becoming important to Lola. Contrary to the widespread opinion that she was wealthy, she had very little left of the fortune she had let slip through her fingers.

The Australian adventure did not replenish her purse. It began auspiciously in Sydney but ended in disaster, with the authorities in several cities branding the Spider Dance immoral and forbidding its performance.

Getting her company back to San Francisco took the last of Lola's resources. Follin held himself responsible for the tragic fiasco into which he had led her. Day after day on the homeward voyage he became increasingly depressed, sitting on deck for hours staring at the sea without speaking. No doubt his despondency irked Lola, who had more reason to despair than he. One morning as they sat together on deck, she left her chair for a turn about the ship. When she returned, he was gone. In her absence he had leaped over the rail and drowned. His death followed the tragic pattern that seemed to be the lot of her lovers. Another chapter was added when Pat Hull, impoverished and a hopeless drunkard, was found dead in a Jackson Street flophouse.

Discouraged, feeling that she could no longer find happiness in California, Lola arrived from Australia determined to dispose of the Grass Valley property and turn her other assets into cash, which would leave her free to return to the East. Her jewels— and they did not include Ludwig's mythical diamond necklace— were sold at auction for a reported figure of $20,000. At Grass Valley she disposed of the furniture and arranged for the sale of the property.[1] The faithful Periwinkle accompanied her. It was the last time they were to be together. The girl was soon to be married and would not leave California.

Late in October, from the deck of the steamer *Orizaba,* Lola caught her farewell glimpse of what was soon to be hailed as the wickedest city in the world.

Save for a brief tour of Albany, Providence and nearby New England cities, with Miriam Follin, Noel Follin's sister, Lola's career as an actress ended when she left California.² Soon after reaching New York, she sailed for Ireland, where, depressed and her health failing, she turned to religion for escape. Whether or not she embraced Catholicism is debatable, but there is evidence that she appeared on the lecture platform in Dublin, offering herself as a repentant sinner whom the Lord had saved from the burning. That these appearances in Ireland were in the nature of an experiment cannot be doubted, for a few weeks later she was touring England, giving a series of religious lectures, appearing on the podium in a classical white Greek gown that fell to the floor in folds. The curious paid their pittance to see this former symbol of unholy love who had turned to the Lord for salvation.

But the financial returns were a disappointment, and after five months of warring on sin, Lola returned to London and hid herself away in a furnished apartment near Hyde Park, where her friends kept in touch with her. But suddenly she disappeared. Months passed before she was heard from. Although no reliable evidence has been produced to confirm the tale, it had been said that during this period when her whereabouts were unknown, she was in Rome with ex-King Ludwig and that they were united in a morganatic marriage.

In November, 1859, she arrived in New York from England. She was greatly changed; her body had wasted away and her eyes had lost their old fire. When a lecture bureau secured a number of engagements for her, she left the city on a speaking tour, using the religious lecture she had given in England. In her weakened condition the strain was too much for her, and she appeared on the platform for the last time at the Melodeon in Boston in 1860. She did not have long to live. Using the name of Fanny Gibbons to avoid publicity, she settled in a boardinghouse in the Prospect Park section of Brooklyn. It was while she was living there that she suffered a stroke that paralyzed her left side and face. For weeks she was unable to speak. News of her condition and real identity reached the newspapers. Her melodramatic life was to remain melodramatic to the very end, for the newspaper stories brought a Mrs. Isaac Buchanan, the wife of a New York florist, to see her. As young girls, the two of them had attended the Montrose Seminary at Bath together. On the strength of that ancient association, Mrs. Buchanan promised Lola that she would take care of her, and a few weeks later had her moved into the Buchanan home. Far from suspecting the rapacity of the woman, Lola deeded over to her all that she possessed. A few days after the papers were signed, she was removed to a squalid tenement bedroom in the West Seventh Street district that was later known as Hell's Kitchen, where she died on January 17, 1861.

Forgotten, unknown, she lies in an unmarked grave in Brooklyn's Greenwood Cemetery.

The Washoe Seeress, Alias Queen of the Comstock

THE PHYSICAL ORDEALS and dangers women faced in crossing the High Plains in the 1840's has become epitomized in the pioneer journey of Narcissa Whitman, the young bride of Dr. Marcus Whitman, and Eliza Spaulding, the ailing wife of the Reverend Henry Spaulding. They were the first white women to travel over the Oregon Trail from Independence, Kansas, to the Columbia River. The fact that all four, and nine others as well, were massacred five years later in an uprising of the Cayuse Indians has given historical and dramatic importance to their Christian venture, but the fate that overtook them at the mission Wailatpu was quite apart from the day-to-day trials and mishaps that were their lot on the long trail west.

In Narcissa's diary and her many letters there are repeated references to Dr. Whitman's concern for the comfort of "we ladies." They rode sidesaddle for part of every day and when they tired, they transferred to the light Dearborn carriage which had been provided for them. They had tents of waterproof osnaburg sheeting to sleep in or provide shelter from the elements when it stormed.

These were niceties not enjoyed by the thousands of women who followed them up the long, jolting miles of the Platte and over the Shining Mountains, who either rode in a covered wagon or trudged along beside it with their menfolk. Many of them were pregnant when they started and many gave birth on the way.

Lacking medical attention when they fell ill, scores died and were buried beside the trail.

It should be remembered, too, that at first the Plains Indians— the Oglalla Sioux, Arapahoes and Northern Cheyennes—were content with running off the emigrants' livestock, but as they saw the ever-increasing streams of white men crossing their hunting grounds and making them untenable for the game on which they largely subsisted, they began attacking the wagon trains, spreading death and destruction. These atrocities reached their peak when in the gold rush to California in 1849-50, thousands of men, and a few women, headed westward over what came to be called the Overland Trail, which from the Missouri River to South Pass and the Continental Divide was identical with the Oregon Trail. Both trails, as far as Fort Laramie, were separated from the Mormon Road only by the width of the North Platte River.

Beginning in 1847, no fewer than twenty thousand women crossed the plains in the fifteen years that followed, some bound for Oregon, some for California, but the goal of the majority was the new Zion of the Mormons in Utah. The wonder is that so many of the latter survived the rigors of the great migration. Of those who had taken part in the forced exodus from Nauvoo, Illinois, whither the Latter-day Saints had fled after being driven out of Missouri, many were ill and all undernourished when they reached Winter Quarters (Council Bluffs) on the Missouri. And yet, after a few months of recuperation, sustained by their faith in the Infinite and spurred on by the driving force of Prophet Brigham Young, they marshaled their fortitude and went on.

But what they did was minimal compared to what was demanded of the several thousand female converts to Mormonism from the mill and colliery towns of England and Scotland who trudged every step of the way on foot from Iowa City to Salt Lake in the annual handcart expeditions that began in 1856. Not only did they walk the thousand miles or more across the plains and over the mountains, taking their place beside their husbands, but they dragged behind them the two-wheeled carts that held all their worldly goods. Remarkably, the great majority got through; but other hundreds died of exhaustion and starvation or froze to death in the snows and below zero temperatures in the early winter storms of Wyoming.

When the fortunate ones straggled into the new Zion on the shores of Great Salt Lake, they were received with rejoicing and a committee composed of the wives of elders and bishops organized to provide them with shelter and sustenance. Directing its efforts was the wife of Bishop Edward Hunter. Although he was a member of the church hierarchy, he was not yet a person of any importance. Nor was his wife who, after ten years of marriage, suffered from the ignominy of being childless, a seeming contravention of the unswerving edict that Mormons must multiply and spread their seed.

If she had not presented Bishop Hunter with a brood of young Mormons, it was not because of any conscious fault of her own, for she craved motherhood. That was just one of the many strange facets of her being that were to lead her to fame and fortune and make her so improbable. It is as Eilley Orrum, not as Mrs. Bishop Hunter, that she had her place in the grass roots history of the Comstock Lode.

In their village in the Highlands of Scotland, Eilley, her sister Betsy and the latter's husband had been converted to Mormonism, largely on the promise of the riches and wonders of America. As guests of the Perpetual Emmigration Fund established by the Church of Jesus Christ of Latter-day Saints, they sailed from Liverpool in company with several hundred other converts and reached Nauvoo in the summer of 1842. She was eighteen, buxom, red-haired and looking for a husband. She found one in then Elder Hunter. She considered herself fortunate, for Nauvoo had more marriageable females than eligible men.

Although the town had no commercial harlots, scandalous tales of adultery were frequent. They reached as high as Prophet Joseph Smith who, it was whispered, absolved himself from misconduct by performing secret plural marriages with the women he took to bed. In the end it led to his being murdered, along with his brother Hyrum, in the Carthage jail. The Book of Mormon had expressly forbidden polygamy, but on July 12, 1843, Prophet Smith had another revelation establishing and approving plural marriages.

This decree was not published, but it soon became widely known and aroused great indignation. It cost him the support of some of his staunchest adherents and drove them into exile and apostasy. Eventually it led to the expulsion of the Mormons from Illinois.

It brought matters to a head between Elder Hunter and Eilley. He expressed a desire to bring out several of his nieces from Philadelphia to live with them. Eilley put her foot down; she would not live under the same roof with what she called "my husband's concubines." After years of wrangling, he brought three of his alleged "nieces" to Salt Lake City and built a house for them. Enraged, Eilley went into another ward of the city and purchased a divorce from the presiding bishop. Free at last, she moved in with her sister Betsy and her husband and found employment in the store of Enoch Reese, selling calico and flannel, bonnets and sewing materials. In the store she came into daily contact with the Argonauts bound for California and listened to their tales. Eilley was sure something good would come of it, for she was convinced that she had the power of second sight and could predict the future.

One day a Yankee limped into the store to trade a plow for bacon and beans and a pair of blankets. Old Reese set out what he was willing to give. After a great amount of haggling a deal was made.

"You can afford to throw in a couple pair of shoelaces," said the stranger.

"Just one pair I'll give you," Reese growled.

"I'll throw in this," the other responded.

From his pocket he produced a glass crystal the size of a duck egg. Eilley gasped when she saw it, recognizing it for what it was —a peep-stone such as were common enough in Scotland. In it, a person with the gift for such things, could read the pattern of things to come.

"I want it," she told Enoch Reese. "I'll work a day without pay for it."

"It ain't worth a day's labor," he said, examining the bauble. "I wouldn't give ten cents for it, but if you say so, it's yours."

To Eilley it was nothing short of a gift of Providence miraculously given to her. In the days that followed she spent hours gazing into the depths of the peep-stone after warming it in her hands. In it she believed she saw a small lake nestling in a green meadow, with snow-capped mountains beyond. When Elder Orson Hyde returned to Zion from a long exploratory tour to the West and announced that it was his intention to establish a Mormon colony in a valley he had discovered at the foot of the eastern slope of the Sierra Nevada that Indians living there called Washoe, she did not doubt it was the very place she saw in her crystal.

She consulted it again and again. She easily persuaded herself that the specks of yellow she believed she saw in the peep-stone were streaks of gold in the gulches and hilltops. Surely it indicated that treasure was to be found there for the seeking. Any doubt of what she must do was quickly erased from her mind; when Elder Orson Hyde's expedition set out in the early spring for the Washoe Valley, she would go with it. She would need a husband to build a cabin and provide a living until the riches began to pour in.

With the practicality of a determined woman, she began looking around and settled on Alec Cowan, a quiet, self-effacing farmer. She had no difficulty in convincing him that they should join Elder Hyde's expedition. They sold the farm in the spring and when Hyde's train of twenty-one wagons set out from Salt Lake City, they were a part of it.

In January, 1854, the Territorial Legislature of Utah had created Carson County as a political subdivision embracing its westernmost fringes and named Orson Hyde probate judge, to preside over it. Johntown, the rag-tag tent settlement of Gentile and Mormon prospectors to which he led his little company, was a bitter disappointment to Eilley. Instead of the sparkling, swift-running stream she had seen in her peep-stone, here was only a sluggish creek, its waters befouled by the runoff from the rockers in which the miners washed their ore.

Elder Hyde announced that he was renaming the place Genoa. Eilley agreed that Genoa sounded better. But she wasn't interested. She told her subservient husband to drive on.

At the base of what was then Sun Mountain they came to Six-

Mile Canyon and the crude beginnings of the town of Gold Hill, which was to become almost as famous as Virginia City, the Queen City of the Comstock, the future site of which lay just over the rise to the north. Gold Hill had a tent saloon already, but no harlots. That was in its favor in Eilley's eyes.

"This might be a good place to work if not to live," Eilley told Alec. "After we get our crops in, we could come back here and open a boarding house to feed these men."

Following the direction they received, they went on, and toward evening she got her first glimpse of little Washoe Lake. It was just as she had imagined it would be—the shaggy green meadow surrounding the lake, hot and cold springs rising like fountains from the earth, the rugged mountain wall beyond with its gorges and gulches timbered with pine and cedar that marched all the way up to the lingering snow patches.

She and Alec walked off the half-section of land they had bought in their brief stop at Johntown. With frantic haste, for the season was getting late, a few acres of land were turned over and seed put in. When that had been done, logs were cut and a cabin began to take shape. He remarked how small it seemed.

"No matter," she said. "Someday I will build a mansion here of many rooms. With its gardens and fountains it will be fit for a queen."

And it came to pass—some years and another husband later. It still stands where she placed it. Its glory is gone and it has grown shabby, but it attracts hundreds, if not thousands, of visitors annually, a solid, two-story castle of dressed stone of Victorian architecture that, with furnishings, cost $250,000 to build and equip. Any Nevadan can direct you to the Bowers Mansion.

Before winter set in that year, Eilley opened her boarding house at Gold Hill in the cabin Alec had built for her. In addition she conducted a laundry service. Instead of trying to use the hard water in Six-Mile Canyon, she bundled her laundry into a wagon and drove to Washoe once a week and did her washing there.

Among her boarders were two young brothers, Hosea and Ethan Grosch. They were the only prospectors in Six-Mile Canyon who had any knowledge of mineralogy. Although much of their talk of fissures and strata was over her head, she was convinced that if anyone made a rich strike in Six-Mile Canyon, it would be the Grosch brothers. In the evening after the other men had left, they silently watched her as she gazed into the depths of her peep-stone in trancelike concentration. "I see the earth full of yellow to the north," she told them. "But there is blood on it. Be careful as you work further up the canyon."

This was just some of her hocus-pocus, but it was what they wanted to hear. If she saw any blood, it must have been the blood of Hosea and Ethan Grosch; both were to die of accidental wounds within the year. And yet—whether they were following their own hunches or Eilley's directions—it was along the last outcropping on which they worked that, a year later, Pat McLaughlin and Pete O'Reilly made the original strike on what was to become the world-famous Comstock Lode. Fifteen cents' worth of gold washed out of a panful of earth was enough to start it. Windy Henry (Old Pancake) Comstock, who was in the habit of claiming everything in sight, talked McLaughlin and O'Reilly out of a half-interest in their claim by insisting that they were trespassing on ground he had previously staked off.[1] In addition to McLaughlin, O'Reilly and Comstock, half a dozen men, including a young teamster named Sandy Bowers, took up claims adjacent to those that had belonged to the Grosch brothers. One of them, a man named Rogers, unable to pay his board bill, deeded over to Eilley his ten feet next to the Bowers claim. Not much, to be sure, but it might amount to something. Eilley consulted her peep-stone. She could see no streaks of gold, just a discouraging band of black.

A call came from Brother Brigham asking all Mormons to hasten back to Zion to defend the city against an impending attack by the army of the United States.[2] Alec pleaded that he must go. "If you do, you'll go alone," Eilley told him. "And don't try to come back to me when the trouble is over; I'll have no spineless fish for a husband."

Cowan took the wagons and livestock, but her release was cheap at the price. After waiting a respectable sixty days, she borrowed a mule and rode to Genoa where a new judge, a Gentile, was holding court. It did not take her long to convince him that she had been deserted and was entitled to a proper divorce.

She was now thirty-two and childless. There was still time, but not for another Bishop Hunter or Alec Cowan. It startled her to see in the clouded depths of her peep-stone the round, bearded face of her young boarder, Lemuel Sanford Bowers. He was eight years her junior and, like herself, a Scot. Believing as she did that the hand of Providence could be detected in everything that happened, she attached great significance to the fact that far up the canyon her claim and Sandy's adjoined. This had to be more than blind chance; they could so easily be made one. In her secret mind she began thinking of that happy union at the Bowers Mine.

Sandy was working up the gulch every day. He was doing as well as other men, but none of them were taking out more than six to eight dollars for a day's hard labor. All were complaining about the "damned black stuff" that clogged their rockers. They tossed it aside, not knowing what it was.

To cheer them up, Eilley gave her boarders a party. Sandy remained after the others had left and, made bold by the whisky he had consumed, he asked her to be his wife. They were married the following day. After spending a week in Washoe Valley, they returned to Gold Hill to find the camp in a lather of excitement. A rancher had sent some samples of the blue-black ore the miners were throwing away to Grass Valley, California, for assay. The ore proved to be sulfurets of silver, assaying as high as $4,790 a ton, along with a trifling bonus in gold. Judge Jim Walsh and lawyer Joe Woodworth, who were the first to hear the news, barely had time to pack a pair of mules and set out pell-mell for the new bonanza before half the population of Grass Valley and nearby Nevada City were on their heels, clogging the road to Placerville and Carson Valley. The great rush to Washoe that was to see thousands of Californians backtracking across the Sierra and would write a new page in the history of the mining West had begun.

In a matter of months Virginia City blossomed into the most important town between San Francisco and St. Louis. Gold Hill was not far behind. Money began rolling in on Sandy and Eilley—

streams of money that he despaired of counting. The Bowers Mine, the Mexican and the Ophir were the first great bonanzas. The Gould and Curry, Norcross, Crown Point and a dozen other fortune-producers were to follow. Eilley reminded her husband of the mansion she had promised she would build in Washoe Valley when the money was available. "Go ahead," he told her. "Hire contractors; get the best. We got money to throw at the birds."

She unfolded her plans to Mr. Dan DeQuille, the editor of the *Territorial Enterprise*. When his story appeared in print, it made a splash that delighted Eilley. She complained to him and his cub reporter, Sam Clemens (Mark Twain), about the harlots who were becoming so numerous. Tongue in cheek, DeQuille and Clemens agreed with her that prostitution was a social cancer and advised her to organize a campaign for its abolishment. They flattered her, however, by publishing her prognostications in their newspaper and knighted her with the title the Washoe Seeress.

These were rich, full days for Eilley. She organized the "good" women of Virginia City and continued her attacks on the bawds who were debauching their sons and husbands. Decency was her battle cry, but she temporarily detached herself from her crusade when she discovered that she was going to have a child. She went to Washoe to rest and relax and watch the masons laying the foundations of the mansion.

In due course a son was born to her, but he lived only a few weeks.[3] To bring her out of her despair, Sandy proposed a trip to (as he put it in his quaint way) "visit the Queen and the other great men of them countries." Naturally Eilley was delighted. It was fitting that the Queen of the Comstock, as some were calling her, should be visiting the Queen of England. Of course there would be a side trip to Scotland, and they would visit Paris and Rome. She could buy some old masters for the mansion and an assortment of rare bric-a-brac such as could not be found in San Francisco.

Julia Bulette—the Queen of Sporting Row

EILLEY and Sandy must go down in history as the two easiest marks that ever crossed the Atlantic. Naturally they didn't get to see Victoria or even Mr. Adams, the American ambassador. But tradesmen and shopkeepers welcomed them. In Scotland, at Eilley's birthplace, they awed the native with their assurance and largesse. They spent the Christmas season of 1861 in Paris, where they became the prize customers of the year. Couturiers, art dealers, jewelers, silversmiths, took them for what they so obviously were, a couple of stupid Americans loaded down with money. One day they did enjoy the satisfaction of seeing the Emperor Napoleon the Third driving by in the imperial coach, attended by outriders and a military escort.

What their European holiday cost Sandy and Eilley must be left to conjecture. It must have been a tremendous sum. Among the barrels and boxes that began arriving at the mansion after their return, there were only two items that had no price tag—ivy clippings from Westminster and broom plants from Scotland.

In their absence Virginia City had doubled in size. Seven twenty-stamp mills instead of two were now crushing ore, and their banging was a saga that went on night and day. The new International Hotel, six stories high and equipped with a steam elevator, gave the Virginia City skyline distinction. Carson Valley had succeeded in detaching itself from Utah and had taken its place in the firmament of the United States as Nevada Territory. Down at Carson

City, twenty miles away, its first governor, James W. Nye, was functioning from his rooms in the St. Charles Hotel until the new state house was ready for occupancy.

Eilley was thrilled by this pageant of progress and prosperity that was transforming what she regarded as *her* Washoe into a booming metropolis. But she was to discover that there were thorns among the roses that had an anesthetic effect on decency and morality.

Preparing for the welcome-home party that she and Sandy were giving, and to which only the "best" people were to be invited, made some shopping necessary. Eilley and her long-time friend Louisa Ellis were on C Street one afternoon and had just hurried past Piper's Opera House, in the lobby of which were displayed several large pictures of a voluptuous female clad in tights, named Adah Isaacs Menken, who was soon to play an engagement there, when a handsome, fashionably attired young woman stepped out of the millinery shop next door. Her bonnet was set at a rakish angle and from it trailed a long ostrich plume that was too scarlet to be virtuous. Her chin held high, she sailed past Eilley and Mrs. Ellis as though unaware of their existence.

"That," Louisa Ellis explained, "is Miss Julia Bulette, the Queen of Sporting Row."

The queen? Eilley refused to recognize that brand of royalty. "That whore," she predicted, drawing herself up in icy rejection, "will come to a bad end."

So the line of battle was drawn. But Eilley was to find that the enemy had become strongly entrenched. Instead of a few scattered shacks down the slope from C Street, the prostitutes of Virginia City now had all of D Street to themselves—two rows of white-washed cottages at the head of the street, the cheaper women in cribs below, farther down the Chinese, and at the bottom of the slope the Indian mahalies. And they had found a spokesman and champion in Julia Bulette, Virginia City's most famous courtesan. About her, as with other noted ladies of the evening, countless tales have found their way into print, most of them exaggerations and filled with misinformation. Many of them have become accepted as legendary, chiefly because so little is known about her

before her arrival in Virginia City that their originators were in
no danger of being called to account.

It has been said of Julia—without any evidence being produced
to prove it—that she was an escapee from the Barbary Coast,
which must be doubted, for she had none of the hardness that was
the trademark of other young women who had served their apprenticeship in that sink of iniquity. She is known to have been
one of the girls in a house of prostitution in Angels Camp, California. The record does not go back beyond that. That she was of
French origin by way of New Orleans has never been disputed.

One of the most repeated tales concerning her is that she was
a madam and regularly imported the fairest frails from San Francisco and Sacramento for her Virginia City establishment, which
was so sumptuous that the public named it "Julia's Castle." This
is sheer nonsense; Julia was never a madam and there was no
"Julia's Castle" unless the name was used facetiously by some of
her ardent admirers to designate her cottage on Sporting Row.

When she came over the Sierras to booming Virginia City, a
gay, laughing strumpet with a merry wit, in addition to her other
considerable charms, she took her place in one of the cribs down
the slope from C Street, no other accommodations being available
at the time for the town's scarlet sisters. She shortly became so
popular with the affluent masculine upper crust that due to her
urging, the meandering path was cut through and D Street formally
established; the twin rows of cabins were built and the old cribs
torn down and replaced with new.

It was a transformation that in Eilley's eyes was the work of
the devil. Going down D Street one morning in search of an Indian
washerwoman, she passed Julia's cottage and gaped in disgust at
the potted roses and geraniums in the windows—ten dollars a pot
at the florist's—and wondered how that Jezebel could afford them.
As a matter of fact there was very little that Julia could not afford.
Wells Fargo, silently discreet in such matters, could calculate her
progress by the increasing number of packages it delivered to her
door, the contents of which were hardly a mystery, seeing that
they came from San Francisco's most expensive furriers and Shreve
and Company, its leading diamond merchants.

Diamonds were for wearing, and Julia displayed them on her person in profusion—rings, bracelets, stomachers and sunbursts. Her admirers were all solvent and growing more so with every passing day. When one of them presented her with a team of prancing white trotters and a gleaming phaeton, the town smiled approvingly and wondered why someone had not thought to do it before. In the late afternoon it became a daily sight to see her tooling her fancy equipage up and down C Street, the common herd of drivers making way for her to pass.

Julia won semiofficial acclaim when she was elected a member of the Virginia City Engine Company Number One. The roaring town had no greater social éclat it could bestow. Behind closed doors the "good" women of Virginia City raged at their lords and masters for giving such recognition to what they dubbed that "vile Bulette creature." But Julia had her badge and provided herself with a uniform, one she felt was fitting for a female firefighter. She marched in all the company parades and responded to every alarm, which occurred with trying frequency in Virginia City, leaving her hospitable bed and customer of the moment whenever the fire bell sounded. When hot water invaded the main shaft of the Mascot Mine and work had to be abandoned, some wag promptly renamed it the "Julia mine"—the obvious allusion being that it was too hot to handle.

But the generosity of her admirers led to her untimely death. One morning the geraniums and roses, brought up from the "city" at some expense, were blooming as gaily as ever in her windows when her maid arrived for the day. In the bedroom she found Julia lying dead on her bed, her furs missing and her jewel cases empty.

The wives and mothers of Virginia City hailed her passing as a blessing and forbade their husbands to march in the funeral procession. But they did, several thousand of them. The story has often been told that one of the mourners, mounted on horseback, plunged through the rotten planking to a mine tunnel beneath the street but, uninjured, rejoined the procession several blocks further on.[1]

Mindful of the storm awaiting them at home, the members of

Virginia City Engine Company Number One met in solemn conclave and decided that although their late honorary member had been one of that class known as "fair but frail," she had always taken so great an interest in the fire department that it was fitting and proper for the company to bury her. And so, the following day, almost to a man, married and single, "the members put on their light blue greatcoats, with pearl buttons like desert lilies and huge manly flaps on their pockets, dusted off their tasseled silver bugles and marched behind the casket from church to cemetery." [2]

From behind their drawn Venetian blinds the "good" women watched from above the most solemn procession the Comstock had ever witnessed. Eilley, although sobered by the fulfillment of her prophecy, expressed no compassion for the dead. "Julia Bulette was an evil woman—a whore," she said with the condemnation of the righteous.

Armed posses took to the hills to kill or capture the man or men who had committed the crime. Three days later a gun battle took place in the salt marsh north of Walker Lake between three men and a sheriff's posse. One of the fugitives named Douglas was killed; a second man by the name of Dillon was mortally wounded. Before he died, he confessed that with his assistance the third man, John Millain, had strangled Julia to death. Her furs and diamonds had been disposed of in Virginia City a few hours after the crime was committed.

Millain—Jean Marie à Millain, a Frenchman who had been drifting around California for ten years—was brought to town and lodged in jail, charged with murder. His capture was openly regretted by many of the wives of Virginia City, Eilley among them, who regarded him as their savoir against such women as Julia Bulette.

The evidence against Millain left no doubt of his guilt. However, the trial dragged on, and as it did, the virtuous wives of Gold Hill and Virginia City deluged the prisoner with fried chicken, pies and assorted homemade delicacies, that his remaining days might be made easier. And then late one night, two weeks later, a rider arrived at the Bowers Mansion with word that Sandy was desperately ill in the cottage at Gold Hill, "where," the *Gold*

Hill News said later, "he has more or less lived for the past year, attending to his mill and the Bowers Mine."

Eilley was happy to learn how her husband had spent his days, but she could not help wondering where and how he had passed his nights.

Sandy breathed his last early on the morning of April 21, 1868. He was a Mason, and his remains were removed to the hall of Silver State Lodge, No. 1, F. and A. M., and lay in state for a day while Eilley arranged a noble funeral that she insisted should be more imposing than Julia Bulette's. On reaching the Ophir Grade, the procession disbanded and only a handful of mourners followed the body to Washoe, where Sandy was interred beside his long-departed infant children. Two days later John Millain was found guilty and sentenced to be hanged.

A scaffold was erected in a ravine on Sun Mountain just below the Geiger Grade, about a mile north of Virginia City. Word of the public hanging spread like the proverbial wildfire, and by noon on Friday, April 26, between three and four thousand spectators were on hand to enjoy the grisly holiday. The condemned man was brought up from his cell in a closed carriage, guarded by the sheriff and his deputies. On reaching the platform, Millain knelt and prayed with two priests. The black cap was pulled over his head and the rope adjusted. Thirteen minutes after he had plunged through the trap, he was pronounced dead. The crowd broke up and moved away, leaving behind it a litter of chicken bones, eggshells and sandwich wrappings. Julia Bulette had been satisfactorily avenged.

Eilley was not present. Poor Sandy was barely cold in his grave when she found herself involved in financial matters which she could not understand beyond the shattering knowledge that the Bowers Mine was no longer hers and that her beloved mansion was about to be taken away from her. With her opaque innocence and stubborn optimism, she had closed her mind to the persistent rumors that claimed the end of bonanza days on the Comstock were in sight; that such big producers as the Bowers Mine—which had netted a million dollars a year—were bringing ore to the surface that assayed a steadily diminishing percentage of high grade.

For the first time she learned that, as profits declined, Sandy had formed a company and sold stock in the Bowers Mine. He had invested the money in other mines, putting up the Bowers Mine and the Bowers Mansion as collateral against his loans. When the legal maneuverings were over, William Sharon, Nevada manager for the Bank of California and later its president, owned the Bowers Mine, and M. C. Lake, the rancher who had made a fortune out of his toll bridge across the Truckee River where Reno now stands, held a $10,000 lien on the mansion, which Eilley could not pay. Mr. Lake gave her the cottage at Washoe and a few acres of land on the shore of the lake; the villainous Mr. Sharon gave her nothing and was not interested in her prediction that in good time she would point the way to a greater bonanza than any the Comstock had known.

Although bewildered and impoverished, Eilley had the spunk to warn him that in her peep-stone she saw a swirling ball of fire on which his name was written. He waved her warning aside with a laugh and showed her to the door. Wealthy, she had been a person of some importance; penniless, she was a troublesome old bore. And yet, on April 7, 1869, fire swept through Sharon's Yellow Jacket Mine and raged unchecked for days, taking the lives of forty-five miners.

Eilley left Washoe and took up her residence in the cabin in Gold Hill where Sandy had died. It had a good address and she placed in the front window a sign:

The Washoe Seeress
Readings Without Appointment

Her charitable patrons always left something on the table before they took their leave. It helped to provide her with a living. In 1869, Mackay, Fair, O'Brien and Flood located the big bonanza she had predicted would be found. Mackay and his partners did not feel it incumbent on them to share their good fortune with her, so in the resulting tumult, with the Comstock booming as it never had in the past, she was overlooked and forgotten. With success now assured, Sharon and D. Ogden Mills, the millionaire

California banker, turned a thousand Chinese loose to hack out a roadbed for the fabulous Virginia and Truckee Railroad, connecting Carson City, Virginia City and Gold Hill by rail with Reno and San Francisco. With the completion of the V. and T., the Comstock enjoyed its gaudiest days. For many years the little Virginia and Truckee was to be the wealthiest and most profitable railroad in the United States, so busy that fifteen trains a day were necessary to transport the ore it carried to the mills. Its bright yellow passenger and baggage cars, its brass-trimmed locomotives were things of beauty and still arouse nostalgia in all railroad buffs.

The millionaires who rode up and down the road in comfort voiced their raucous approval when someone in authority—it could not have been Sharon or Mills, who had ice water in their veins— named its fanciest club car *Julia Bulette*. Eilley had returned to Washoe Lake. The trains passed directly in front of the mansion. She looked the other way when the *Julia Bulette* passed.

The Bowers Mansion stood empty for several years. It was of no use to its new owner. When Eilley approached him with the idea of renting the place and making it a picnic and day-excursion resort for lodge, Sunday school and union parties, he was agreeable. All the financial backing Eilley had was that of old friends. She hired two or three acquaintances to help her and, overcoming her aversion to drinking, installed a small bar in the former library.

The V. and T. obligingly stopped the excursion trains at her door. The crowds came and enjoyed the hot baths, the flowers and the goldfish in the pools. However, the operation did not pay and had to be abandoned.

The great fire of October 26, 1875, that destroyed Virginia City was the first of three catastrophes of the year. It was followed by the crash of the supposedly all-powerful Bank of California. Closely related was the panic that struck the Comstock. Ophir fell from $300 a share to $8. Eilley, despite the reverses she had suffered, hurled herself into the breach and, based on the information she received from her contacts in the spirit world, issued a stream of optimistic predictions and revelations. Miffed by the small amount of attention they aroused, she recklessly announced that by following the advice she had received from the world beyond, she could lead the way to a deposit of silver richer than anything the Lode had hitherto known.

She was not leaving herself an out this time, something she had never done before. Several gentlemen were interested enough to put her in a carriage and, following her directions, drove her two miles northwest of town, when she ordered the driver to stop. "The deposit lies in this long ravine below," she said, indicating the depression in which the idle Wells Fargo Mine was located. Claims were staked off, including fifteen hundred feet for her, and the necessary monuments erected. It is not of record that a glory hole was ever dug in the ravine to make the claims legal. The Washoe Seeress was further chagrined by the lack of confidence the community showed in her predictions.

Going to Reno, Eilley established herself as a professional clair-voyant. When her predictions came true, she made much of them; when they failed, she made excuses, as all good mediums soon learn to do. When business began to taper off, she went to San Francisco. The newspaper publicity she received brought her clients, among them Sarah Althea Hill, William Sharon's "rose," then suing him for divorce and a share of his immense fortune.

An opportunity to contribute in some way to the downfall of the wily Sharon who had done her out of the Bowers Mine called for a supreme effort on Eilley's part. She consulted her peep-stones, of which she now had six. Under the circumstances it was im-material to her that Sarah Althea was a siren and adventuress. It is unlikely, however, that the advice and revelations of the Washoe Seeress materially affected the course of the legal proceedings that followed. But Eilley thought so. She was in court every day and was delighted when the court ruled in Sarah Althea's favor and was likewise chagrined several months later when Justice Field reversed his decision and branded the alleged marriage contract fraudulent.

Sometime later Eilley returned to her toehold in Washoe Valley and lived alone in the cabin by the lake. She had long been a member of the Adah Chapter, Order of the Eastern Star, in Reno. The charitable sisters of that organization decided in 1901 that she would be safer and more comfortable in an Eastern Star home in California.

Eilley was seventy-seven when she entered the Home of the King's Daughters. The Comstock had come on lean years—the government had closed the Carson City Mint and the V. and T. was running only two through trains a day. But she was convinced that the decline was only temporary; that the Comstock would come back and that Virginia City would boom again. She even spoke vaguely of returning to Bowers Mansion. She was to come home to the Washoe in 1903, but not as she would have wished. On November 15, with snow already covering the hills, an honorary committee from Adah Chapter and former governor of Nevada, Jewett Adams, who had often been her benefactor, accompanied her ashes to the Washoe Valley and interred them beside Sandy and the children. She had outlived all but one or two of her contemporaries. She had played her part in the rise and fall of the great Lode and brought to it her ideas of elegance and gentility. That was all in the past now—along with Julia Bulette. The Washoe Seeress was dead and so was the Comstock.

Alias Madame Moustache

WHEN ONE OF JIM BIRCH's northbound Sacramento-Marysville stages pulled up at the Shasta House in Nevada City to discharge passengers, among the three or four who got down that April afternoon in 1854 was an exceedingly attractive, smartly attired young woman. The way she carried herself and the smiling dignity with which she met the stares of the male onlookers bespoke a cultured background. At the hotel desk, she signed the register: Madame Emma (Eleanora) Dumont, of New Orleans—which may or may not have been her true name. But she was undeniably French and very likely from New Orleans, from where the great majority of California's growing French population had come.

Identifying herself as Madame Dumont, rather than as Mademoiselle, raised some piquant questions, but Nevada City, with its ore mills, two newspapers and growing prosperity, beginning to regard itself as a sophisticated town rather than the brawling mining camp it had so recently been, put aside its questions and welcomed the new and charming arrival. It was to have good reason to congratulate itself on its wisdom. Madame Emma Dumont was to become a legend in the gold and silver camps in her lifetime and she still retains a prominent place in the galaxy of notorious women of the mining West, for she was the tragic and unforgettable Madame Moustache.

A tremendous amount of sensational nonsense has been written about her. Actually no one has produced any evidence to throw any light on who she was and what her background was before she arrived in Nevada City in 1854. She was an experienced and expert gambler was evident when she opened what she called a *vingt-et-un* (popularly known as twenty-one or blackjack) parlor. That was her only game, and throughout her career she played no other.

The novelty of playing against a "lady" dealer, and a pretty one at that, appealed to the miners who put their dust on the table. One declared that he "would rather lose to the Madame than win from someone else." She lost with a smile and won with a deprecating movement of her beautiful shoulders. The odds of the game being with the dealer, she won oftener than she lost.

She had been in Nevada City only a few weeks when she rented a place across the street from the hotel and proceeded to make it over to her taste, furnishing it with rugs on the plank floor and installing candle chandeliers. Over the front she had a modest blue-and-white sign placed, naming it the *Vingt-et-Un*. The establishment had an air of elegance about it. No women were allowed, nor was any rowdyism permitted. To those of her patrons who cared to indulge, she offered champagne—and it was "on the house."

Nevada City approved of the way she ran her establishment and conducted herself. She continued to live quietly at the Shasta House, her virtue questioned only by the cynics who refused to believe that a young woman as attractive as Emma Dumont did not have a man in her life. But that unknown stranger failed to put in an appearance.

It is generally agreed among old-time mining camp commentators, such as Thompson and West, that the sobriquet "Madame Moustache" did not come into use much before 1871, when Emma Dumont's face had coarsened and she had become a tragic figure, drifting from one camp to another. As a young woman, she had what was described as "blonde peach fuzz" on her upper lip which was not regarded as a disfigurement.

In 1855, Nevada City's gold production fell off drastically for the first time since the founding of the camp. It gave rise to the rumor that the diggings were worked out. That was not true, but it gave the town a warning that resulted in a tightening of the belt. The *Vingt-et-Un* felt it. Madame Dumont was considering closing up and moving on when Lucky Dan Tobin, a card sharp and professional gambler, temporarily footloose and looking for a spot in which to light, rolled into town. He looked the *Vingt-et-Un* over and liked what he saw, including the proprietor.

Tobin must have been a persuasive talker. The fair Emma was in trouble and needed help, so she listened. The following day the town learned that she and Tobin had joined forces. Tobin brought in poker tables, a keno outfit, chuck-a-luck and a faro-bank. Madame Dumont had made some stipulations, which he ignored. But there was one on which she was adamant: women were to be barred from the premises.

Over their liquor the cynics said that Tobin and the Madame were more than partners; that he was her long-awaited lover. They were mistaken; Tobin found his pleasure elsewhere and his partner remained aloof from the entanglements of sex.

With diversified entertainment to offer, the *Vingt-et-Un* became prosperous again. Nevada City experienced another boom, but this time it was the feast before the famine. In 1856, the partners closed up shop and went their separate ways. Tobin headed east—some say as far as New York—while Madame Dumont, a bird of passage, moved from one camp to another and finally established herself in Columbia, which after the great fire of 1857 that leveled it, became the most prosperous and hell-roaring town on the Mother Lode. The new town of brick and stone that replaced the one that had gone up in flames was so stoutly built that some of its storied buildings are occupied today. The builders had good reason for their optimism, for gold was close to the surface all around Columbia. In the late fifties and early sixties $87,000,000 worth of the yellow metal was mined within its corporate limits.

From what is still visible today, one can believe that Columbia was the most beautiful as well as the wealthiest of all California hill towns.[1] A multitude of stately trees, Lombardy poplars, locusts and weeping willows, recovering from the damage the fire had inflicted, gave the town a false air of tranquillity. On Broadway, its principal thoroughfare, there were two solid blocks of saloons, some of them extending all the way through to Main Street, which paralleled it in the rear. In every one there was a faro-bank or other games for separating the customer from his money.

Madame Dumont set up her *vingt-et-un* table in George Foster's City Hotel, where the food and the stock of wines and liquors were the best in town. Columbia could take anything in stride, even a lady gambler, but it went wild when John Strain dug up a nugget on Kennebec Hill on the outskirts of town that broke all known records. The group of exuberant miners who accompanied Strain to the Wells Fargo office gaped in silent amazement when Will Daegner, the express company agent, placed the nugget on his gold scales and announced that it weighed thirty pounds and was valued at $7,438.50.

In any town where men outnumbered women ten to one, prostitution was considered a necessary adjunct. Columbia was no exception to the rule. It was tolerant of its whores, but no one paid much attention to them as they came and went. Its twin diversions were whisky and gambling. With money so abundant, it followed that Madame Dumont prospered. In fact, it would appear that the year and a half she spent in Columbia was the most prosperous period in her life—or in that part of it of which there is any record. But it was a hard, aging life, an endless matching of wits with rough men, none of them saints, that had no compensations other than the money it produced. She sought to soften it by being generous to the unfortunate. How many miners she staked to a second chance in their quest for gold is unknown, but it occurred often enough to give rise to the comment in the saloons along Broadway that "the Madame is an easy touch."

Why she left Columbia and the prosperity she was enjoying there to join the great "rush to Washoe" in 1859-60 can be explained only as a reflection of the mass hysteria that sent thousands of men and women over the Sierra Nevada when the cry of "bonanza" was raised. It happened time after time whenever word of a rich new strike came winging over the mountains, whether in Nevada, Montana or elsewhere. People dropped whatever they were doing and on foot, horseback or wagon headed

Beautiful Ah Toy, the most famous of all the slave girls (prostitutes) of San Francisco's Chinatown, who became an importer of girls herself, amassed a fortune and returned to China to enjoy it. *(Courtesy Mercaldo Archives)*

Mammy Pleasant. From a photograph taken in 1901, when she had passed her eighty-fifth birthday. *(Courtesy San Francisco Examiner)*

1661 Octavia Street—the "House of Mystery." *(Courtesy San Francisco Examiner)*

Lola Montez, the Countess Landsfeld, Munich, 1848. From the command portrait by the noted German artist Wilhelm Kaulbach.

Eilley Orrum, shortly after her
marriage to Sandy Bowers.
*(Courtesy Nevada Historical
Society)*

Julia C. Bulette, the Courtesan
Queen of the Comstock.
*(Courtesy of the Mercaldo
Archives)*

The queen of the lady gamblers—Madame Eleanora Dumont, alias Madame Moustache. *(Courtesy Mercaldo Archives)*

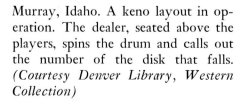

Madame Moustache dealing *vingt-et-un* at Pioche, Nevada, in 1861. *(Courtesy Harolds Club, Reno, Nevada)*

Murray, Idaho. A keno layout in operation. The dealer, seated above the players, spins the drum and calls out the number of the disk that falls. *(Courtesy Denver Library, Western Collection)*

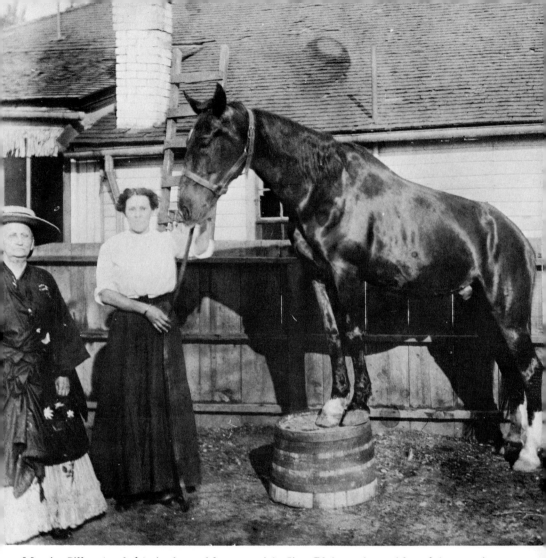

Mattie Silks (at left) in her old age, with Jim Blaine, the pride of her racing stable. *(Courtesy Denver Library, Western Collection)*

Deadwood, South Dakota, soon after its founding in 1875. Below, the booming gold camp a year later. *(Courtesy Mercaldo Archives)*

Jennie Rogers, the only madam who successfully contested Mattie Silks' claim to the title of Queen of Denver's Red Lights. An original painting. *(Courtesy of Mercaldo Archives.)*

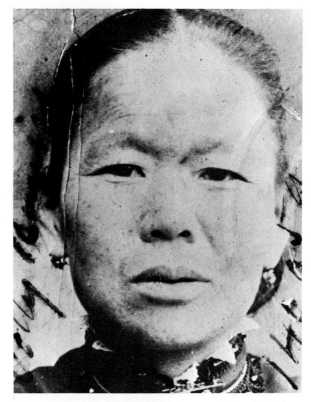

China Polly Bemis. The myth persists that as a young and beautiful slave girl she was the stake for which four gamblers played during the Salmon River gold rush. *(Courtesy Denver Library, Western Collection)*

Belle Starr, the Bandit Queen, and Blue Duck, her "husband" of the moment, who was killed a few weeks after this photograph was made. *(Courtesy Oklahoma Historical Society)*

Pearl Starr, Belle's daughter, at right, and two of the inmates of her Fort Smith bordello. *(Courtesy Oklahoma Historical Society)*

Poverty Gulch, the slum of Cripple Creek's tenderloin in 1894. *(Courtesy Library of Congress Collection)* Below, Meyers Avenue, Cripple Creek— where the girls were. *(Courtesy Denver Library, Western Collection)*

Horace A. Tabor, richest of the Silver Kings. *(Courtesy Denver Library, Western Collection)*

Augusta Tabor, the Silver King's discarded wife. *(Courtesy Denver Library, Western Collection)*

The young and beautiful Baby Doe Tabor. *(Courtesy Denver Library, Western Collection)*

Silver Dollar, the daughter of Horace A. Tabor and Baby Doe. *(Courtesy Denver Library, Western Collection)*

Harrison Avenue in Leadville, 1878. *(Courtesy Mercaldo Archives)*

Calamity Jane (Martha Jane Cannary)—a rare photograph. *(Courtesy of Mercaldo Archives)*

Jim Averell and Ella Watson, who were lynched on the Sweetwater, Wyoming, in 1889. *(Courtesy Mercaldo Archives)*

Annie "Pegleg" Morrow, heroine of Idaho's gold-rush days, who lost her feet from freezing when she and her companion were caught in a blizzard as they trudged over Bald Mountain from Atlanta to Rocky Bar. *(Courtesy Denver Public Library, Western Collection)*

Evelyn Hildegard, the original Diamond-tooth Lil, who was born Katie Prado, in Vienna, Austria, in 1882. *(Courtesy Mercaldo Archives)*

over the trails to the scene of the excitement. It was a phenomenon that continued into the twentieth century when—in the saline reaches of southern Nevada—Tonopah, Goldfield, Rhyolite and a dozen more ephemeral towns blossomed into the headlines. By then the rushing hordes were stampeding across the barren wastes in their Fords and Stanley Steamers.

The lurid, allegedly "true tales of the West," centering on the woman they identify as Madame Moustache, have very little to say about her in the year she was in Virginia City. Actually, nothing is known about her activities in the brief time she was on the Comstock. Presumably she was gambling, but while it was the custom for gambling establishments to insert a card (a small paid advertisement) in the columns of the *Enterprise*, her name does not appear. If she was a stranger in Virginia City, so was everyone else. Certainly she was not unknown to the hundreds of miners from Columbia, Nevada City and other California camps, who had preceded her across the Sierra, and with whom she had been popular. Why she seemingly made no impression on the town and left it unnoticed for greener fields in eastern Nevada remains a mystery.

The Comstock so overshadowed the less important mining districts of Nevada in the 1860's and 1870's that they have been largely ignored. They were strung out from west to east like pods on a pea vine—Austin, Eureka, Hamilton, Ely, Pioche, the wildest of them all, and half a dozen other camps that faded almost as quickly as they flowered.[2] Some of them have survived. Hamilton, the gaudiest, perched so high on Treasure Hill that it was often lost in the clouds when viewed from below, is gone, leaving nothing to remind the visitor that its population once numbered a boasted fifteen thousand and that it was the site of the greatest find of surface silver chloride the world has ever known.

But it was Pioche, a hundred miles across the wastelands to the southeast, that outdid them in the amount of wealth it produced and in the violence of its citizenry. Pioche was the center of a surrounding mining district. Disputes that began anywhere in the Ely Mountains were brought to town to be settled, and without benefit of law. There was constant strife, most of it due to accusations of claim jumping. Destroying another man's monuments and taking possession of the claim he had staked was not a common occurrence in other Nevada camps, nor is there any evidence that it was actually widespread at Pioche. But the suspicion that the big owners had banded together to drive the little fellows out by one means or another was there, and it was enough to keep the partisan feud burning. The situation was not helped when the Pioche Consolidated, the district's biggest producer, imported cheap Mexican labor to work its ore.

The *Pioche Record* noted Madame Emma Dumont's arrival in September, 1861, adding the information that "the noted lady gambler has engaged space in Handsome Jack McKnight's popular emporium and will be found there nightly from now on. If you enjoy a fast game of twenty-one, pay the little lady a visit."

Pioche was destined to become the turning point in Emma Dumont's life. Not since Columbia had she been so well received. The town was tougher than any she had known, but the men liked her, and in her presence they seemed to forget temporarily the violence that swirled about them. She had not been there long when the *Pioche Record* had occasion to mention her again. It related how she had run out into the street one night and confronted a mob of jobless miners who were on their way to wreak vengeance on the Mexicans who had replaced them. With her laughter and good sense she made them realize that their quarrel was with the owners of the Pioche Con, not with the Mexicans who had been brought in to replace them.

For years she had lived almost exclusively among men, and it might have been expected that she had learned how to judge them. She now proved that she had not, for she fell in love with Jack McKnight and married him. He was handsome, debonair, popular —and worthless. That she hoped to find peace and quiet and divorce herself from the life she had led for the past ten or more years is indicated in her purchase of a ranch "in eastern Nevada," according to that compendium of grass-roots history *Pioneer Nevada*, published in Reno in 1951. Unfortunately no further information is given regarding its exact location. The best ranching country in that part of the state was in White Pine County, particularly in the valley of the Shell Creek Range, so it may be presumed that it was there that she and McKnight settled down.

It was not to be for long. The isolation and pleasant monotony of ranch life that his wife found so satisfying did not appeal to McKnight. He had married her for her money, after convincing himself that she possessed a tidy fortune. Biding his time for some months, he got his hands on it in some manner and promptly deserted her. All she had left was the unimproved ranch, which was a liability rather than an asset.

Apparently she sold the ranch and, using the money as her grubstake, returned to her old trade of dealing vingt-et-un, moving on from one camp to the next as fortune dictated. Speaking of McKnight's desertion and treachery and the effect it had on her, Thomas Wilson, the editor of *Pioneer Nevada*, says:

"From the profound emotional shock, a change took place in the fortunes and appearance of Madame Moustache. Until then the records indicate she had a fresh, girl-like beauty and vivacity. Now her features coarsened, and a growth of dark hair, previously absent or virtually invisible, appeared on her upper lip, from which she derived the name of Madame Moustache.

"Her old light touch, and her skill as a gambler, seemed to desert her and she failed to rise from a grinding poverty that followed her from mining camp to camp. Hairy-faced, her features coarsened, and now in her late forties, she became an outstanding object of pity."

In summing up in this fashion, Mr. Wilson is covering a period of sixteen years. But Emma Dumont's slide downhill into obscurity was gradual. She was in Fort Benton, Montana, in 1866, three years after Jack McKnight robbed and deserted her, and she was far from being an object of pity during her stay there. Fort Benton, the head of navigation on the Missouri River, was booming. Gold had been discovered in quantity in Alder Gulch in June, 1863. Virginia City (Montana) had grown mushroomlike into a city of fifteen thousand. Fort Benton was the easiest and quickest way of reaching the Montana diggings. Once only a fur-trading post, it was now thinking of itself as the great inland seaport of America.

Some of this optimism was warranted. In 1863, after several years of trying, seven steamboats succeeded in making it all the way up the Missouri to Fort Benton; by 1865, the arrivals numbered forty. They arrived in the late spring in the season of high water and left on the return voyage to St. Louis several weeks later, or before the run-off from the melting snow in the mountains had passed and the river was dropping, a seasonal occurrence that annually made the upper reaches of the Missouri unnavigable.

In that year of 1865, 1,000 passengers, 6,000 tons of merchandise, and 20 quartz mills were received at Fort Benton. The ultimate destination of the newcomers and the mountains of freight piled up on the riverbank (the raw town had no levee or manmade landing as yet) was Virginia City and the Alder Gulch diggings. Freight was forwarded by bull teams; human beings got where they were going by being bounced around in one of Oliver and Company's stages (not Concords; they came later) for twenty-four hours, when the mud was not too deep. Anyone who wanted to eat on the journey brought his own food, for not so much as a cup of coffee could be purchased between Fort Benton and Virginia City. The fare was a modest $30.

As it was only a way station or port of entry for the hordes of men and women the steamboats were bringing up the Missouri, Fort Benton was shaped to suit the needs of transients. They had no money to spend on reaching Montana, and when they left several years later—the lucky ones, that is—they were too busy arranging passage downriver and putting their gold in the steamboat's strong room to have any time for whoring. As a consequence, although every other building on Front Street housed a combination saloon and gambling parlor, prostitution never flourished in Fort Benton.

The fanciful story is told that Emma Dumont did so poorly in Fort Benton that she turned from gambling to operating a bordello, offering herself to the trade along with her "girls." Although she was now fat and fortyish, drinking heavily and unquestionably going downhill, she retained the respect of the town, for when word was received that the steamboat *W. B. Dance* was coming up the Missouri with smallpox aboard, she led a group of men to the riverbank and at pistol point forbade the captain of the boat to land. Fort Benton had been scourged by smallpox on several occasions in its past. In the great epidemic of 1837, in fur-trading days, an estimated 6,000 Indians had died.

After a few tense minutes the captain of the *W. B. Dance* swung the wheel and the steamer retreated downriver to Cow Island, one hundred and thirty miles below, where it remained for four weeks, by which time the epidemic had disappeared.

For five years after she left Fort Benton, Madame Moustache—the name was beginning to have some publicity value—wandered from one Montana mining camp to another. In 1870, she was in Virginia City (Montana), dealing twenty-one in a Jackson Street gambling house. Later she was in Helena, the booming camp in Last Chance Gulch, far to the north. Of course by now she was merely chasing rainbows, satisfied to be earning enough to keep her supplied with brandy and to have a roof over her head. Whenever a new gold strike was rumored, she was ready to hit the trail.

She was in Bannack when word came over the mountains that a bonanza had been uncovered at Salmon, Idaho, on the other side of the Bitter Root Range, no more than twenty-five miles away as the crow flies but close to two hundred miles by way of Monida Pass, which was the only way of getting there. Although it was late spring, there was so much snow on the ground in the high places that coach travel was impossible. But Oliver and Company, always ready for such emergencies, provided the travelers with horse-drawn sleds and guaranteed to get its patrons through to Salmon. They did, despite frequent upsets that pitched the travelers into the snow and froze the marrow in their bones in the makeshift stations where they were forced to spend the night. But the pioneers from Bannack reached Salmon in time to stake claims along the Salmon River.

The Salmon River Mining District soon petered out. It was on to Lewiston for Emma Dumont, and from there to the Coeur d'Alenes. On and on—Murray, Eagle City, Idaho City—a dozen places. She had not been looking for gold or even modest riches for a long time. What kept her going was the hope that somewhere, sooner or later, she would cut Jack McKnight's trail. She was prepared for that moment, her pistol never being far from her hand. But as she went on, almost a penniless wanderer, it began to seem that the West was too big, too wide, for her.

In 1878 she was back in Nevada. Gamblers and bartenders who had known her in happier days befriended her. Some of them had known McKnight, but they couldn't tell her where she would find him. In Reno, an old-time barroom "professor" (piano player) whom she had known in her flush days in Columbia gave her a dollar and told her to get a "reading" from the Washoe Seeress. Eilley gazed into her peep-stones at length, but the best she could tell her caller was that her quest would end somewhere in California—which was taking in a generous amount of territory. Miraculously, it was to be fulfilled, but scarcely in the manner implied or in the way Emma Dumont interpreted it.

Bridgeport, the seat of Mono County, lies in a pleasant green valley crossed by sparkling creeks. With its Gothic courthouse and steepled church it is more typical of New England than California. Four miles to the south a weed-grown road takes off to the east. Fifteen miles on that now unused road brings you hard up against the Nevada line. There you will find what is left of "bold, bad Bodie of the 1860's and '70's," which, but for Wells Fargo's ancient vault and cellars filled with broken bottles and rusted iron doors, is nothing at all. Today Bodie is the ghostliest of all ghost towns.

No cow town or mining camp was ever tougher than Bodie or more boastful of its wickedness and horrendous number of homicides. Not to be outdone by the Comstock, the Esmeralda Mining District, which included Bodie and adjacent Aurora, claimed to have a population of 20,000. But mining statistics are always suspect, and there is no reason to believe that the true figure ever exceeded 12,000. By way of Sonora Pass, which was kept open most of the year, it was only a hundred and thirty miles to Sacramento. It gave the state capital such a vested interest in Bodie that the *Sacramento Union* stationed a permanent correspondent there and printed the latest tidings in every issue.

Wells Fargo records disclose that the express company suffered more from the depredations of road agents on the Bodie run than elsewhere. This was due to the fact that the Esmeralda District was shipping bullion rather than ore. Flowing over Sonora Pass, a stream of bottled luxuries and crated comestibles passed unmolested. With thirty saloons, ranging from such posh caravansaries as the Occidental and the Bodie House down to the groggeries where miners off duty congregated, with three breweries going full blast, Bodie was a bibulous town. With honest pride it could say that there were no delicacy a man could find in Virginia City that couldn't be found in Bodie. It couldn't brag about the quality of its whores, who were the overage castoffs of other camps, but with two newspapers and a railroad of its own, the little narrow-gauge Bodie and Benton which brought up timber for the mines from the low country to the east, it was self-sufficient.

How she got there does not appear on the record, but in September, 1879, Madame Moustache appeared in Bodie. From some unknown source she had garnered a little money. In the Grand Central she stepped up to the bar and sipped her brandy. Only a few of the old-timers remembered her. No one could tell her anything about Jack McKnight.

After a few days she disappeard from Bodie. On the morning of September 8, her dead body was found beside the road, two miles from town, an empty vial of poison clutched in her hand. She had taken the only escape left to her.

In its self-righteous hypocrisy Bodie buried its prostitutes in what was called the "outcasts cemetery." When it appeared that Madame Moustache would have to be buried at the county's expense and interred in the "outcasts cemetery," money was raised in the saloons and she was buried in consecrated ground farther up the hill.

Those pioneer Nevada historians, Thompson and West, append a fitting epitaph to her passing: "Let her many good qualities invoke leniency in criticising her failings."

—◦✦{ X }✦◦—

The Creole Belles and Some Others

THE FASHIONABLE COUPLE who came up the gangplank as the steamer lay at the levee in New Orleans were down on the passenger list as Mr. and Mrs. This-or-That, although their relationship had never been sanctified by the so-called holy bonds of matrimony. There were others on board whose status was the same as theirs, for in the golden age of steamboating, roughly from 1847 to 1870, it was the custom of wealthy Southern planters, bound up the Mississippi to St. Louis on business, to be accompanied by their mistresses.

Such *filles de joie* had no social standing ashore or afloat, but they had luxury as a pleasant and apparently satisfactory substitute. Almost without exception they possessed at least a veneer of culture and conducted themselves with decorum. And needless to say they were vivacious and remarkably attractive, with the flawless skin and classic features so common among young women born in Louisiana of white French ancestry and identified as Creoles.

Their presence on the grand packets may have contributed to the slanderous whispering in the North that the steamboats, no matter how big and luxurious, were nothing but floating bordellos. Unquestionably some of the steamboats carried prostitutes, who with admirable discretion plied their trade. Since the captain was usually the owner of his boat, it was he who decided whether to bar them or permit them aboard. A score of names come to mind of captains who would have no part of what one of them, Captain Samuel Rider, called "the whore trade." Captains E. W. Gould, W. J. Kountz and James Good were religious men and strict disciplinarians. Prostitutes and crooked gamblers found it unprofitable to ride their boats.

There were captains who viewed the presence of bawds on board in a different light. They contended that with the big packets engaging in costly competition with one another for the approval of the traveling public, which was 75 per cent male—five-piece orchestras, the finest wines and liquors and a table groaning with an assortment of delectable viands, the like of which was not to be found in any fashionable restaurant ashore—there was no point in denying them the additional "convenience" of a woman.

No courtesan could "work" a steamer for more than a trip or two without becoming known to its officers. If she was detected aboard a boat that did not tolerate her ancient trade, she was put ashore at the nearest landing. That happened frequently enough to acquaint the profession with which were the so-called "closed" boats and which were "open." It is inescapable that when these ladies of the evening boarded a steamer at New Orleans, it was after some arrangement had been made between the captain and them or through their pimps. Though he might deny it, and usually did, the captain was responsible for their presence, and it was he who restricted them to certain parts of the deck, assigned them to staterooms abaft the wheels, and compelled them to dine by themselves before the dining room doors were opened to their fellow passengers. Drunkenness and disorderly conduct automatically meant being put ashore at the next landing. It was a penalty that seldom had to be enforced. Having paid the full first-class fare to St. Louis, the river frails could not afford to be dumped along the way or gain the reputation of being troublemakers.

On the whole, their conduct must have been admirable. Captain Gould in his *History of River Navigation* mentions their "ladylike" deportment. "Families traveling together," he says, "were seldom aware that there were scarlet sisters among their fellow passengers."

There were never more than four and oftener only two or

three professional harlots on a boat. Travelers from the North, to whom the term Creole mistakenly meant a woman of mixed blood, referred to them as "Creole belles." Actually they were quadroons, the offspring of a mulatto and a white. They were tall, long-legged, graceful creatures possessing the beauty that in antebellum days became celebrated in the annual New Orleans Quadroon Ball. Judged by the standards of the times, they earned "big" money, and after a few years on the river they could have retired with a competence. But very few did, for while the steamboats on which they traveled up and down the river did not share in their earnings, invariably some man ashore did and, following a practice as old as prostitution itself, spent their money on some other woman.

When the railroads began reaching the Mississippi and its principal tributaries, the steamboats were confronted with competition they could not meet. It is generally agreed that the pageant of the packets reached its high point in 1870 in the famous race between the *Natchez* and the *Robert E. Lee*. But as the romance of the rivers began to fade, it had no immediate effect on such sinks of iniquity as Natchez Under the Hill and the red-light districts of New Orleans and Memphis. During the war, when the siege of Vicksburg was taking place, Union General Sherman, commanding at Memphis, in an effort to curtail the spreading of venereal disease among his troops, had deported several hundred whores by steamboat to the north. The Ohio River towns at which they were to be put ashore refused to permit them to land, and it was not until the steamer *Washington* reached Cincinnati that the consignment of tarts was landed. At Nashville, Brigadier General John D. Morgan gathered up a similar number of prostitutes for the same reason and deported them down the Cumberland River aboard the steamboat *Idaho*. The infuriated camp followers strenuously objected to being shipped away from their market, and for days they smashed furniture and crockery before they were finally subdued at gunpoint. But after the *Idaho* steamed up and down the Ohio for two months without being able to discharge its unwanted cargo, the order deporting the women was countermanded and the battered boat reluctantly returned them to Nashville.

Long before the War Between the States, the myth was widespread that there was something unduly attractive about the bawds of the Mississippi River towns. It was current when the big rush to the California gold fields occurred in 1849, and it was still being accepted as late as 1868, when Abilene, the first of the Kansas cow towns, really got going, and the "fair Cyprians," as Kansas newspapers made a practice of calling the harlots, came flocking in.

Actually the women that the steamboats brought up the Red River to Preston, Texas, in 1849 to intercept the thousands of gold seekers about to take off for California were the overage off-scourings of Natchez and other Mississippi River towns. They and the criminal scum that accompanied them—pimps, gamblers and cutthroats—turned quiet, frontier Preston into a deadfall where no man's life or property was safe.

Cowboys with money to spend were a new experience. The St. Louis underworld was quick to realize that the market for Texas cattle Joseph G. McCoy had opened at Abilene, Kansas, in 1867 presented it with a golden opportunity for its enrichment. Although the first herd had not reached Abilene until September 1, by the end of the season 35,000 head of Longhorns had been shipped out over the rails of the Kansas Pacific Railroad. With McCoy's idea a proven success, it was predicted that as many as 200,000 head would be shipped in 1868. That meant that there would be upward of two thousand cowboys coming up the Chisholm Trail who would be paid their wages in Abilene.

A word about the Texas cattle trade is necessary for the few who may be uninformed. At the conclusion of the War Between the States an estimated ten to twelve million Longhorns were running wild on the plains and in the brush country of Texas. Less than half of them were branded. They were next to worthless. Thousands were killed, but only for their hides and tallow. It was the custom for a group of men to go on what was called "a cow hunt," kill as many animals as they desired, strip the hides, render the tallow, and then cart the results of their toil to Corpus Christi or one of the Gulf ports to be shipped by boat to New Orleans for sale. After five to six weeks of waiting they could expect to receive payment in Yankee dollars, the return averaging out at about $3 a head for each animal killed.

It was miserable pay for the time and work involved, but there was very little "hard" money in Texas, and a dollar could be stretched a long way. With the economy of the Lone Star State in collapse, young McCoy reasoned that if he could provide a market in Kansas at which the Texans could be guaranteed a minimum of $15 a head for their cattle and up to $25 for first-grade beef steers, they would be eager to make the long drive north. Being a member of the firm of McCoy Brothers of Springfied, Illinois, cattle dealers doing a gross business of a million dollars a year, he was acquainted with the needs of meat packers and feed-lot operators in the Midwest and was confident they would flock to his Kansas market to buy cattle at such attractive prices.

McCoy was setting in motion a chain of events that were to change the face of Kansas and result in the greatest mass movement of cattle the world has ever known. Before it was all over and embargoes were placed against the entrance of Texas cattle into Kansas and Colorado, upward of two and a half million head of Longhorns, and half as many mustangs, had been trailed north. Millions of dollars had changed hands and 90 per cent of the money had been carried back to Texas. Kansas could point to a number of empty stockyards bleaching in the sun, and not much more; the cattle trade built no schools, churches or roads. That was left to the granger, the farmer, to do.

With the first sign of spring in 1868 an army of carpenters and laborers from St. Louis and Kansas City arrived in Abilene. The Kansas Pacific began dumping carloads of lumber beside its tracks. The place had no depot, no depot platform, just a signboard to indicate that it was Abilene. And now began a frantic sawing and hammering that went on day and night. The saloon interests and the vice lords of St. Louis—and they were closely allied—were gambling that Joseph McCoy's cattle market would line their pockets with gold.

The local citizenry, numbering not more than two hundred, gaped in wonderment as two parallel lines of flimsy eight-by-ten shanties were hastily knocked together and more substantial buildings began to take shape on what was to become Texas Street, the heart of cow-town Abilene. Jake Karatofsky, the ubiquitous frontier merchant, arrived with a carload of merchandise and opened his Great Western Store. McCoy himself was spending a small fortune building a hotel of eighty rooms, the Drovers' Cottage, soon to become famous as the finest caravansary on the prairies.

The first herds of 1868 were not expected before the end of June. Abilene was ready for them. A trainload of whores had moved into the cribs. They were a coarse, tough, belligerent lot. Painted and perfumed, they paraded about town in their finery, the mode of the moment requiring white kid tasseled boots. These provided a handy carrying place for a derringer, with which many went armed.

The spirit of adventure may have tempted some to quit their comparatively comfortable existence in the red-light district of St. Louis for the rigors of a raw cow town, but for many it was the bitter realization that they could no longer meet the competition of their younger and more attractive sisters that had set them adrift.

There was nothing glamorous about prostitution in a town where the sanitary niceties were limited to a washbowl. But Texas cowboys, denied the sight of a woman for three or four months and with money in their pockets, were not inclined to be critical. By mid-July, according to McCoy's estimate there were, between outfits arriving and those about to depart, upward of fifteen hundred to two thousand cowboys camped on the prairies surrounding Abilene. The town was as lawless as a town could be. It had no courthouse, no jail, a Town Board that could not enforce its dictums, and a deputy sheriff for marshal whose chief concern was to keep himself out of trouble.

In a town where there was no restraint and there was seldom a night that was not punctuated by gunfire, it was remarkable how few killings were recorded. If a cowboy was wounded, he usually could make his way out to where his outfit was camped. If he died, he was buried on the open prairie and his death was not reported. The first female killed in Abilene was a prostitute who called herself Louisville Lou (Luella Hines on the coroner's death certificate). The shooting was the culmination of a quarrel with another inmate of the cribs named Jenny Lyons, the trouble stemming from the dead woman's attempt to replace Jenny in the affections of one Quade Hill, a gambler who conducted a faro-bank in the Applejack Saloon.

There was an investigation of a sort in which it was disclosed that Louisville Lou had threatened to do Jenny bodily harm, so the inquisitors decided that the shooting was a clear case of self-defense. But that was not the end of it as far as Quade Hill was concerned, for it appeared that he had transferred his affection to the slain girl. To prove it, he gave Jenny a good slapping around and informed the lady that he was through with her.

Abilene had no dance halls, so the harlots did their hustling in the saloons. The Applejack was crowded a few nights later, when Jenny sauntered in and began using her trusty pistol. She was there to usher Mr. Hill into that same nebulous Valhalla to which she had dispatched Louisville Lou. But she had been drinking and her aim was so poor that Hill escaped the fusillade of shots without damage. However, she shattered two expensive back-bar mirrors and a hanging ormolu lamp before she was subdued.

The incident produced an unexpected semblance of authority, and it came from the saloonkeepers. Although they were bitter competitors, they could unite when their business was threatened. To prevent a recurrence of the trouble in the Applejack, they posted notices barring women from their premises. Their action was not popular, but they made it stick.

With the close of the shipping season in mid-October, stores and saloons were boarded up and a general exodus of the gamblers, pimps, saloonmen and whores occurred. The native population, now grown to five hundred, could venture outdoors without being confronted by a bunch of drunken cowboys firing their pistols as they raced their broncs up the street. It was to be a brief reprieve, for with the coming of spring another frantic rash of building began. More stones, saloons, a dance hall and a vaudeville theater were run up. Abilene had elected a town council and a mayor. They decided that the cribs would have to be moved to a new location north of town. That put them close to McCoy's home. It wasn't long before some wag nicknamed the new district "Mc-Coy's Addition."

When the Texans returned in 1869, they found that Abilene had built a small jail. Tom Sheran, the grocer, had been named town marshal. He was an inoffensive man and wanted no trouble with the Texans, but one of his deputies arrested two drunken cowboys and lodged them in jail. That night friends of the two men pulled the roof off the jail and freed them. Mayor Henry asked the St. Louis chief of police to send him two men who could maintain law and order. The two officers arrived. After looking the town over, they took the next train back to St. Louis. The country over, Abilene was deservedly winning the reputation of being the wickedest town in the United States. The Topeka *Commonwealth* commented in late summer, "At this writing, Hell is now in session in Abilene."

The year 1870 was notable in Abilene for two things. It produced in burly, soft-spoken Tom Smith, the ablest frontier town marshal the West has ever known, including those motion-picture and television dandies Wild Bill, the Earps and the Mastersons. Although he killed no one and went unarmed save for his fists, he brought law and order to Abilene.[1] Notable, too, in an unrelated way, was the arrival of the irrepressible Mattie Silks, then a young woman of perhaps twenty-three, whose boast it was until she died at the advanced age of eighty-one, "I never was a prostitute. I was a madam from the time I was nineteen years old, in Springfield, Missouri. I never worked for another madam. The girls who work for me are prostitutes, but I am and always have been a madame." She gave Abilene its first parlor house. Who put up the money for her establishment has never been disclosed. It was a large, square, two-story house of some elegance, its back yard screened from public gaze by a high board fence. It stood on the corner of Cedar and Texas streets, almost opposite the schoolhouse. Resplendent in its bright yellow paint, it was an object of speculation by the children, who quickly surmised the nature of the business that was conducted within.

Mattie's "house" was intended only for the élite or, in more practical language, for wealthy Texans. She furnished it in fashionable style, served only champagne, and her ten "boarders" were the youngest and most attractive Abilene had seen. Among them was a dark-eyed brunette named Jessie Hazel. Over her Phil Coe, the blond six-foot-four Texas gambler, and Wild Bill Hickok were to lock horns a few months later. "Two handsome, magnificent bulls," they have been called.

That summer Abilene was, as this writer described it some years ago, "an island in a sea of cattle." For the first time the number of cattle shipped climbed to 200,000 head. The season was over and the annual exodus of the sporting element had taken place, when the town was stunned by the killing of Marshal Tom Smith out on Chapman Creek, three miles east of Abilene. A settler named McConnell had quarreled with a neighbor and shot him to death, after which he and his friend Moses Miles had forted up in McConnell's dugout and refused to submit to arrest. Sheriff Cramer returned to town for help. Marshal Smith volunteered to go out to Chapman Creek with him and a deputy. At the last minute Sheriff Cramer manufactured an excuse for remaining in town, and Smith left Abilene accompanied only by Deputy Sheriff McDonald. At the first blast of gunfire from the dugout, McDonald turned and ran. Smith fought his way into the dugout, only to stagger out a few moments later, mortally wounded, Miles followed him out and finished him off with an ax.

McConnell and Miles fled and were pursued by a posse that captured them three days later. When tried for murder, they escaped the death penalty but were sentenced to long prison terms.

Although merchants and property owners had profited from the Texas cattle trade, rumblings against it were heard in Abilene that winter. Dickinson County was filling up with grangers and new and stringent herd and trespass laws were being put on the books, all aimed to curb the Texans. The grangers had the votes, and the judges that were elected were prejudiced in their favor. But while the pot simmered, nothing came of it.

With the coming of spring, the first order of business was to appoint a new town marshal. Wild Bill Hickok, recently marshal of Hays City, Kansas, which he had left hurriedly after killing two troopers stationed at nearby Fort Hays, had come to Abilene. He had a fearsome, dime-novel reputation as a scout, mankiller and expert pistoleer, dating back to the McCanles affair at the Rock

Creek Station on the Overland Express in 1861. On April 10, he was appointed to succeed the late Tom Smith.

It was evident almost at once that he did not intend to police the town as Smith had done. He made the Alamo Saloon his head-quarters. Through its plate-glass doors he could observe what went on along Texas Street and, other than his nightly stroll up and down the length of that thoroughfare of violence, let his two deputies do his legwork. As the Texans began arriving, he made no effort to enforce the "no gun" law that Tom Smith had made the town obey.

It was a new and resplendent Hickok who, with his back to the wall, ran his restless eyes over Texas Street from his comfortable chair in the Alamo Saloon. He had shed his fringed buckskins and replaced them with a frock coat, ruffled shirt, string tie and red sash. With his blond hair falling to his shoulders, he was the Beau Brummell of Texas Street. Not being a fool, he realized that he was in greater danger of being cut down by some rash young punk, eager to make his own reputation, than by an experienced gunfighter against whom he could be on guard. There were a number of the latter in Abilene, including Wes Hardin, the young Texan who claimed that the score of "credits" on his gun had been honestly earned. And there was five-foot-six Ben Thompson, he of "the great inky black mustache, a gunslinger second to none that Texas ever produced," as Eugene Cunningham described him long ago. Thompson and Phil Coe were partners in the Bull's Head Saloon. Having such a partner may explain why Coe never found it necessary to go armed.

Hickok may have had some value as a tourist attraction, but when Susanna Moor stepped down from a westbound train, it was not as a tourist. She was an old flame of Hickok's. Over her he had shot and killed Dave Tutt in Springfield, Missouri, in 1865. If Susanna had come to Abilene hoping that she and Bill might resume where they had left off, he disillusioned her; his current romantic interest was centered in Jessie Hazel, Mattie Silks' star "boarder."

Hickok believed he had the inside track with her. But she was playing fast and loose with him; her real heart throb was handsome Phil Coe. The situation boiled over one afternoon when Mike Williams, the special policeman at the Novelty Theater, whispered in Hickok's ear that Jessie and Coe were spending an hour together in the wine room of the Gulf House, a block up Texas Street from the Alamo and across from Coe and Thompson's saloon. Bill rushed in on the lovers and found the fair Jessie in Coe's arms. The latter leaped to his feet and for a moment the two men stood glowering at each other like two rutting bulls.

If Phil Coe went unarmed, he could use his fists. Blows were struck, but it could not have been much of a fight, for as Hickok reeled backward, Ben Thompson and Bud Cotton, another friend of Coe, rushed in and separated the two men. No shots were fired. But threats were made and they may explain what occurred at the end of the shipping season. Coe heaped further indignity on Wild Bill by taking the lovely Jessie out of Mattie Silks' bordello and establishing her in his cabin as his exclusive property.

The Marshal's regrets over losing Jessie Hazel were dissipated when Lake's Olympiad and Mammoth Circus arrived in Abilene in mid-July. Alice Thatcher Lake, the famous equestrienne and animal trainer, was not only its star performer but since the death of her husband, Bill Lake, its owner. She appears to have taken Hickok's eye at once. She was a buxom forty, six years older than he, but had a voluptuous figure which was displayed to advantage in tights. He helped her select a site on which to pitch her tent, and during the week attended every performance, ostensibly to maintain order.

There is little doubt that she was as much smitten with him as he with her. As Charles Gross, one of the town's local historians, wrote in the Abilene *Chronicle* some time later: "She fell for him hook, line and sinker, all the way to the basement and wanted to marry him and make him manager of her circus." Very likely it was Alice Lake who first implanted in Hickok's mind thoughts of a career in the arena and on the stage. He resisted the temptation and, when the circus left town for its next engagement in Topeka, he did not accompany it.[2]

From the Kansas line north, the number of fines levied against trail drivers for damages, real or fancied, caused by their herds—

trampling growing crops and knocking down fences—had tripled. By the end of August the trail drivers were being confronted by armed groups of grangers who were making them detour to the west. Despite all these difficulties, it was apparent by the first of October that it was to be the greatest year in Abilene's history.[3] In Abilene itself the uproar against the violence and obscenity of the cattle trade could not be silenced. McCoy could not believe that his market was finished. But it was, and any doubt of it vanished when the Kansas Pacific Railroad dispatched a corps of engineers to lay out a trail from Pond Creek Ranch, below the Kansas line, directly to Ellsworth, fifty-nine miles west of Abilene. It clipped thirty-five miles off the old route, which was equivalent to three days' driving.

The annual exodus began, as had those that preceded it; the girls from the cribs gathered up their personal effects and, with a collection of pimps, gamblers and underworld hangers-on, departed for the East. But there the similarity ended. Mattie Silks crated up her expensive furniture and "art" collection and shipped it to Ellsworth; saloonkeepers packed their fixtures and potables and had them freighted to the same destination. Regretfully, it seems, the *Chronicle* commented: "Abilene is painfully quiet."

Phil Coe had taken time by the forelock and dispatched his Jezebel to St. Louis, well-supplied with money. She was to remain there until he was able to tell her where to meet him. It was a promised rendezvous that he was not going to be able to keep. Ben Thompson was already on his way back to Texas, via Kansas City, with his wife, having instructed his partner to dispose of the Bull's Head for whatever it would bring. Whether Coe sold the place to Tom Sheran or not is disputed.

Coe had arranged to ride back to Texas with a score of his friends. On their last night, October 5, they were in town for a final spree before leaving. Coe joined them and, as was not his custom, he was armed. They soon got out of hand, yelling and trooping from one of the saloons that were still open for business to the next. Hickok came through the back door of the Alamo and from inside the front plate-glass doors had them in view most of the time.

There are two versions of what followed—pro-Hickok and anti-Hickok. Both are prejudiced and as irreconcilable today as they were in 1871. But the provable facts add no luster to Wild Bill's reputation as the Prince of the Pistoleers, the man with ice water in his veins who, it is said without justification, "tamed Abilene"— an honor that belongs to Marshal Thomas Smith.

Unquestionably the Texans knew that the man they had nick-named the "pimp marshal" was watching them. To bait him into tak-ing some action, a shot was fired into the air. Hickok bounced out and confronted Phil Coe, who acknowledged having fired the shot at—as he said—a stray dog, which brought a loud guffaw from his friends.

The two giants stood facing each other, eight feet apart. At that moment it would have been strange if Hickok's thoughts had not gone winging back to the afternoon in the Gulf House when he had caught Coe with Jessie Hazel in his arms and Coe had struck him. Believably, to have been shamed over a whore must have left its sting. Suddenly the two men began firing, Hickok with a .44 caliber derringer in each hand. His first shot struck Coe in the abdomen, inflicting a mortal wound. Altogether he must have fired four or five times, for several of the Texans were slightly wounded. When Hickok saw an armed man come running around the corner, he whirled and killed him, not realizing that it was his friend Mike Williams, the special policeman, coming to his aid.

Coe fired twice, one slug passing between Wild Bill's legs and the second plowing into the door frame at his right elbow.

Phil Coe died two days later. His friend Bud Cotton took the body to Texas for burial. He (Coe) and Mike Williams were the only men Wild Bill killed in his tenure as marshal of Abilene, and that ended on December 13, when the Town Council discharged him "for the reason that the city is no longer in need of his ser-vices." There was no word of commendation, no thanks expressed for what he had accomplished in the eight months less two days that he he had served.

As though to prove that vice and violence had been permanently routed, Abilene tore down the several hundred empty cribs out on the prairie, and eager hands carted the lumber away to serve— hopefully—more moral purposes.

Scarlet Sisters of the Cow Towns

"If it [prostitution] can't be routed out, the vicious vocation should be made to contribute to the expense of maintaining law and order."

Thus spoke the Ellsworth *Reporter* in May of 1873. For the past year the hard-hitting, independent semiweekly *Reporter* had successfully spearheaded a campaign to control the excesses of the Texas cattle trade. Saloons had been put under a heavy license fee of $500, in addition to the federal excise tax of $25 and a local business tax of $10. As a result, Ellsworth was forced to get along with only thirteen saloons. A tax was put on gamblers and, as a further safeguard, prostitution was confined to a district half a mile from the center of town down in the Smoky Hill River bottoms, which some unknown savant in such matters had named Nauchville. Now the *Reporter* was demanding that the whores be taxed. Backed by Arthur Larkin, Ellsworth's leading merchant, and other prominent citizens, the city council enacted the suggestion into law.

The money collected from such licensing and fines amounted to more than all municipal expenses. It led the caustic Topeka *Commonwealth* to comment: "The city [Ellsworth] realizes $300 per month from prostitution fines alone. . . . The city authorities consider that as long as mankind is depraved and Texas cattle herders exist, there will be a demand and necessity for prostitutes, and that as long as prostitutes are bound to dwell in Ellsworth it is better for the respectable portion of society to hold prostitutes under restraint of law."

Nauchville had its own saloons, gambling joints and a half-mile race track. Ellsworth made no attempt to police the district, contending that no man wandered into it by mistake; if that was where he wanted to be, he was on his own.

Mattie Silks tried to crack the ban against conducting a bagnio on South Main Street in what Nauchville called "uptown." When she failed, she built a house down in the district. But she was too elegant for it, and before the season closed, she packed up and went on to Dodge City. Her departure left Lizzie Palmer the undisputed queen of Nauchville. Lizzie was an aging, hard-bitten ex-St. Louis whore. Her "strong man" was Mike Donovan, a gambler. He had put up the money for her ten-room bagnio. Her broads were a tough lot, no better than the women in the cheaper cribs. One of her better known girls was the much-traveled Molly Brenan, who was in bed with Bat Masterson one night in the spring of 1876 in what was then Sweetwater, Texas, and later renamed Mobeetie, down in the Texas Panhandle, when the Army's "bad boy," Sergeant King, burst in on them and lamed Bat with a bullet below his right knee.[1]

Shootings, stabbings and other forms of mayhem were a nightly occurrence in the district, but the killings took place "uptown," in the continuing feud between the Texans and the police. Ellsworth had a force of five men, aided when necessary by the sheriff and his deputy. The five policemen were corrupt and ran the town for their own profit. Late in August word spread among the Texans that the leaders of their faction were to be deported. Ben Thompson was in Ellsworth. He knew that his name would head the list. He left for Kansas City at once and advised his friends Cad Pierce, Neil Cain and John Good to leave with him. They refused.[2] The following afternoon they stopped Marshal Hogue on the street and questioned him about a list of men marked for deportation. Hogue denied that such a list existed. Patrolman Ed Crawford came along and got into the argument. Eyewitnesses testified that when Cad Pierce put his hand to his back (he was not armed), Crawford drew and fired, the bullet striking Pierce in the left side. Pierce then ran into Beebe's store, Crawford following him and firing again.

Cad Pierce lived only a few minutes. His killing was described on all sides as cold-blooded murder. And now it was Crawford, not the Texans, who fled from town. Policeman Happy Jack Morco left with him. They went no further than Salina, thirty miles to the east. To still the rising clamor, the city council fired Crawford and Morco and appointed J. C. (Charlie) Brown and John DeLong to take their place. Dick Freebourne was named city marshal in place of Ed Hogue.

The new men were a great improvement on the old, especially Charlie Brown. He was cut to the same pattern as Marshal Tom Smith of Abilene—strict, fair and incorruptible.

The taunt that he had been run out of Ellsworth and was afraid to go back was too much for Happy Jack Morco. Grabbing a freight train, he arrived in Ellsworth in time for breakfast and afterwards was parading South Main Street, armed but causing no trouble, when Brown encountered him and ordered him to give up his gun. Instead of complying, Happy Jack started to draw. Brown beat him to it and killed him with a bullet in the heart.

Ed Crawford waited until he believed the Texans were gone before he ventured back to Ellsworth. Several nights after his return he went down to Lizzie Palmer's house in Nauchville. As Crawford stepped inside he was confronted by four young Texans, among them the two Putnam brothers, Sam and Oliver, brothers-in-law of Cad Pierce. As Crawford turned back to the door, he was riddled with lead. It was never learned who killed him, but it was generally believed that it was the Putnams, to avenge the killing of Cad.

Ellsworth called it good riddance. As a cattle market, 1873 was the only profitable year it enjoyed, and it was not a full year at that. The panic of 1873 was sweeping the country and cattle prices were plummeting. There was a second reason. Sixty miles to the south of the Kansas, Pacific and roughly paralleling it the Atchison, Topeka and Sante Fe Railroad had been building westward across Kansas in a frantic race with time to reach the New Mexican line to claim the federal and state land grants that would enable it to satisfy its clamoring bondholders. In 1871 the railroad had reached the Newton prairies. A signboard was put up here to designate the place Newton and name it a division point, which it still is. There were no facilities there for handling cattle, but by the end of the season Newton had shipped forty thousand head, all weaned away from herds that had been bound for Ellsworth. The figures for 1872 were much greater. But that was all; before the season of 1873 arrived, Newton was finished as a shipping point; the infant Wichita and Southwestern Railroad (twenty-odd miles) had been completed between Newton and Wichita. Although incorporated by Wichita men, it was obviously a Santa Fe subsidiary. The myth that it was locally owned had been employed by the promoters to insure the passage of a $700,000 bond issue for building it.

Although Newton's star had set so soon after rising, even before the tall grass on Main Street had been chewed to mud, the town had compiled a history for depravity and bloodletting un-equaled by its rivals. "Bloody Newton" was the cry that echoed across Kansas. "Another killing in Newton" became almost a standing "head" with some newspapers. How many men met a violent death in Newton is not known. In the volume devoted to Kansas in the American Guide Series, the number is placed at fifty. R. W. Muse, in his *History of Harvey County*, accounts for only twelve. A tabulation of the available evidence shows that at least twenty-five men were killed—five of them on the night of August 19, 1872, in a gun battle in Perry Tuttle's dance hall in "Hide Park," the town's red-light district several blocks from the heart of Newton. This was the bloodiest twenty minutes in cow-town history.

"Hide Park" was exactly what the name implies, a collection of several hundred white, Negro and Mexican bawds culled from the lowest strata of whoredom. When not otherwise employed, they hustled drinks in Ed Krum's dance hall or the more popular establishment conducted by Perry Tuttle. They received brass checks for the liquor they induced their companions of the mo-ment to buy. This is the first recorded instance of the brass check being used in the cow towns, although it had long been the practice in the melodeons and cowyards of the Barbary Coast. It spread to hurdy-gurdy saloons all over the West. Later, in Denver, some madams gave their "boarders" a brass check every time they ascended the stairs with a customer. When the night was over, the checks were redeemed for cash. It did away with much tiresome bookkeeping.

When Newton faded, the next stop on the trail to which the bawds of "Hide Park" were committed was Delano, the wild, lawless settlement that sprang up across the Arkansas River from Wichita. Not being within the town limits, it had no law, other than the shadowy government of Sedgwick County, nor did it want any. Being on the side of the river on which the bed grounds for all herds coming up from Texas were located gave the vice lords of Delano first crack at a constantly changing army of cowboys.

Usually cattle had to be held from three or four days to a week before they were driven across the Arkansas to the stockyards in Wichita, with the crew not being paid off until the herd was put aboard the cars.[3] As a consequence most of the Texans were strapped for cash while they waited on Cowskin, Gypsum or one of the other creeks for their turn at the shipping pens. They spent what they had. When their money was gone, Rowdy Joe Lowe and Red Beard, the rival kingpins of Delano, and their followers, had no further immediate interest in them. Being strictly hard cash men, no one meant less to them than a cowboy without money in his pocket.

Between Rowdy Joe Lowe and his rival Red Beard there was an implacable enmity that only the death of the other could satisfy. Their dance hall saloons were but a few yards apart, the upper floor of each being divided into cubicles in which the bawds employed by the two establishments plied their trade. When one of Rowdy Joe's girls committed suicide by taking an overdose of morphine, he had her buried without ceremony in back of his place. Months later a woman died in Beard's place. Whether to shame Rowdy Joe or because there was some human compassion in his make-up, Beard had her buried in a Wichita cemetery.

Beard was an educated man and ordinarily well-behaved; Lowe was a squat, ignorant, black-haired tough with a bullet-shaped head. When he was in his cups, he was a wild man. The only person who could control him in his drunken rages was his wife, Kate. It was well-known that he had killed Jim Sweet, a gambler, in Newton in the fall of 1871, and was reputed to have killed several others. Among Texans his place in Delano was known as "the swiftest joint in Kansas." During the trail-driving season its receipts seldom fell below a thousand dollars a week.

Joe Lowe can be dismissed as no more than the typical illiterate, supercharged and successful thug. Kate was something else. She was a small, handsome woman with traces of an education. Although the sobriquet of Rowdy Kate was fastened on her, she was not rowdy, just cold and hard. Living in an atmosphere impregnated with vice, violence and depravity, partly of her own making, she seemed immune to it and was unquestionably a virtuous wife.

From its inception as a shipping point, it was obvious that Wichita meant to be different from the cow towns that had preceded it. It embraced the cattle trade with open arms and convinced the Texans that in Wichita the Longhorn was to be king. The City Commission designated Douglas Avenue, the town's principal street, as the thoroughfare by which cattle coming off the bridge were to be driven to the shipping pens. It meant that 2,500 head of Longhorns would be passing every day, but no one registered a complaint against the clouds of dust they kicked up, the incessant bellowing, the accompanying profanity, or the accidental knocking down of a post that supported a wooden awning along the way.

At all the principal entrances into town, signs were posted reading:

> Everything goes in Wichita. Leave your revolvers at Police Headquarters, and get a check. Carrying concealed weapons strictly forbidden.

A carnival spirit pervaded Wichita. The town grew rapidly— half a dozen hotels, two theaters, a multiplicity of big stores. The hub of the town was the intersection of Main Street and Douglas Avenue. There, on the northwest corner, Whitey Rupp, the Kansas

City gambler, built his two-story gambling casino, the famous Keno House, where all games of chance were played. Perched on its upper balcony, the brass band he imported tootled from midday to midnight. By the end of the 1873 season Wichita had thirty-one licensed saloons.

It was all very gay. Cattle prices were up again, and it was estimated that upward of 400,000 head of Longhorns reached Sedgwick County before the end of the shipping for 1874.

If it was a woman a man wanted, he did not have to go more than two blocks from Douglas Avenue to find one. Wichita's "line" was located on Water Street, a score of brothels rubbing shoulders all the way down to Emil Warner's beer garden. The house at Number 33 did not rate comparison with the elegant establishment of Miss Dixie Lee, Wichita's most popular madam, but it deserves a word or two in passing, for it was the establishment of Bessie Earp, the wife of Jim Earp, the elder brother of the much-publicized Wyatt Earp. Jim was employed as a bartender in Ab Pryor's saloon, next door to the Keno House, which put him in position to steer customers to Number 33. Though he tells it differently, Wyatt sought refuge in Bessie's place on the night that Manning Clements and his three brothers (cousins of Wes Hardin and just as tough) were gunning for him.

Soon after the close of the War Between the States the most popular alias adopted by the women of the red lights was Dixie Lee. It was not because so many of the soiled doves had been followers of the Lost Cause; rather it was because Dixie and Lee (Robert E.) were the two most romantic names to come out of the great struggle. When Wichita's Dixie Lee died in 1875 of what used to be called "galloping consumption," she was twenty-seven or older, which indicated that she had not been born Dixie Lee. She left a considerable estate, exaggerated estimates running from fifty to a hundred thousand dollars. A long search ensued for her heirs. Lawyers finally located her father, a country minister in southern Missouri. He was shocked on learning how his daughter had amassed her fortune. But he took the money, which led the caustic Whitey Rupp to observe that "the wages of sin are a damned sight better than the wages of virtue."

The toughest dive on Water Street was conducted by Mag Woods. She was arrested innumerable times and fined for conducting a disorderly house. Her husband, George Woods, an unsavory saloon character and two-bit gambler, ran her errands and did her bidding. Mag—coarse, pugnacious, hard as nails—might have been a transplant from a Barbary Coast cowyard. The success she enjoyed in Wichita was as nothing compared to the splash she made five years later when she moved down to Caldwell, the so-called Border Queen, which almost straddled the Kansas-Indian Territory line. There her combination, saloon, dance hall and bordello, appropriately named the Red Light, with its killings and depravity became as notorious as Rowdy Joe Lowe's Delano deadfall had been.

The previously mentioned feud between Rowdy Joe and his competitor Red Beard came to a head on October 27, 1873. "Beard was in his dance house, indulging in a drunken frolic with a group of his Delano friends, when it occurred to him that it would be a good idea to step next door and break up the festivities in progress in Rowdy Joe's place. For some inexplicable reason Red disdained the sawed-off shotgun he had carried for months and led the way armed only with a pistol.

"The fiddlers were sawing away and a dozen couples were dancing when Red and his friends burst in. Whether by accident or design, he fired into the crowd. The bullet struck one of Rowdy Joe's girls and she ran screaming to the rear of the building. The musicians scattered, and so did the other girls. Rowdy Joe and a half dozen of his stalwarts rushed up to do battle. In a moment the shooting became general, revolvers and shotguns being brought into play."

The foregoing was written by the author in 1960 and accurately describes what took place. When the shooting was over, it was remarkable that so many of the combatants were still alive. Red Beard and his friend Bill Anderson were dead and two other attackers wounded. Rowdy Joe had been shot in the back of the neck, the slug not doing any serious damage. Two of his friends needed a doctor's attention, as did the strumpet who had been shot by Beard.

Rowdy Joe crossed the bridge in the morning and surrendered himself to John Meagher, the sheriff of Sedgwick County.[4] Bail was set at $2,000 but Lowe was never prosecuted.

In response to the hue and cry being raised throughout Kansas for legislation to control the spreading of Texas (or tick) fever, to which the Longhorns were immune but which was fatal to domestic stock, an embargo against the entry of Texas cattle east of the 99th parallel between May 15 and October 15 (in effect the entire trail-driving season) was voted into law. The Santa Fe Railroad hurriedly built down to Caldwell on the Kansas-Indian Territory line, where it could load Texas cattle and circumvent the Embargo Act, leaving Wichita dangling on the vine as it had Newton.

Rowdy Joe closed his place in Delano and took off for Denison, Texas, where hell was popping. Kate turned westward to Dodge City. Calling herself Rowdy Kate, she built and operated a dance hall on the South Side, where the pursuit of pleasure was the principal business. You may read that Joe and his wife parted in anger. But no evidence to that effect has been produced. They were back together briefly in Dodge before he joined the gold rush to the Black Hills, where he was killed.

The Missouri, Kansas and Texas Railroad had been built down through the Nations (Indian Territory) and bridged Red River. On the Texas side, some five miles from the Red, it had built its temporary terminus and named it Denison for George Denison, the Katy's vice-president.

The Houston and Texas Central Railroad, building all the way north from Houston, got there about the same time and drove on the few remaining miles to Red River, where it began a railroad-owned town of its own. The Katy made things as difficult as it could for its rival. Several hundred armed men were posted to prevent the H. and T. C. from laying its rails across the Denison town site. Peace came when the Katy was given permission to lay out a switching yard on the other road's right of way. With other accommodations being made, the way was now open for freight and passenger traffic direct to Kansas City. It meant that the Kansas towns were going to be hurt; that thousands of Longhorns would be leaving the Chisholm Trail and pointing for Denison.

When the town had a population of 2,000, it was still without a charter. There was no law other than the little the railroad supplied. Casting about for a man who, conceivably, might give Denison some semblance of decency, the Town Commission settled by happy chance on ex-Texas Ranger Captain Lee (Red) Hall.

Lee Hall has never received the acclaim he deserves. As the first "sheriff" of Denison he was confronted by such a collection of thugs, criminals and "wanted" men on the dodge from the Texas Rangers on the one hand, and federal marshals scouring Indian Territory on the other, as no other peace officer ever faced. He was ambushed on several occasions and survived innumerable face-to-face "showdowns." Because he was fearless and never drew a gun without using it, he won a grudging respect from the several hundred desperadoes who would have considered it a signal honor to blow him down.

Shortly it became reasonably safe to walk on Main Street, Denison's principal thoroughfare, and to patronize the saloons and gambling dens. That immunity did not extend to Skiddy Street, which paralleled Main, one block south.[5] There, in that ravine of sin and depravity, with its twin rows of tents and board and cloth shacks, were housed the hurdy-gurdy joints, the cockfighting pits, low-class groggeries and a shameless assortment of whores imported from Joplin and Kansas City. The noisiest and most troublesome of the latter was a hard-drinking, hatchet-faced woman named Millie Hipps.

Millie had conducted a bordello in Sedalia, Missouri, catering to railroad construction workers, for several years and had then moved on to Joplin to continue her career as a madam. When the Katy began building south through the Nations, she kept pace with it. Appearing at the various railheads with her tarts, she was ready for business as soon as her tent was put up. As long as she confined her capers to Skiddy Street—already referred to locally as Skid Row—Sheriff Lee Hall did not bother her, but when she began running people down on Main Street with her high-stepping team, rented from French's Livery, he dragged her off to the calaboose, an eight-by-ten adobe with one barred window that had not been designed to hold female prisoners. It gave Millie the distinction of being the first woman arrested in Denison.

In the morning, she was brought before Justice of the Peace Owings (later the town's first mayor), who fined her ten dollars for disorderly conduct and breaking the peace.

"Why don't you make it twenty?" she retorted saucily.

"All right, twenty," he agreed. "And the next time you are brought in for the same offense, I'll have you deported."

That was talk of a kind she could understand. Denison was booming—carloads of lumber were arriving every day, buildings were going up right and left and the stockyards were jammed with Texas cattle. She didn't want to be run out of a town where the pickings were already so good and sure to get even better. It was a feeling shared by other Skid Row venders of debauchery, among them Rowdy Joe Lowe. In the criminal fringe of raw, brawling Denison he found himself in his own element. His crude board and canvas saloon and dance house, which he had brazenly named Lowe's Crystal Palace, although there was already a Crystal Palace Saloon on Main Street, was a popular resort. With his iron fists rather than with his gun, he maintained order of a sort. A quick blow to the jaw and an even quicker kick in the groin invariably sufficed to take the fight out of an obstreperous patron.

Rowdy Joe remained in Denison for at least five years, when the town outgrew him and his "improved" Crystal Palace. But just when he dusted off his money and left was not noted by the Denison *News*. He is known to have been in Silverton, Colorado, in 1880, the year in which Mag Woods, the former Wichita madam, found herself in serious trouble in Caldwell.

Her notorious Red Light resort had had a long history of violence. Two town marshals, one of her bawds and her husband, George Woods, had been slain there. Its close proximity to the Indian Territory line, beyond which the law could not—or did not—follow, made it a gathering place for wanted men. That, as much as its blatant immorality, led to the action the City Council took to close it. The Red Light's liquor license was revoked and Marshal Hendry Brown ordered the place to be boarded up. Policemen were stationed there to bar anyone from entering or leaving. Mag screamed for justice, but to no avail. Marshal Brown informed her that she and her bawds had twenty-four hours in which to leave Caldwell voluntarily or be forcibly deported.

The following afternoon the two-fifteen northbound local for Wichita stood at the depot, ready to pull out. Several hundred spectators had gathered to watch the exodus of Mag and her whores. From where they stood, they could see the Red Light. It got to be two o'clock without any sign of movement in that direction. And then they saw the women coming down the slope carrying their suitcases, hurling a stream of obscenities and profanity at the gaping crowd. The conductor signaled the engineer several minutes later, and the train pulled out. Only then was the smoke rising from the Red Light noticed.

Mag wasn't there to enjoy the satisfaction of watching the place burn to the ground. But she had had the last laugh; before leaving, she had set the Red Light afire.

Dora Hand—Saint or Sinner?

SONGS AND COUNTLESS MAGAZINE PIECES have been written about the young woman who called herself Dora Hand. She has even been enshrined in a motion picture purporting to be the story of her life. But the two German tanners in Philadelphia who invented a process for turning heretofore worthless buffalo hide into serviceable shoe and boot leather, and as a result changed the economic history of white men and the Plains Indians, remain unknown.

For several decades professional buffalo hunters had been interested in killing the animals only for meat and robes, the skinned hide having little value. The extent of the business in buffalo robes cannot be estimated with any great measure of accuracy, but it was a time when no sleigh or buggy was thought to be properly equipped for winter driving without a buffalo robe to protect the feet and laps of the occupants. Add to that the thousands of buffalo overcoats that were worn by men in all walks of life, and the total becomes staggering.

The annual slaughter made no impression on the vast herds of shaggies moving back and forth, north and south, in their seasonal migrations. Witness after witness reports climbing a hill and finding the plains "black with buffalo as far as the eye could see." Of course to the Indian the buffalo was his principal source of food, shelter and raiment. The great herds were in no danger of extermination from him; he killed only what he needed. Naturally he regarded the activities of the white hunters with hostility, but was reassured by the fact that all their slaughtering did not seem to diminish the number of buffalo roaming the plains.

The situation changed drastically when it was discovered that buffalo hides were marketable. W. C. Lobenstein of Leavenworth and other fur and peltry dealers spread word that they were paying two dollars for a flint (dry) hide. The price quickly rose to three dollars, and the slaughter began. An experienced hunter could kill a hundred animals a day or more, depending on the ability of his skinners (usually two) to keep up with him. As news of the great bonanza spread, every Kansas Pacific and Santa Fe train west was filled with would-be buffalo hunters, some of whom had never fired a rifle in their lives.

The Santa Fe Railroad put its rails into what was to become Dodge City on September 19, 1872. When railroad surveyors laid out the townsite, five miles west of Fort Dodge, it encompassed a total of less than a score of crude adobe and brush-roofed human habitations, the only reason for its existence being a stopover for civilian and army freighters going or coming from Hays City, ninety-odd miles to the north. It was not a cow town in the making. Texas cattle were being driven up the Jones and Plummer Trail from Camp Supply, in Indian Territory, but they crossed the Arkansas four miles west of the future Dodge City. They were stock cattle, bound for Ogallala, Nebraska, or up what came to be called the Texas Trail into Wyoming and Montana.

Dodge was strategically located for what Wayne Gard, the Texas historian, has aptly called the Great Buffalo Hunt. To the south it had an open door to the Texas Panhandle, where the southern herd was sure to be found on its yearly northward migration. It was in that vast region of rolling, treeless plains that white hunters were most likely to lose their hair. The difficulty is said to have stemmed from the great peace powwow the U.S. Indian Commissioners held with the Comanche, Kiowa, Cheyenne, Arapaho and White Mountain Apaches at Medicine Lodge Creek, in southern Kansas in October, 1867. The Indian depredations would continue and there could be no peace on the plains, said the chiefs, unless white hunters were forbidden to roam south of the Arkansas River. The Commissioners signified their agreement orally, but it was not incorporated in the signed treaty. Had it been, it would have made no difference. After being confronted with an opportunity to make two to three hundred dollars a day, nothing could have held back the buffalo hunters swarming into Dodge City and Fort Griffin, down in Texas.

Season after season, the wanton destruction of the buffalo increased until no matter where he looked, the Indian saw the plains dotted with rotting carcasses or the bleaching bones the wolves had stripped clean. Naturally he struck back, killing the hunters when he could and mutilating the bodies of the slain to express his wrath. But he was fighting a losing battle. The military took the field against him. Hunted down, given no respite, he accepted the final degradation and consented to being cooped up on a reservation as a ward of the nation.

One has only to gaze at old photographs of piles of flint hides, stacked up eight to ten feet high beside the Santa Fe tracks in Dodge City and extending for a quarter of a mile or more as they awaited shipment, to realize the extent of the carnage. Unbelievably, it seems not to have occurred to the men who were profiting most that the slaughtering of the great herds could not go on forever. There were so many buffalo, they were deceived into believing that the natural increment would keep pace with the number being killed.

Although Dodge City was growing, spreading out, and bulging with prosperity, it remained crude and ugly. The merchandising establishment of Rath and Wright was housed in the only brick building in town. With the whisky barrels filled with water, placed along the plank sidewalk at convenient intervals, the only protection against fire, the rest of Dodge presented an invitation to a holocaust that could sweep it away in a few hours. In due course that happened. The ashes were scarcely cold when a new Dodge began rising that promised some permanency. For the first time several of its leading saloons could claim some measure of elegance. But beyond their usually open doors the white dust still swirled as the wagons and two-wheeled carts piled high with their odorous loads of hides passed up Front Street. The citizenry welcomed the dust and smell, for Dodge was a buffalo hunters' town.

From east to west the railroad cut the town in two. A so-called plaza, several hundred yards wide, separated Front Street, the business section, from the South Side, where the dance halls, cheap saloons and the whores were located. Actually the plaza was just a wide strip of unimproved land cluttered with sagebrush. And it remained so for years. After night fell, there was an endless going back and forth across it, the women leaving their dens and doing their hustling in the saloons along Front Street, only one or two of which barred them from their premises.

Naturally any place where men were making so much money that they were reckless about how they spent it was an irresistible magnet for gamblers, saloonkeepers and the entrepreneurs of vice. Dodge was no exception. But the bawds who were brought to Dodge were of the lowest order—coarse, overage haybags from the cheapest dives of Kansas City. Cowboys, and they were not finicky where the women of the cribs were concerned, would have walked away from them. The hide hunters, perhaps because of the debasing nature of their occupation, found them acceptable.

Apparently fastidious Mattie Silks had taken one look at Dodge and continued on to Denver, where her peculiar talents as a madam were to attain a lasting celebrity.

There were signs as early as the fall of 1874 that, eventually, Dodge was to undergo the metamorphosis from buffalo hunters' town to queen of the cow towns—the Cowboy Capital—but the businessmen of Dodge refused to believe that it could compete with Wichita for the Texas cattle trade. Being far to the west, its freight rates to Kansas City were higher. Stockyards would have to be installed, costing money that no one was prepared to pay. The Sante Fe took matters into its own hands. In a move to divert the herds going north to the completed Kansas Pacific west of the proscribed area, it equalized its freight rates to Dodge City and began building the required shipping facilities at its own expense. By the end of the 1875 season 80,000 Longhorns had been put aboard the cars, all of them coming up the Cut-Off Trail, which broke away from the Chisholm Trail at Turkey Creek, Indian Territory, and followed the Cimarron River to Longhorn Crossing and then the old Jones and Plummer Trail to Dodge.

It was only the beginning. Whether Dodge City liked it or not, cattle were becoming more important to its economy than hides. The face of the town changed. Over on the South Side the Lady Gay Theater and Comique were built; the number of saloons, gaming establishments and dance halls multiplied. New bands of younger and more attractive tarts moved in and forced the old hay-bags into exile. Soliciting was forbidden on Front Street. An ordinance prohibiting the carrying of a gun north of the tracks was enacted. A serious attempt was made to enforce it, but the killings and gun battles continued. Over on the South Side every man went armed.

It does not matter that it was not until the spring of 1879 that the buffalo hunters in Dodge, Fort Elliot, Rath City and Fort Griffin waited in vain for their scouts to bring in word that the great herd had been sighted. Only scattered bunches had been found; the millions of shaggies that had once blackened the plains had been all but exterminated. It does not matter, because the future of Dodge City had been decided two years earlier, when "Maxwell and Morris, with a big herd of stock cattle from South Texas, bound for Ogallala, Nebraska, left the Chisholm Trail at Belton (below Waco) and, striking northwest, followed the Leon River . . . with the North Star their only compass—and reached Fort Griffin." [1] They crossed Red River at Doan's Store, and, in turn, the Washita, Canadian, North Canadian and the Cimarron, where they struck the Camp Supply–Fort Dodge Trail that brought them to Dodge City. If a trail can be measured by the number of animals that passed over it, then Maxwell and Morris had blazed the second most important American cattle trail—the great Western Trail—a direct route from South Texas to the wide Arkansas River bottoms at Dodge.

Dodge City began to boom, the prosperity of its buffalo hunting days forgotten, and arriving on the crest of its rising importance came the beautiful young woman who called herself Dora Hand. She found employment as the star of the "Fairy Belles" who danced and sang at the Lady Gay Theater.

Today's Dodge City has its Wyatt Earp Boulevard, Masterson Street and Tilghman Room, in the Lora-Locke Hotel, but it is the mention of Dora Hand that brings the warmest response. Among the romanticists who have told her story countless times, not one has cast a stone at her. To them she is always a blameless, tragic figure, and they scoff at the suggestion that she may have been an unfortunate frail who fell by the roadside. The most widely accepted story of how she happened to be in Dodge City is that she was a young operatic soprano in Boston when her career was menaced by the sudden inroads of tuberculosis and that she had come west in the hope that the dry air of the high plains would arrest the disease. Another version is that she left Boston because of an unhappy love affair. Either may be true, but no evidence has ever been uncovered to that effect. Indeed, it is equally uncertain that she came from Boston.

Brushing aside the fanciful for provable fact, Dora Hand was born Fannie Keenan. She was not young, in the generally accepted use of that word. When she arrived in Dodge City in 1877, she was thirty-four. She had been married and divorced from a honky-tonk musician named Theodore Hand, with whom she had appeared for years in variety theaters in New Orleans, Memphis and other Southern towns, using the stage name of Dora Hand. For several years prior to coming to Dodge, she was employed off and on at Esher's Varieties and the Tivoli Varieties in St. Louis. She is known to have had a trained soprano voice, which was not a requirement of singers appearing in Western variety theaters of the period. It is the peg on which the widely accepted tale of her having been an operatic soprano in Boston is hung.

The most puzzling facet of the Dora Hand story is why Fannie Garretson, her closest friend, with whom she had worked and lived for two years in St. Louis, and who could have cleared away the mystery, refused to speak. Obviously she was shielding some-one—and who more likely, it has been asked, than Dora's parents? But shielding them from what? Their daughter had not been lead-ing a sheltered life, but hardly what used to be called "a life of shame." It is far more reasonable to believe that Fannie Garretson remained silent because Mayor Jim (Dog) Kelley admonished her to do so.[2]

The popular Kelley, three times mayor of Dodge and half owner of the Alhambra Saloon and Gambling Rooms, was well known to have been one of Dora Hand's admirers and her unofficial sponsor. That their relationship may have reached an intimacy beyond the bounds of friendship is not unlikely. If so, it would have been reason enough for imposing silence on her friend Fannie.

Ostensibly Kelley lived alone in his three-room cabin up the road a short distance to the rear of the Western Hotel. It was his habit to leave the Alhambra about three in the morning, cross the plaza to the South Side and drop in at the Lady Gay for a few minutes before proceeding home. The regularity of his irregular life was directly responsible for the tragedy that occurred in the early morning hours just before daylight on October 4, 1878, which resulted in the killing of Dora Hand. It had its beginning on the night of August 17, when Kelley ejected young Spike Kenedy from the Alhambra and tossed him out on the sidewalk. Though he was drunk, Kenedy fought back, but he was no match for the robust Kelley. He swore that he would get even. It was taken as a drunken man's threat and no one thought any more about it.

James "Spike" Kenedy was the son of Captain Miflin Kenedy, the Quaker cattleman of Corpus Christi, Texas. He and his neighbor and former partner, Captain George King, owner of the famous Santa Gertrudis Rancho, were the two wealthiest and most powerful cattle barons in the country. The two captains had grown rich steamboating on the Rio Grande during and after the war with Mexico and plowed their money into Mexican land grants, acquiring tens of thousands of acres of range, an empire of grass that dwarfed such great spreads as John Chism's Jingle Bob and the X I T.

There was nothing Quakerish about Spike Kenedy. He was born of a Mexican woman, and he was ruled by the wild recklessness of his maternal ancestors. After his trouble with Kelley, he hung around the South Side for a week, watching his man carefully until he was sure of the routine the other followed—undressing as soon as he reached the cabin and sleeping in the front room. A man on horseback could ride up to the front window and kill him as he slept. Determined to square his account with Jim Kelley, Kenedy took the train for Kansas City to buy the fastest horse he could find, a horse that would outdistance pursuit and speed him in safety to Texas. He completed the cast of principal players in a drama that might well have been designed for frontier style grand opera.

In an effort to separate fact from fiction, the place to begin is with the arrival in Dodge in May, 1877, of Fannie Garretson and four other young women, singers and dancers, who had been brought out from St. Louis by the management of the Lady Gay Theater at a salary of $40 a week, which was twice what they had been earning in the Mound City. A few weeks later, with the arrival of the first herds from Texas and business booming, Fanny induced Dora to join her at the Lady Gay.

These young women were seasoned honky-tonk troupers and their morals may not have been any better than they should have been. But they were not prostitutes. The Lady Gay was a free-wheeling resort, with its bar at the rear of the auditorium doing a land-office business between acts. Whenever a hilarious cowboy put a bullet into the ceiling, it caused only momentary concern. Occasionally barnstorming actors played the Lady Gay. Young Eddie Foy, the comedian, later to become a nation-wide celebrity, played there for an extended engagement. For the most part, however, the Lady Gay had to depend on its own talent. That gave Dora her opportunity. Pressed into service as a soloist one night, she became an instant hit. The cowboy audience knew little or nothing about music, but it appreciated the bell-like melody of her voice.

The management quickly realized that she could be developed into a popular favorite. Presently, as a featured soloist, she was being paid $75 a week. It was noticed before long that Jim Kelley was often seen in her company. On occasion when he went out to run his hounds, she accompanied him, or they went driving together behind his pair of fancy trotters.

Until it was forbidden by law some years later, it was the custom in Dodge for the leading saloons, such as the Long Branch and the Alhambra, to employ a singer during the rush hours of the evening. In some way Kelley worked out an agreement with the Lady Gay by which Dora Hand was free for two hours, five nights a week, to sing in the Alhambra, the saloon providing her with a piano accompanist. This arrangement must have added considerably to her income, for she now turned in earnest to succoring the poor and unfortunate, and it is as an angel of mercy that Dodge remembers her. She was often observed setting out in the late morning, modestly dressed, with a market basket bulging with groceries on her arm. Somewhere in its depths there was likely to be found a toy or bit of candy she had promised an ailing child—white, black or Mexican.

Despite its brashness, no place ever responded more quickly or generously to an appeal for its charity than cow-town Dodge. But it had done little or nothing for its unfortunate poor until Dora Hand's ministering called attention to their needs. Some of the members of the Ladies' Aid Society of the First Methodist Church resented being shown their duty by "such a woman." The Reverend Mr. Wright confounded her critics by inviting Dora to appear as soloist at the Sunday evening services. When she took her place beside the organist, the church was crowded to the doors, which was something of a phenomenon. An hour later she was back on the stage of the Lady Gay. These dual appearances at church and on stage were repeated as summer waned and the shipping season reached its height.

In mid-September Jim Kelley took to bed with an intestinal affliction. When informed by his doctor that surgery was necessary, he decided to go to Fort Dodge and have the operation performed by the post surgeon. Before leaving for the fort, he invited Dora and her friend Fannie Garretson to occupy his cabin until his return. This the girls did, for it was far more comfortable than their own quarters. What followed is history. Spike Kenedy returned to Dodge between three and four o'clock in the morning of October 4. Ignorant of the fact that Kelley was five miles away, he rode up to the cabin and fired four shots through the window. Fannie Garretson was asleep in the front room, Dora in the rear. Two of the bullets plowed into the floor; the third knifed through the mattress in the front-room, barely missing the Garretson girl; the fourth slug pierced the thinly plastered partition between the two rooms and struck Dora in her right side under the arm, killing her instantly.

Shooting at that hour of the morning attracted attention even on the South Side. Men rushed out of the Western Hotel and caught a glimpse of young Kenedy fleeing up the river or, in other words, to the west. Fannie Garretson had run into the road and was able to confirm the suspicion that Kenedy had done the shooting. When it was discovered that Dora Hand had been killed, Sheriff Masterson hastily organized a small posse consisting of himself, Deputy Sheriff Bill Tilghman, ex-Sheriff Charley Bassett and Assistant City Marshal Wyatt Earp.

Earp has left an account of what followed. Aside from giving himself all the best of it, which was characteristic of him, it belies the known facts. It was Bat's idea, not Earp's, that heading up the Arkansas was a ruse on Kenedy's part to throw off pursuit, and that as soon as he was clear of town, he would swing around it and line out for Wagon Bed Springs Crossing on the Cimarron, seventy miles to the southeast. Also, Bat was in command of the posse, not Earp.[3]

The four men drove through a driving rain that turned to hail shortly after noon. The storm was severe enough to make them seek the shelter of a cut-bank for an hour. They had seen nothing of young Kenedy throughout the day. On reaching the crossing about five o'clock, they examined the approach without finding fresh tracks in the mud. It convinced them that they were in time to intercept him if they had guessed right about the route he was taking.

There was a dugout near the ford. They talked with the farmer who lived there. He told them he had seen no one heading south. All they could do was conceal their horses and wait.

The gray afternoon was merging into evening when they saw their man coming. Apparently satisfied that he had eluded pursuit, he turned toward the dugout for food for himself and a bait for his horse. He was within fifty yards of the waiting men when he saw what he was riding into. Before he could swing around, Bat fired, the rifle bullet shattering Kenedy's right arm. But he held his seat and was getting away when Earp shot the horse out from under him. He expressed no regret as they gathered around, believing they wanted him for killing Jim Kelley. He was astounded when informed that they were taking him in for the killing of a young woman, not "Dog" Kelley.

When the posse got back to town with the prisoner, they found Dodge preparing to give Dora Hand such a funeral as the town had not witnessed since the slaying of Marshal Ed Masterson, Bat's elder brother.

Several members of the Driskill clan were in town, as were the Dewees brothers and other wealthy Texans, all staunch friends of Captain Miflin Kenedy. To save Spike's arm, they had an operation performed at once. He had been charged with murder in the second degree and was being held in the Ford County jail, a room with barred windows in the rear of the sheriff's office. On October 28—twenty-four days after the killing of Dora Hand—he was physically able to undergo a preliminary arraignment. It was conducted in Sheriff Masterson's office, with Judge R. G. Cook presiding. No spectators were permitted and no record made of the evidence offered, the official report of the proceedings being limited to one sentence: "Prisoner acquitted for lack of evidence to convict."

Dodge roared its disapproval and the talk was general that Captain Miflin Kenedy's friends had "dug deep into their pockets to save Spike." His father arrived in Dodge City on December 8 and had his son removed to Fort Dodge for a second operation, which was performed by Dr. B. E. Fryer, who had been brought from Fort Leavenworth, and Dr. McCarty, of Dodge City. Fragments of bone were removed from the damaged shoulder. A month later, via Kansas City and Denison, Captain Kenedy took his son back to Texas by rail. Spike never appeared in Dodge City again. When he died three years later, he had already been forgotten. But not Dora Hand. With the passing years the legends about her began to multiply—the honky-tonk singer by night and the angel of mercy by day. The myth-makers are not likely to allow her memory to die.

Mattie Silks—Queen of the Red Lights

IN THE 1880's Larimer Street was Denver's principal thoroughfare. Paralleling it one block to the west was McGaa Street, on which the stables and barns of Ben Holladay's Leavenworth City and Pikes Peak Express Company had once been located. When the railroads ushered the express company into oblivion, the complexion of McGaa Street changed and it became the heart of the town's sprawling Tenderloin. For four blocks it was lined with cribs and parlor houses. Along Hop Alley, the narrow passageway at the rear, were clustered the opium dens, gambling joints, and the shops of Denver's Chinese colony, which numbered as many as eight hundred, including not more than fifty slave girls at any one time.

Why so few Oriental prostitutes were brought to the Mile High City has never been satisfactorily explained. But the total number of harlots of other colors practicing their profession in the McGaa Street district often exceeded one thousand.

If it could not compare with the Barbary Coast in numbers, it equaled it in its vice, depravity and violence. Nowhere else did the bunco steerer, the thimblerigger and the con man ply their trades so brazenly. In no other American city, including New York, were such fortunes wagered nightly on the turn of a card. With the gold and silver mines of Colorado pouring a seemingly endless stream of riches into Denver, it was not only the bonanza kings who could lose $50,000 in a night's sitting and be back a

night or two later for more. The whole town was dizzy with
recklessness. The municipal government was corrupt, the courts
venal. But little was done about it. The population had mush-
roomed from nothing to 35,000 by 1880, and two years later was
well on its way to its first 100,000. With five railroads serving it
and a sixth, the Chicago and Rock Island, nearing Colorado Springs,
to give it still another outlet to the East, Denver had become the
transportation center of the West, second only to Kansas City in
importance. With such a backlog of prosperity to attract them,
it followed, as night follows day, that the number of McGaa
Street bagnios multiplied, with several of the madams who operated them achieving a tarnished fame that few of the scarlet sister-
hood have enjoyed.

The McGaa Street cribs were no different from the cribs of
other red-light districts—a succession of wooden cubicles standing
shoulder to shoulder, each barely wide enough for a door and
front window, and ten to twelve feet deep, the standard rental of
which was $25 a week, paid in advance. In them dwelt the street-
walkers and what were known as the "dollar" and "four-bit
whores"—a dollar if white and four bits if black. Between such
women and the girls in the parlor houses there was a wide social
gulf, no madam permitting her "boarders" to associate with the
crib women. This enforced segregation was undertaken for the
economic purpose of convincing the patrons of the parlor houses
that the quality of the merchandise they had for sale justified their
higher prices.

Young Denver's love affair with Big Ben Holladay, the "stagecoach king," has been told so often that only the pertinent facts
need be repeated here. When he acquired the bankrupt Butterfield Overland Dispatch, the town's only direct express, mail and
stagecoach service to the East, and announced that the line was to
be restocked with new equipment and six hours clipped off the
running time between Leavenworth and Denver, he was hailed in
the Colorado capital as its great benefactor. But later, when he
took over the Central Overland Company from Russell, Majors
and Waddell, he promptly scrapped the old Butterfield line and
Denver found itself at the end of a stub line running down from

Julesburg, where mail often piled up for a week to ten days before it was forwarded.

Denver's love for Ben Holladay changed to hate. To show its displeasure, it renamed McGaa Street Holladay Street. Naturally it was delighted when Holladay Street became synonymous with depravity throughout the West.

After enduring the jibes about Holladay Street for nine years, in 1889, Big Ben's heirs, one of them a judge of the United States Circuit Court, petitioned the Denver board of aldermen to change the name. This was done, and Holladay Street became Market Street—which some sarcastic wit must have convinced the board was particularly fitting in view of the merchandising in which it was engaged.

The proper place to pick up the trail of the much-traveled Mattie Silks, the golden-haired miniature Lily Langtry of the Colorado gold camps, is mountain-rimmed Georgetown. Fortunes were being washed out of the surrounding hills of what, with Central City and Blackhawk, was often described as "the richest square mile on earth." That was taking in considerably more than a square mile, but the exaggeration was excusable. There, in 1876, Mattie operated one of the town's five parlor houses on Brownell Street. It was in Georgetown that she put together the small fortune that was to launch her into underworld fame as the Queen of the Denver Red Lights. It was also in Georgetown that she met Cortese D. Thomson (commonly called Cort), who was to become her "solid man" for most of her life.

Cort Thomson was a sandy-haired Texan, barely six feet tall and lithe and lean. He was a year or two younger than Mattie, a handsome physical specimen who spoke with a pleasant Texas drawl, his masculinity emphasized by a pinkish bartender's mustache which he tended with loving care. By trade he was a professional foot racer. As a sporting event, foot racing had largely disappeared by the turn of the century, but there was a time when every Western town and mining camp had its champion, who almost invariably came from the ranks of the local volunteer fire company. Thousands of dollars were waged on a contest that pitted a local champion against a touring professional such as

Cort Thomson. Naturally, with so much money involved, the gamblers moved in. As a consequence many of the races were "fixed," the backers of a professional using "ringers" or secretly betting against their own man, who had been instructed to lose, which made their wagering a sure thing. Cort's boast that he had ridden with Quantrill's raiders during the war can be dismissed as fiction.

According to the evidence, Mattie fell for Cort Thomson like the proverbial ton of bricks. She remained loyal to him even after he had proved himself to be utterly worthless, a fool who believed he could match wits with the gamblers who quickly relieved him of the thousands of dollars she lavished on him. He added insult to injury by being unfaithful to her, a break of trust that enabled the Denver underworld to snicker at her behind her back.

Estimates of the amount of money she squandered on Cort run as high as $75,000, which does not appear to be an exaggeration. She was twenty-nine when she left Georgetown for Denver in 1876. Cort Thomson accompanied her, as did a gambler named George D. Silks. Because of the similarity in names, he is believed by some to have been her husband, which is not true. Silks disappeared from Denver a year later and his path never again crossed Mattie's. Back in Springfield, Illinois,[1] where she ran her first brothel in 1864, she was known as Mattie Silks, a name she had coined for herself because of her love for silks. Of her childhood nothing is known, and she died in January, 1929, at the age of eighty-three without revealing her true name, which was only one of many secrets she carried to the grave.

Her first venture in Denver was in rented premises on what was then McGaa Street. Presently, she bought the property at Number 501, which she was to occupy for years. She stocked it with twelve young "boarders," reputed to be the "fairest frails in town." Money was rolling in, and what she called her "money pocket," on the left side of her expensive de Medici gown, direct from Kansas City, was usually bulging with twenty-dollar gold pieces, despite Cort's frequent "borrowings." In the other pocket she carried an ivory-gripped pistol. He won a race on which Mattie had wagered a thousand dollars. To celebrate, she invited

all the leading personages of the Row to a champagne party at
the Olympic Gardens, later known as Denver Gardens. The resort
was owned by the Denver Brewing Company and located on the
west bank of the South Platte River, just beyond what was then
the city line. It was there, during the course of Mattie's wild party,
that the celebrated "duel" between Mattie and Katie Fulton, a rival
madam, occurred.

Katie Fulton, a dashing brunette with a fiery temper, had been
trying for weeks to supplant Mattie in Cort Thomson's affections.
Mattie was evidently aware of it. Whether it was something she
saw or some word that passed between the two women which led
to the pass-at-arms is unknown, but Mattie challenged Katie to
a showdown with pistols. Seconds were named and thirty paces
stepped off between the duelists. At the count of three the antag-
onists turned and fired. Mattie had often boasted that when she
was in Abilene and Wild Bill was town marshal, he had taught
her how to handle a pistol. Her markmanship as she faced Katie
Fulton reflected no credit on herself or her instructor, Hickok or
whoever he was, for the bullet she fired buried itself in the trunk of
a nearby cedar. Katie squeezed the trigger of her pistol almost
simultaneously and Cort Thomson grabbed the back of his neck
and fell screaming to the ground, blood oozing out between his
fingers.

It was only a superficial flesh wound. Mattie tried to stanch the
flow of blood with her lace handkerchief, which was inadequate.
Someone produced a towel. She snatched it away and refused to
permit anyone other than herself to touch Cort. When the wound
continued bleeding, she had him placed in a hack and rushed to
the Denver General Hospital, where a surgeon dressed the wound.

The affair left the underworld with a question that was never
resolved to its satisfaction. Had Katie Fulton, in her infatuation
with Cort, decided that if she couldn't have him no one else
could, and had she tried to kill him? One side contended that the
wounding of Cort Thomson was purely accidental, but the majority of the eyewitnesses were just as strongly convinced that she
had deliberately tried to kill him.

Mattie bought three other houses on the Row and leased them

to other madams. She was becoming plump, which distressed her, for she knew the facts of life well enough to understand that she could hold Cort only as long as she remained desirable in his eyes; that just supplying him with money and taking care of his gambling debts would not be enough. She stopped guzzling champagne and called in a Swedish masseuse to rub and knead the flabbiness out of her pampered body. What she needed was exercise, but there was little opportunity for getting it. While she cherished her unofficial title of Queen of the Red Lights, it had its handicaps; she was so well-known that she couldn't leave the Row without being recognized wherever she went. Although shrewd and hard, she realized that even in wide-open Denver there were two worlds, one of which was closed to her. It was the old story of not being able to eat your cake and have it too. She had been eating hers for a long time.

For a reprieve from the routine of McGaa Street she went to Kansas City, accompanied by Cort, and bought a new wardrobe. She had no taste for clothes, which was not surprising, for to her unsophisticated eyes the bizarre and tawdry passed for elegance if it were expensive. In her photographs she appears to be in Victorian costume, her skirts, decorated with rows of lace, trailing the floor. Suspended on a gold chain about her neck was the diamond cross that Cort bought for her with his own money on one of the rare occasions when he had been lucky at poker.

Mattie returned from Kansas City imbued with the idea of establishing her own racing stable, a costly hobby that she pursued for years. She became a fixture at Overland Park during the racing meets, in which her horses lost oftener than they won, with the exception of Jim Blaine, a fine, rangy chestnut gelding.

For five years Mattie had reigned unchallenged as Queen of Denver's underworld. When she leased the sporting house at 527 Holladay Street to Jennie Rogers in 1881, it could not possibly have occurred to her that she was opening the doors of her bailiwick to the woman who was going to dethrone her—at least temporarily.

Tall, cultured Jennie Rogers—her legal name was Leah J. Fries—reached Denver by way of St. Louis, where she had conducted an upper-class bagnio. A dashing brunette, with a sparkling wit and a sense of elegance that Mattie strove for but never achieved, Jennie Rogers was by all accounts the most beautiful woman who ever appeared on the Row.

She was no sooner in possession of the house at Number 527 than she had it painted and papered from the cellar to the roof, making a clean sweep of the old furnishings in the meantime and replacing them with new ones that suited her taste. Although the distance between the two cities was great, she was visited every five or six weeks by a gentleman from St. Louis. He was her sweetheart, not her "solid man," not a pimp. The Row soon discovered that he was the respected chief of police of St. Louis. That he had any "connections" in Denver is open to question, nor is there convincing evidence that he concocted the bizarre blackmail plot against one of the city's politically ambitious millionaires, several years later, that supplied Jennie Rogers with the money to build her fabulous "House of Faces and Mirrors." That the alleged plot had any more substance than was to be found in a newspaper reporter's imagination is also to be doubted.

Jennie soon bought the house she had leased from Mattie and expanded further by buying an adjoining house and making them one by knocking out the connecting wall. She added a third house a year later. It was the almost invariable rule in the so-called "parlor" houses never to open a window and to keep the shades drawn. As a result, the air within was foul with the mingled stale odor of alcohol, tobacco and perfume. Jennie changed that; she put bars on her windows and gave the premises a daily airing. The barred windows also discouraged robberies and put an end to the well-known practice of some "boarders" of admitting men through their window and conducting business on the side, in which the madam did not share in the profits.

Jennie gave herself a daily airing as well. Every afternoon, the weather being favorable, her two-wheeled trap and matching pair of grays was brought to her door. Modestly attired, she set out for an hour's drive. She was recognized wherever she appeared, and although she pretended not to be aware of the attention she attracted, it must have pleased her. Undoubtedly that was why she drove through the wealthiest parts of town, conscious of the feminine eyes behind the curtains that were tearing her apart.

In 1889 at about the time the name of Holladay Street was changed to Market, Jennie Rogers purchased the house of Minnie Clifford at Number 1942 and rebuilt it inside and out. She intended it to be the most elegant sporting house Denver had ever seen. The hand-hewn gray stone house had a sculptured façade on which were carved five human heads, rumored to be likenesses of the five people who had figured in the unbelievable shakedown plot. It was the most luxurious establishment of its kind in the West, San Francisco included. The carved furniture, the bird's-eye maple tables with their inlaid mother-of-pearl tops, the three grand pianos and the paintings and bric-a-brac scattered about, the rich oriental rugs made a picture that was the embodiment of a harlot's dream. In the ballroom, a circular, sixteen-foot mirror was attached to the ceiling.

If the gentleman visitors—some of them muckers yesterday and millionaires today—blinked their eyes, it was understandable. Madame Rogers, ravishingly gowned, and her twenty strumpets, most of them new girls recruited in St. Louis, waited beneath the crystal chandeliers to greet them. Mattie heard all of the ghastly details before the night was over. But she continued to smile. The name of the business was money, and she had it.

With her new palace of sin formally opened and business booming, the police chief from St. Louis, who is supposed by some to have produced the money for Jennie, disappeared from her life, which is additional proof to this commentator that the blackmail plot was imaginary. Further evidence is found in the fact that Jennie married a bartender at the Brown Palace Hotel three months later. He wasn't around long. Although she set him up in the saloon business, he expressed his gratitude by tom-catting with another woman. When she caught him, she whipped out a pistol and fired with deadly intent, but her marksmanship was so poor that he received nothing more serious than a flesh wound. Jennie filed for a divorce, which she was granted, but not without the embarrassing details appearing in the newspapers.

Undoubtedly Mattie Silks found some pleasure in the discomfiture of her rival and congratulated herself on having a man like Cort Thomson. Of course he drank too much and had no head for business. Providing him with a life of ease was costly, but she didn't mind; he was kind and faithful—or so she believed. Somewhere in Texas he had a wife and married daughter whom he had not seen in years. That impasse was broken when he received word in July, 1884, that his wife had died. He and Mattie were free to marry at last. They lost no time about it, and on July 6 they were wed at Peru, Indiana. As so many others were doing, they went on to Niagara Falls for their honeymoon.

She must have had a reason for having the ceremony performed in the little town of Peru, Indiana. What better reason can be suggested than that she was returning to claim respectability in the eyes of her home folk? Her first known connection with the world of the red lights was at Springfield, Illinois, only several hundred miles to the west on the Wabash Railroad.

When the honeymooners returned, they found Denver emerging from one of its periodic slumps. Old frame houses on Market Street that had been thought good enough for their purpose in previous years were being torn down and replaced with brick and stone structures that were still flourishing when prohibition and a reform government dimmed the red lights forever in 1915.

Her racing stable and the money she was wagering and losing on her horses, coupled with Cort's increasing extravagances, were making a serious dent in Mattie's finances. A further problem came when Cort received a telegram in 1886, informing him that his daughter, who had been deserted by her husband, had died, leaving an orphaned grandchild to be cared for. Cort did not feel that it was his duty to step into the breach. Mattie insisted that it was. If they had a farm, she said, it would give her a place to keep her string of horses and provide a home for the child. A woman could be hired to look after her. Her proposal was not as unselfish as it sounded. For one thing, if she could get Cort away from Denver, he would not have an opportunity to do so much drinking and, what was far more important, it would put an end to the whispers that he was spending a great deal of his time with

Lillie Dab, a little redheaded tart in Belle London's house, who was young enough to be his daughter.

The upshot of the matter was that Cort bought three pieces of land on the Burlington Railroad several hundred miles east of Denver near the little town of Wray. He put up a house and bought a small herd of cattle with the announced purpose of running a ranch. In Pigfoot Charley Grant's speakeasy in Wray he hired a couple of cowpunchers to work his place. One of the men was married, and his wife was hired as cook and housekeeper. When Cort's granddaughter Rita arrived, the woman was given the responsibility of looking after her.

Cort soon won an evil reputation around Wray, his neighbors accusing him of running off stock and altering brands. Mattie came out to visit him and didn't like what she saw. At her insistence he discharged his foreman, known locally as Dirty Face Murphy, and hired Handsome Jack Ready, a mountain of a man, in his stead. In time, Ready was to play an important role in Mattie's life.

Cort thoroughly enjoyed the reputation of being a *bad hombre* that he acquired around Wray and Laird, the next town to the east, and on his visits to Denver he swaggered about his old haunts on Larimer Street. If he fooled no one else with his boldness, he fooled himself and no longer found it necessary to clothe his relations with Lillie Dab in secrecy. Unbelieving Mattie refused to credit the tales that reached her ears, but as January and February dragged by, she realized that the rumors were true; that Jennie Rogers and every other rival Market Street madam, all anxious to topple her, were gloating over her shame.

On the night of March 13, 1891, she caught Cort and Lillie together in an Arapaho Street assignation house. She was armed with her pistol. Her first shot clipped off one of Lillie's curls; the second thudded into the door as Lillie fled the room, which was preliminary to her hurried departure from Denver.

Before Mattie could turn the gun on him, Cort wrenched it out of her hand and gave her an unmerciful beating. The following morning Mattie filed suit for divorce in the Arapaho County court. She also petitioned for an order restraining him from disposing of the ranch property, its improvements, horses, cattle, all of which had been purchased with her money. A temporary restraining order was granted and a day set for the divorce proceedings.

It brought Cort Thomson to his senses, such as they were. Faced with the prospect of losing his meal ticket, he was contrite and filled with remorse. Without contest, he deeded the ranch and appurtenances to Mattie. Both were aging. Undoubtedly that had something to do with Mattie's decision to forgive him and take him back, which obviously was the best means of saving face. Whatever her reasons, eleven days after the divorce suit was filed, she instructed her lawyers to ask the court to dismiss it.

Mattie had been on the Row for twenty years when she announced in 1897 that she and "Mr. Thomson" were going abroad to attend Queen Victoria's Diamond Jubilee. It put Market Street on notice that she was still its leader. With a million people from around the world heading for London to witness the spectacle, it was bound to be an expensive junket, but as Sandy Bowers had told his Eilley, "money was no object."

They returned in late summer from what Mattie spoke of as their "second honeymoon" to find the Denver red-light district deserted by hundreds of its gamblers, bunco men, madams and tarts who had joined the great rush to Alaska and the Yukon, where one of the world's richest gold strikes had been made in the Klondike. Soapy Smith and his gang, who had been run out of Creede, had seized control of Skagway; Wyatt Earp, the Dodge City and Tombstone "marshal," had opened a saloon and gambling house at Nome. The newspapers were filled with tales of the fortunes being made in the Far North. Mattie couldn't resist the lure of easy money. In the spring of 1898 she closed her house and, accompanied by a dozen of her "boarders" and Cort, she set out for Dawson City on the Yukon. The railroad between Skagway and White Horse had been completed and the rest of the journey could be made by steamboat.

Although she had to pay $400 a month for the house she rented in Dawson, and $50 a day protection money to the police, never in her long career as a madam had she made so much money so quickly as in Dawson City. But the weather was foul—rain and mud almost every day. Cort developed a heavy cold that could not be doctored with whisky. Suspecting that it was the first stages of pneumonia, which was prevalent, and dreading the approaching long winter that would put an end to river travel and make it impossible to get "outside," she pulled up stakes and returned to Denver and reopened her establishment at 1922 Market Street. She had been away a little more than three months and returned with a net profit of $38,000. But she had no regrets for having turned her back on such a bonanza. The dry air of Denver restored Cort to health and he went back to the ranch at Wray. He left it to Handsome Jack Ready, the foreman, to do the work and run the place.

In April, 1900, Cort came to Denver to demand that Mattie give him $5,000 with which to buy cattle. For some unknown reason she refused to give him the money. Perhaps it was just a case of the pitcher going to the well once too often. But she compromised by giving him her check for $1,500. Two days later she learned that he had scattered the money in the bars and Larimer Street gambling joints and had had to borrow money to get back to Wray. Fearful that in his need for quick cash he would sell her favorite horse, Jim Blaine, she wired the sheriff of Yuma County to take him into custody and hold him until she arrived.

The sheriff took her to the old Commercial Hotel, where she found Cort in a rocking chair, writhing in pain. A doctor was called in. He diagnosed the trouble as a severe attack of stomach cramps. Doubtless cirrhosis of the liver, due to excessive drinking, would have been a more accurate pronouncement. He gave Mattie a bottle of laudanum and told her to lace Cort's whisky with it as needed; that it would ease the pain he was suffering.

Throughout the night Mattie dosed Cort with whisky and laudanum. The doctor was summoned at daybreak. He pronounced Cort dead. There was no investigation, it being generally believed that he had eaten something that had poisoned him. Mattie buried him in a plot she owned in Fairmount Cemetery, in Denver.[2]

For twenty-five years he had lived on her bounty, a worthless weakling. Over the bars and gaming tables he had squandered the thousands of dollars he had received from her. He had lied to her, beaten her and shared the beds of other women. Her only excuse for what she had endured was that she loved him—which leads one to ask why such women, hard, wise in the ways of the world, invariably put their trust in such men.

The death of Cort Thomson left Mattie with the problem of caring for his granddaughter, now nearing sixteen. She solved it by legally adopting her. Rita married at eighteen. Mattie then sold the ranch and brought Handsome Jack Ready to Denver and installed him as bookkeeper and bouncer in her house. He found that being the bouncer in a sporting house, even one run as sedately as Mattie Silks', was not a sinecure. Obstreperous drunks walked in three or four nights a week. It was his job to eject them. He was big and strong enough to make it no contest. A more difficult task was to keep peace among the nymphs who were the attraction. Twice that first winter he helped the police to carry out girls who had swallowed bichloride and place them in a police van for a quick trip to the hospital. Unfortunately the trip was not quick enough. A perusal of the daily police news revealed that Market Street averaged about one suicide a month. Being unpleasant news, the Denver papers held their coverage of it down to a few lines.

Jennie Rogers, still an important woman on the Row, stole away to Hot Springs, Arkansas, and in April, 1904, secretly married Archie T. Fitzgerald. It was a marriage that was as unreasonable as prosperous sporting women had been making for years, even more so, for Archie Fitzgerald, it might have been presumed, was the last man in the world to appeal to the fastidious Jennie. He was a former Chicago underworld politician, less than six feet tall, paunchy, his fat face rimmed with sagging jowls. His carefully clipped mustache and his diamonds further identified him as a "sport"—a man whose existence centered on the saloon, gambling room and the bordello. And yet from such unpromising material Jennie Rogers fashioned a seemingly satisfactory husband, the result, perhaps, of some form of osmosis.

When Jennie died in 1909, she left an estate in real and personal property amounting to $40,000, naming relatives in Pennsylvania and Ohio as her heirs. They hastened to Denver to claim their share, unmindful of the stigma attached to how the money had been earned. Archie Fitzgerald produced proof of his marriage to Jennie and claimed his half of the estate as her husband. But he settled for $5,000 in cash and the house at 1942 Market Street. In 1911 he sold the property for $14,000, and the purchaser was Mattie Silks. She was triumphant at last. Before she took possession of the famous premises, she had the name M. SILKS inlaid in white tile on the doorstep—presumably to leave no doubt that she still was Queen of the Red Lights.

In addition to Number 1942, she owned the houses at Number 1916 and Number 1922. But money was not rolling in as it had in previous years. Pioneer Denver was a thing of the past, and in its place was rising a great Western metropolis. The growing clamor to abolish legalized prostitution would not be stilled. Police raids became frequent and on several occasions the houses were closed, only to reopen a few weeks later. But property values were falling and when the final curtain fell in 1915, Market Street soon became a blighted area.[3]

Mattie was forced to concede that the good old days were gone forever. She removed some of the costly furnishings to the cottage she had bought on Lawrence Street, two blocks away, and had the balance sold at auction. She was seventy-seven when she fell for the second time and fractured a hip. To have someone to care for her in her old age, she married Handsome Jack Ready. He remained with her to the end, and when she died in 1929, at eighty-three, he and Cort's granddaughter had been named to share her estate. More than a million dollars had passed through her hands, but by the time the public administrator and the lawyers got through, it had dwindled to $1,922.

Incredible? So was she. Visitors to Fairmount Cemetery pass a modest stone inscribed Martha A. Ready unnoticed, for she belonged to an age that was gone before most of them were born.

Lady with a Past

TO ANYONE ACQUAINTED WITH THE STORY of old Fort Laramie, the name of John Hunton, rancher and grass-roots historian, will be familiar. One spring day in 1876, he encountered a wagon loaded with a dozen females that had just pulled away from the Hog Ranch, a crude frontier saloon with several prostitutes in attendance, three miles west of the army post.

"What have you got there, Dave?" he inquired of the driver.

"A load of whores headed for Deadwood," was the laconic answer.

Those words accurately disclose the lowly position such women occupied. They were just cattle, necessary and serving only one purpose. It makes no difference that in this instance one of the tarts in the wagon was Martha Jane Cannary—Calamity Jane.

Gold had been discovered in the Black Hills of South Dakota by the so-called "Scientific Expedition" led by Lieutenant Colonel George Armstrong Custer in 1874. The Black Hills was the homeland of several of the Sioux tribes. Under the terms of the Treaty of Laramie, the United States was obligated to bar white men from settling in the Black Hills. A feeble attempt was made to live up to that commitment, but where there was gold, there was no holding back the swarms of prospectors who rushed in. By the spring of 1874, the town of Deadwood had been established and was booming. The two nearest railroad points were Sidney, Nebraska,

225 miles to the south, and Cheyenne, Wyoming, 250 miles to the southwest, by way of Fort Laramie.

Denver was only three hours by rail from Cheyenne. When anyone got the itch to join the stampede to the Black Hills, it was comparatively easy to get there. No great amount of preparation was necessary. A traveler could catch a morning train out of the Denver Union Station, be in Cheyenne before noon and if he were lucky enough to be able to crowd into or on a Cheyenne-Deadwood stagecoach, he could be well on his way by evening.

The Cheyenne–Black Hills Trail was to become famous, but in early 1876 there was nothing but a few scattered stage stations north of Fort Laramie. It was Indian country, and the Sioux and Cheyennes were leaving their reservations and gathering in the hills south of the Yellowstone River. Army scouts reported that in every camp on the lower Tongue River, the Powder and Rose-bud, the war drums were thundering night and day; that as many as 5,000 Indians were massing to throw the whites out of the Black Hills, their holy land.

The gold seekers in Deadwood and out in the gulches refused to take the threat of an Indian uprising seriously. The military did. From three directions—east, south, and west—troops took to the field to scatter the massing Sioux. The situation exploded June 25 on the Little Bighorn in the annihilation of General (Brevet) Custer's immediate command. The nation was stunned, but the influx of whites into the Black Hills region continued to soar. From Denver alone an estimated 2,000 men and women joined the rush to the Dakota diggings in 1876. So many of them were products of its underworld—gamblers, whores, madams and saloon characters—that the Denver Tenderloin showed signs of becoming depopulated. Steely-eyed Ed Chase, its undisputed gambling czar, held fast, insisting that Deadwood was only a flash in the pan. He did not waver even when Madame Vestal, perhaps his most important competitor, pulled down her canvas gambling hell across Blake Street from the Palace, Chase's citadel of chance, and joined the exodus to the north.

Madame Vestal (her current name; she gave herself many) was a beautiful dark-eyed brunette in her early thirties, with a charming manner and intriguing smile. Between bartenders, dealers, spindlemen and bouncers she had upward of a dozen men in her employ. Like Madame Moustache, she was an expert dealer herself, specializing in Spanish *monte* and blackjack.

After several weeks of planning and preparation, she avoided breaking up her organization by taking her employees with her. Instead of entraining for Cheyenne, the expedition covered the entire distance to Deadwood by trail, and it was a caravan the like of which the Cheyenne-Deadwood Trail was never to see again. She had purchased a secondhand yellow omnibus [1] and re-modeled it into a comfortable home on wheels, with bed, alcohol stove for light cooking, curtained windows and a shelf of books. When she tired of riding inside, she rode up on top with the driver. Her maid traveled in the wagon that followed, along with her staff. Behind it rolled a sort of commissary wagon, which also transported the personal effects of the party. In a fourth wagon were stowed the large tent and gambling paraphernalia.

In Deadwood she set up her tent on Main Street in the center of the town's growing red-light district, appropriately called the Bad Lands. A few hours later she was open for business, but not as Madame Vestal. She had adopted a new name for herself—Lurline Monte Verde, very likely pilfered from some romantic novel she had read. She had used other aliases before this, for the obvious purpose of concealing her true identity. With Deadwood over-flowing with male and female stampeders from Denver, she could hardly have hoped to go unrecognized no matter what name she gave herself. If it aroused enough comment, it would stimulate business. That may have been her purpose. From a woman auda-cious enough to couple such opposites as madam, with its red-light connotations, and vestal, a temple virgin, into a name for herself, anything might be expected.

By her maneuverings she had so completely erased her back trail that very few people knew who she really was. Perhaps smiling Ed Chase, the gambling overlord of Denver, knew her story and respected it. It would explain why he departed from his practice of crushing his competitors and permitted her to prosper. Her life divides into two parts, the second half beginning when she first appeared as a dealer in a New Orleans gambling house in 1869. It was unrelated to the period that preceded it, when as the daughter of a well-to-do Jefferson City, Missouri, family she attended and graduated from the Missouri Female Seminary at Lexington, Missouri. She was the niece of Governor Claiborne Fox Jackson, the last elected governor of the state prior to the outbreak of the War Between the States, whose Secessionist policies led to his removal from office.

Missouri was about evenly divided in its loyalty to the Union and to the South. St. Louis was strongly Republican, and it became the headquarters of the Union Department of the Mississippi. It was also a hotbed of Southern sympathizers. The young, petite graduate from the Missouri Female Seminary at Lexington was one of them. The junior officers of Major General Halleck's staff escorted her to the opera house and danced with her at social functions. Thrown off their guard by their charming companion, they talked too much, and military secrets, invaluable to the enemy, found their way into the hands of Rebel General Sterling Price.

In December, 1862, Union General Newton M. Curtis ordered the arrest of the fascinating young woman. She fled on horseback but was captured as she reached Ste. Genevieve on the Mississippi, fifty miles to the south. Documentary evidence was found on her person, leaving no doubt of her guilt. Brought back to St. Louis, she faced Provost General John M. Schofield defiantly and readily admitted that she had supplied Rebel General Nathan B. Forrest with the information that had enabled him to thwart General Grant's attempt to cut the Memphis and Mobile Railroad.

Sentenced to the Gratiot Street prison for Rebels, she was incarcerated for only four months when she was given her freedom, on condition that she leave the state and not return for the duration of the war. Scandalous tales were whispered of the type of persuasion she had used on the provost marshal, but no evidence to her discredit or Schofield's was ever produced.

She was, of course, Belle Siddons, the famous Confederate spy. She went to Texas and continued her service to the South. After the war she returned to Jefferson City and became a professional lobbyist at the state capitol. In 1868, in Jefferson City, she met and married Dr. Newton Hallett, an army surgeon of Kansas City. When he was ordered to Fort Brown, Texas, down on the Rio Grande, she accompanied him.

In that forlorn post, garrisoned by two companies of Negro troops, he is said to have taught her the rudiments of medicine and dissection. More likely, he taught her the rudiments of gambling as they sought relaxation across the river in Matamoros, Mexico. In any event, he contracted yellow fever in the epidemic of 1869 and died. A few months later she appeared in New Orleans, dealing Spanish *monte* and blackjack.

In Deadwood, about four o'clock in the afternoon of August 2, 1877, within five hundred yards of her gambling tent, Wild Bill Hickok was shot to death as he was playing poker in Carl Mann's Number Ten Saloon.[2] The assassin was Jack McCall, a faceless, unimportant saloon character. He was tried at once, acquitted and deported. Subsequently, he was arrested at Laramie City, Wyoming, and returned to Yankton, South Dakota, to be tried in a federal court. Since the murder of Hickok had occurred in Deadwood, an "outlaw" town on an Indian reserve, the local, or vigilante, court that had tried and acquitted McCall had been without jurisdiction. A second trial took place. The verdict was guilty, and on March 1, 1877, McCall was hanged at Yankton.

The killing of Wild Bill created a greater furor in Deadwood than the Battle of the Little Bighorn. No incident in Western history has engaged the attention of more commentators and writers. The evidence has been sifted and resifted. It reveals the surprising fact that less than fifty dollars were at stake in the game in which Hickok was sitting. Having lost twenty-five dollars the previous evening, he had to ask Mann's bartender to loan him fifteen dollars' worth of bar checks to enable him to continue to play.

Wells Fargo arrived in Deadwood in 1876 and opened an office for forwarding gold to the outside world. When spring came and the Cheyenne-Deadwood Trail was open again, the express company had $200,000 accumulated over the winter in its cast-iron safe awaiting shipment. In the fall of '76 there had been frequent holdups. The express company had lost several treasure chests,

The local agent was relieved when Wells, Fargo's Chief of Detectives James B. Hume arrived and took charge of getting the accumulated gold safely through to Cheyenne.

Lucius Beebe, Wells, Fargo historian, is authority for the story that when Wyatt Earp and his brother Morgan, who had been prospecting without much luck around Spearfish, informed the man at the counter that they wanted to buy passage for Cheyenne, Hume spoke up.

"Wells, Fargo will give you and your brother free transportation and fifty dollars in gold to boot if you'll ride shotgun for us tomorrow."

The deal was made, and a sign soon appeared in Wells, Fargo's window announcing that "The spring cleanup will go out on Monday's stage, with Wyatt Earp, of Dodge City, Kansas, riding shotgun."

The coach got through without being stopped. Beebe says Earp told him it was the easiest fifty dollars he had ever earned.

Deadwood was a town without law. If a man made a killing in Lurline Monte Verde's place or in one of the half dozen other gambling "casinos," he was very likely to be robbed before he was a block away. She was never molested or her safe rifled, for her dealers and bartenders could double as bodyguards at a moment's notice.

She had always made it a cardinal rule never to become involved personally with the men who patronized her establishments, knowing that romance and gambling did not mix. All her resolves and good sense seemed to desert her when young Archie McLaughlin sat across the table one night until he was broke. He had an engaging crooked smile and lost with a laugh. She offered to stake him, but he refused and promised her he would be back. She didn't see him a second time until a week later. He was plentifully supplied with money. He was gay, carefree. Reading the unasked question in her eyes, he told her he had made a strike.

He had, but not the kind of "strike" she imagined. The night before he, Billy Mansfield, Jim Brown, Alex Casswell and Jack Smith had held up the Sidney stage and relieved the passengers of over nine thousand dollars.

His luck was better this evening, perhaps because her mind was not on the cards. Before leaving, he pressed an invitation on her to be his guest at dinner the following day. She said no, but he was persistent, and she dined with him at the Tivoli. Though he had arranged for a private room, there were too many wagging tongues in Deadwood to keep such a meeting secret. The tale reached the ears of Art Donovan, her head bartender. He felt he should tell her that Archie McLaughlin was the head of a gang of road agents.

The information came too late to make any difference to the sloe-eyed Lurline, with her enigmatic smile. She knew she was in love with Archie McLaughlin. As their relations ripened, it is reasonable to suppose that she confronted him with what she had learned and that he readily admitted the truth. Something in his recklessness and devil-may-care attitude appealed to a streak in her that had long been dormant.

It seems unquestionable that she was soon supplying him with valuable tips as to who was leaving for the south with a considerable amount of money on his person. Holdups multiplied and for Archie and his gang there were few dry runs. That he was grateful to her can be taken for granted. There is even some reason to believe that he was actually in love with Lurline. At least, he was no longer a nightly frequenter of the brothels, where he had cut quite a figure. But Wells, Fargo detectives were keeping a close watch on him. Inadvertently Lurline let word slip about a planned holdup in Whoop-up Canyon between Deadwood and Rapid City. It was all Hume's men needed to take steps to prevent it.

On the night of July 2, 1878, the scheduled Wells, Fargo stage for Rapid City and Sidney left on time. It carried a sizable amount of treasure from the Homestead Mine. A few minutes before its departure the passengers were removed and their places taken by a number of armed company deputies. For the greater part of the distance to Rapid City, the trail followed Box Elder Creek. Where it dipped down into Whoop-up Canyon, with its trees and high brush, was an ideal place for a surprise holdup. The coach had not proceeded far down the canyon when the expected happened. A man, Alex Casswell, broke from cover and, seizing the bits of the lead team, ordered the driver to reach. Archie Mc-Laughlin and the other members of the gang rushed into the open as soon as the coach stopped rolling. They were greeted by a blast of gunfire.

Casswell went down, shot through the head. A slug in his thigh doubled up Jim Brown, and he staggered away into the brush. Archie McLaughlin received a superficial wound. Jack Smith and Billy Mansfield survived the hail of lead without being touched. They picked up Brown and fled. The night stage then proceeded to Rapid City without further incident.

Archie and his surviving companions holed up in a cabin in the timber within a few miles of Deadwood and did what they could to relieve Brown's suffering. He had great need of a doctor but, knowing the hunt for them was on, they feared to contact one. A week passed and Brown's condition became critical. As a last resort Archie sent Billy Mansfield into town to ask Lurline to come to the cabin and see what she could do to save Brown's life.

Obviously she must have revealed some of the secrets of her past to Archie, especially of her days in Texas as Dr. Hallett's wife. Otherwise he would hardly have turned to her for help. When she learned what he wanted her to do, her first reaction was to say no; not only would she be jeopardizing her own safety in consorting with wanted men, but she had no surgical tools.

When Billy Mansfield told her that Archie was depending on her to do something, he played his trump card. Armed with a wire loop used in probing for an imbedded bullet, no doubt borrowed from some Deadwood doctors, she left with Mansfield for the bandit camp. With such skill as she possessed, she removed the slug from Brown's hip and saved his life. She soon had reason to regret it, for Brown was arrested shortly thereafter and confessed his part in the attempted Whoop-up Canyon holdup and impli-cated Billy Mansfield, Jack Smith and Archie McLaughlin. The three men fled the country but were captured north of Cheyenne a few months later. On their way back to Deadwood to stand trial, the stagecoach in which they were traveling was stopped by a party of masked vigilantes north of Fort Laramie on the night of November 3. The prisoners were taken to a grove of cotton-woods, where ropes were looped about their necks and they were lynched.

Lurline-Belle—call her what you will—was an adventuress and undoubtedly had had love affairs with other men besides Archie McLaughlin, but with his death her life began to go downhill. She had planned at their last meeting to join him in San Francisco. Perhaps that is why she went there eventually. She turned to drugs and alcohol for escape from fits of depression. The relief they gave her was only temporary.

Deadwood had become hateful to her. She disposed of her business and went to Cheyenne. After a few weeks, she went on to Denver. Several months later she was operating a dance hall in Cripple Creek. It was on to El Paso, Texas, next and then to Tombstone, Arizona. She was on a seemingly endless trail that led nowhere. Her health was failing, and dissipation was not improving it. She arrived in San Francisco some time in 1880. In a police raid on the Chinese opium dens of Grant Avenue, she was arrested in October, 1881, and gave her name as Lurline Monte Verde. On examination, a police department doctor found her in the last stages of cancer. She was removed to the police ward of the general hospital, where she died, the minor charge of inhabiting a proscribed opium den having been dropped.

Her passing rated only half a dozen lines in the San Francisco papers.

China Polly, the Poker Bride

THE LIFE AND DEATH of most Western mining camps followed an inescapable pattern; in response to the cry of Gold they blossomed full-blown almost overnight, had their brief hour of hell-roaring prosperity and then faded into oblivion when it became apparent that the treasure in the surrounding streams and hillsides was exhausted.

Always it was the gamblers and prostitutes who were the first to leave, followed closely by the saloonmen. The others, even the diehards, soon drifted away to try their luck elsewhere. If what they left behind escaped quick destruction by fire, it became another in the long list of deserted ghost towns, with sightless windows and crumbling shacks. Although many have disappeared completely, one link remains to connect the Old West that is gone with the West of today. It is the myths and legends that refuse to die.

One of the hardiest of such tales is the story of China Polly, the beautiful young Chinese slave girl. Allegedly, she was the stake for whom four men—three Chinese and a white man, Charley Bemis the gambler—played a hand of poker in the booming camp of Old Warren, in the rugged, almost inaccessible Salmon River country of central Idaho in 1872.

At the time, Warren boasted a population of 3,000, a third of whom were Chinese. If the ratio of yellow men to white seems high, it held true in many Idaho gold camps, where placering as well as quartz mining were pursued. Thousands of Orientals had been imported into the United States to build the western half of the first transcontinental railroad. When the rails of the Union Pacific and the Central Pacific met at Promontory Point, Utah, the Chinese laborers, finding their occupation gone, turned to mining as their only means of making a living. It led to almost continuous strife and blood-letting.

In its majestic, downstream plunge of a hundred and twenty miles across central Idaho from Salmon City, in the shadow of the Bitterroot Range, to Riggins, where it is joined by the Little Salmon, sixty miles from its confluence with the Snake, the Big Salmon was aptly dubbed the "River of No Return." Heavy, flat-bottomed scows, guided by sweeps in the hands of experienced rivermen, could negotiate the frequent stretches of dangerous white water and succession of falls. But having reached Riggins, there was no way of getting back by water.

There are houses standing in Riggins today that were built of lumber salvaged from dismantled boats.

With its size and violence, Warren dominated the region. Even after it was three years old and booming, its singular distinction was that there wasn't a white woman in camp. The only females were the Sheepeater (Lapwai) Indian girls, who had been purchased or stolen from their tribe, and the stable of Chinese prostitutes owned by Big Jim, the boss of the Chinese colony. Until she became the common-law wife of Charley Bemis, China Polly was big Jim's property. He had bought her and four other women in San Francisco and he brought them first to Idaho City and eventually to Warren.

Undoubtedly the difficulty of getting into that wild, remote, roadless country along the Big Salmon was responsible in some measure for keeping white women out. When Warren began to fade and men were pulling away to other diggings, there was no reason for bringing women in. After the exodus was over, only a scattered handful of people remained, living on small ranches on the sandbars or creeks in the great canyon. One of the very few was China Polly. She stayed on at Bemis Point, a favorite stopping place for rivermen. They traded their game for the vegetables she raised. By then the story of the "poker bride" was already in circulation, and like most legends that endure, it was founded on half truths and imagination.

Jay (or Jake, as he was better known) Czikek, one-time State-Mine Inspector for the Salmon River District, was rated until his death twenty-five years ago the best-informed survivor of the old days in historic Warren. He was China Polly's dependable friend for well over half a century, and he always ridiculed the story that Bemis had won her in a poker game.

"The folks who put that yarn together got their facts mixed up," he told a correspondent for the Portland *Oregonian* when they had met at the Idaho County Hospital at Grangeville, where Czikek had come to visit Polly. Then in her eighties, she had only a few weeks to live. Friends had brought her out of the mountains, strapped to the back of a horse, and taken her to Grangeville.

"Warren did have a 'poker bride,' if you want to call her that," Czikek recalled. "But it was a young squaw named Molly, not Polly Bemis. There was so few women in Warren that you had to take what you could get; you couldn't be particular. In the spring of '79 the Sheepeaters made off with a horse belonging to a man named Pony Smead. He and a couple friends set out to get the animal back. They caught up with the Indians out in Chamberlain Basin and got the horse so easy they figured they was entitled to some booty. They saw this girl Molly and decided she would do. They brought her to Warren. All three of them wanted her, so they agreed to play a hand of poker and whoever won would be the man she belonged to. Smead won. He married Molly and they raised a big family, half a dozen children. Some of them are still living around Shoup and Salmon City. I suppose because Molly and Polly sound so much alike that whoever started the story about the poker bride got the names mixed up."

He was asked if the two women were acquainted.

"I doubt it. Polly has been telling me for years that she never knew Molly. And I believe her. It was in 1872 that Charley Bemis took her down to what came to be called Bemis Point, a few miles below Warren, and she never left there until after he died in

1923. It was not until 1879 that Pony Smead married the Indian girl.

"Bemis was a strange, unfriendly man. He always went armed. If you stopped at his place at Bemis Point, he usually showed up carrying a shotgun. He treated Polly good enough, taught her to speak English and didn't work her to death in their garden, which was a big one and the best producer on the river. Of course he spent most of his time working his sluice boxes and making a good living.

"Their nearest neighbors were a couple young Germans who were mining back in the hills, three or four miles away. Whenever they had to go to town for supplies, they always stopped by for an hour. After Bemis died, they sorta took it on themselves to look out for Polly. It was them, Pete Klinkhammer and Charley Shepp, who brought her down here a few weeks ago. She's nothing but skin and bones today, but she was always a little thing, no taller than a broomhandle, as the saying goes. I don't suppose she ever weighed over eighty pounds."

Czikek was asked how China Polly had got away from her Chinese owner.

"Big Jim was sitting out in front of his place one afternoon, sunning himself, when he suddenly toppled over. He was dead when he was picked up. The doctor said it was his heart. No regrets were expressed. We hated him because of the way he treated his girls. They were just cattle to him. I don't know how the Chinese handle their business affairs, but Polly and the other girls no longer belonged to anyone. For four of the five it was just a matter of changing hands, and they continued their whoring; Polly opened a little restaurant and did well until she fell in love with Charley Bemis."

In Jake Czikek's mind (himself then a grizzled veteran of eighty-five) no doubt existed but what Bemis was as deeply in love with her as she with him. The turn of events seemed to prove it. Bemis had an argument one evening with a halfbreed Lapwai by the name of John Cox, in a poker game. Cox caught him the next afternoon lounging on the porch of Polly's restaurant and sent a bullet crashing into his left cheek and down through the mouth and out under the ears. The wound was not serious, but it left him disfigured for life. Polly nursed him back to health. In return, he gave up gambling as a profession and, making her his common-law wife, he took her down to Bemis Point and established the little ranch that was to be their home for years. In 1894 he made her his legal wife, "with papers," as the old saying put it. When he died in 1923, China Polly had seen nothing of the outside world for fifty-one years.

She grieved so much over his passing that Czikek and his wife got her down to Riggins by boat and took her on to Boise, hoping to cheer her up. But the wonders of Boise—dazzling electric lights, motion pictures and radio—frightened rather than excited her, and she asked to be taken back to the lonely canyon of the Big Salmon. There she remained alone for the last ten years of her life, seeing no one but her German neighbors and the passing boatmen.

China Polly died on November 5, 1933. Old friends insisted that Bemis Point should be her final resting place. Now that power boats ply the Big Salmon, more people pass, and the captains of such craft point out her grave to tourists and sightseers. The real "poker bride" is forgotten, but China Polly Bemis is a living legend.

--⊰{ X V I }⊱--

That Taylor Woman

IN THE HISTORY of the mass movement of the Longhorns out of Texas to the Kansas cattle markets and beyond, Nebraska has seldom been accorded the importance due it. Using government figures as a guide, the difference between the number of cattle received at such places as Abilene, Wichita, Dodge City, and the number shipped out by rail justifies Joseph McCoy's statement that 40 per cent of all such Texas cattle (and mustangs) were driven on north to stock the empty ranges of Wyoming, Montana and Dakota or to supply the government beef issue at the northern Indian reservations. In either case, they had to cross Nebraska to reach their destination.

When the big herds left the Chisholm Trail in the 1870's for the new Western Trail, which crossed Red River at Doan's Store and struck almost due north to Camp Supply in the Oklahoma Panhandle, trail drivers bound for the northern ranges found they had made a saving of several hundred miles. At Camp Supply they turned into the old Jones and Plummer Trail which, crossing the Arkansas River three miles west of Dodge City, opened the way northward to Ogallala, Nebraska,[1] a shipping point on the Union Pacific Railroad. Over this route passed thousands of Texas cattle and mustangs. It acquired the name "The Texas Trail," and it was so called up through Wyoming and deep into Montana.

By 1877, so many native and foreign-born settlers, the latter largely Welsh, Bohemian and Slovenes, had taken up government land in Nebraska that hostility against the Texans approached open warfare. It was a repetition of the trouble that had occurred in Kansas—the grangers demanding toll for permitting a trail herd to cross their land or to "water" at a pond or creek on which they claimed ownership. Having the votes to control the State Legislature and the local courts, they put stringent herd laws on the books and enforced them. Since the cattleman was held to be the common enemy, it was considered less than reprehensible to steal from him. Stealing a Longhorn or two, butchering them and selling the meat as elk meat became an organized business. The situation got so bad that the big Texas outfits began penning their cattle and horses at night.

When a trail outfit got as far north as the Platte, the stock had to be held and given a week to ten days in which to recruit its strength for the rest of the long journey across Wyoming and Montana. The pens were just big corrals. In the morning, Longhorns and mustangs were put on grass, under guard. This practice reduced the amount of range thievery but it did not stop it, although holding pens were built on the South Loup River, the Republican and South Platte.

Just why Print Olive took it upon himself to spearhead the drive against the rustlers has never been satisfactorily explained. His outfit, Olive Brothers of Austin (Print, Bob, Ira and Marion), was a big one, with three to four herds on the trail at the same time, and undoubtedly suffered more grievously from range depredations than other trail drivers. In any event, he swore he would stop it. He was a rough, violent little man. His first move was to get his brother Bob appointed stock inspector, which gave him the legal right to investigate and question all suspected range thieves. He gathered information on two men named Ketchum and Mitchell that left no doubt about their butchering Olive steers. Accompanied by one of the brothers' cowpunchers, Bob Olive managed to catch the two men ripping the hide off a Longhorn wearing the Olive brand. There was gunfire, and Bob was killed.

Fearful of Print Olive's vengeance, Ketchum and Mitchell surrendered to the sheriff and were lodged in jail. Print's vengeance was swift and terrible. As Ketchum and Mitchell were being taken to Hastings to stand trial, he and a bunch of his men took the prisoners away from the sheriff and his deputies and hanged them from the limb of a lone elm on Plum Creek. As the two bodies were swaying in the breeze, Print emptied his gun into them to make sure the rustlers were dead.

The hanging of Ketchum and Mitchell touched off a reign of violence, lynchings and black hatred that snuffed out the lives of eleven people before it ended. Alive, Ketchum and Mitchell had been regarded as dubious characters by their neighbors. In death, the Texas haters exhibited their remains around the state and proclaimed them martyrs who had given their lives in the farmers' battle with the cattle barons. The papers were silent, but by word of mouth the story was circulated from town to town that the two men had been doused with coal oil and burned alive as they were swung up. This fantastic tale gained credence when the state's attorney reported that he had had the dead men's clothes analyzed and that traces of coal oil were found on them.

Reason fled when such inflammatory talk came from a public official. It could have been pointed out that it would have been all but impossible to have found a homesteader in Nebraska whose clothes did not bear traces of coal oil, which was in daily use. At the trial, the prosecution put numerous witnesses on the stand who described the condition of the bodies of Ketchum and Mitchell when they were cut down. All swore to the grievous burns the two men had suffered, it being the purpose of the prosecutor to establish that death had resulted from incineration rather than by hanging. This was an appeal to popular prejudice against all Texans and calculated to guarantee conviction.

The defense attorneys admitted that the two men had been burned but contended that their clothing had caught fire from the powder flashes of Print's gun after they were dead. That was the contention of several hundred cowpunchers who had come in for the trial, including the men who had taken part in the lynching. Since they could not testify without incriminating themselves, they were not called to the stand.

Print was found guilty and sentenced to a long term in the state penitentiary. Mrs. Olive, a gentle, cultured little woman, had come north for the trial. Only her presence and persuasion prevented the enraged Texans from taking Print away from the authorities and spiriting him out of the state. Various appeals were made, and after spending two years behind bars, Print was given his freedom on a writ of error—which indicated that much of the testimony given in Hastings was both perjured and prejudiced.

The outcome satisfied no one and it was to produce ugly repercussions long after the farmers had pushed the trail driver and cattleman out of Nebraska. Hatred and suspicion took the place of reason and turned neighbor against neighbor. Caught in the vortex of the contending factions were the non-English-speaking settlers from Europe. But to no one did the circumstances bring greater tragedy than to a young woman named Elizabeth Jones Taylor. She was twenty-five in 1879 and had been living on the Little Blue River in what was then known as Spring Ranch Precinct, Clay County, Nebraska, with her husband, children, three brothers and father and mother since 1872. They were Welsh and spoke and read English. The elderly John W. Jones, Elizabeth's father, had migrated to America with his family in 1868 and settled in Pettis County, Missouri. Two years after Elizabeth's marriage to James A. Taylor, a Welshman, and the birth of her first child William, she and her husband removed to Nebraska and took up land on the Little Blue. The other members of the family soon followed. As settlers in a pioneer country, they were in far better financial circumstances than most of their neighbors. As they took up additional land, their cattle, horses and mules were free to roam almost at will as they gorged themselves on the lush grass along the Little Blue.

Elizabeth was described by the "sports" who gathered on a Saturday night in the nearby village of Harvard as a plump, pretty blonde. She was obsessed with a driving ambition to better her lot and her children's, the older heads observed, and that perhaps is what made them question her. Ambition in a man was to be admired; in a woman—it was questionable. Across the road from the Taylor sod house on the Little Blue lived Rees T. Rees, a bachelor and a man of some importance in Spring Ranch Precinct. He had an eye for Elizabeth and made no secret of it. Undoubtedly she compared him with her husband. He was aggressive and domineering. The man to whom she was married was spineless and too obliging to get ahead. She had borne him three children and had always been a faithful wife.

The Print Olive trial had made their neighbors aware of the rights and privileges granted them by the Nebraska Herd Law. Now, when the Taylor cattle, mules or horses broke fence and wandered across planted fields, apologies were not enough; claims for damages were presented. Elizabeth refused to pay them. To avoid trouble, her husband did. Even though he, their hired man and Elizabeth and the children walked fence on their three-quarter section spread and corralled the stock at night, the animals sometimes strayed.

In the spring of 1881, despite his wife's objection, Taylor plowed under a quarter-section of good grazing land and put it under cultivation. No rain fell for twenty-six days that year, and although he had planted drought-resisting Turkey Red wheat, it died without breaking through the dry soil. It meant that no return could be expected that year. The crop failure came at a time when money was needed to pay for the new T-shaped frame house the Taylors had built a hundred yards up the road from their original soddy. If the quarter-section had been left in grass, it would have supported an additional number of cows—Guernseys and Holsteins —for which there was always a ready sale.

The financial pinch in which they found themselves convinced Elizabeth that unless she gained control of their real and personal estate, the course her husband was pursuing would cost them everything they had worked for since migrating to Nebraska. Before the year was over, Taylor capitulated and placed everything in her name. Under the provisions of the Nebraska statute commonly referred to as "The Married Woman's Property Act," this gave her the right to sell, dispose of, make business deals and have recourse to the courts to collect moneys due, without her husband's consent.

Spring Ranch Precinct quickly became aware that they now had an aggressive, determined woman to deal with. When money was due her, the promises of future payment that Jim Taylor had accepted would not suffice. They no longer had any respect for him and dismissed him as just his wife's hired man. On her they focused their venom, manufacturing scandalous tales about her and seeing that they got a wide circulation. Oblivious of her detractors, she drove about Clay County buying and selling stock and prospering.

On May 27, 1882, Jim Taylor died under peculiar circumstances. A Bohemian neighbor was fishing at the river when, in the late afternoon, Taylor came pounding up to the bank, flung himself from his horse and, rushing to the river, began gulping the water and gasping for breath. A minute or two later he fell face downward into the Little Blue. When the Bohemian pulled him out, he was dead. At the inquest the coroner rendered a verdict of death from natural causes. The matter would have ended there had not one of Elizabeth's Welsh neighbors set the tale in motion that he had seen her purchase a bag of Paris Green at the general store in Clay Center. Paris Green was a deadly poison used for dusting potato plants. The feeling against her being what it was, the tale quickly spread that she had bought the Paris Green for another purpose than to rid her potato plants of bugs.

No official investigation was ever made and no incriminating evidence was produced against her, but Spring Ranch Precinct filed the story away for future use. When her father was taken ill a few weeks later, it was whispered that she had poisoned him, too. Inquisitive neighbors visited the sick man and a doctor was called in. He pronounced the old man to be dying of cancer. This put to rest for the time being the rumor that Jim Taylor and his father-in-law had been poisoned.

Thomas Jones, Elizabeth's twin brother, came to live with her, old Mrs. Taylor and the children. He enjoyed an excellent reputation and was a Master Mason of Juniata Lodge. Reversing her role of being in personal command of her business, she put the management of her affairs in her brother Tom's hands. He proceeded to work his ranch and hers as a joint holding, well over a thousand acres in all.

With Elizabeth approving, he hired a full-time fence rider. When the stock had to be watered in the evening, the new man,

Tom Jones and the two young Taylor boys drove the animals down to the Little Blue. With constant fence surveillance the complaints against the trespassing of the Taylor stock decreased. They stopped altogether when Ed Proust, the line rider, caught two of John Llewelyn's sons tearing down a piece of their father's fence. When Llewelyn came storming up to the Taylor house to claim payment for the downed fence, Elizabeth snapped her fingers in his face and told him to file a complaint; that she had a witness to what had happened. Llewelyn called her some ugly names, but he did not file any complaint.

Elizabeth had another visitor, Rees T. Rees, the bachelor from across the road. After several visits, she knew the American-born Welshman was about to ask her to be his wife. His eagerness defeated him. Had he waited a decent interval after she had buried her husband and father, her answer might have been yes. But she said no, and in doing so created an implacable enemy who was not to be satisfied until she had paid with her life for scorning him.

In Hastings, on March 27, 1883, three masked men held up a grocery store and killed the owner, Cassius Millet. The crime and the manner in which it was avenged were tragic enough in themselves, but they were only the forerunner of the greater and more brutal tragedy that was to descend on Clay County two years later. They were not unconnected, for in each instance men ignored constituted law and order and resorted to vigilante or mob law.

A number of crimes had been committed in or near Hastings, many of which had gone unpunished. In the case of the killing of Grocer Millet the evidence pointed unmistakably to three local characters named Ingram, Greene and Babcock. The sheriff swore in deputies and proceeded to the Charles Kohl farm south of Hastings, where the three men were drilling a well. They were taken into custody and lodged in the Hastings jail. In the meantime a number of prominent businessmen had organized a committee to put an end to the reign of terror that was gripping the town. They answered a summons to meet at night in the local lumber yard, where it was decided to take the prisoners out of the hands of the authorities and lynch them. Donning masks and armed with a heavy timber, they proceeded to the jail, bashed in the door and led Ingram, Greene and Babcock to the St. Joseph and Grand Island Railroad bridge. The three men were stood up side by side, a noose placed around the neck of each and the other end of the ropes fastened to a bridge tie. A signal was given and they were pushed off.

This triple lynching (one man was breathing when he was cut down but failed to survive) caused no outburst of public indignation, the consensus being that when the law was ineffectual and slow to act, the public was justified in taking matters into its own hands.

There was further trouble between the Taylor and Llewelyn boys in 1884. This time the Taylor boys were found guilty and an indictment was lodged against them charging that they "wantonly and maliciously lay down, prostrated, defaced and injured a fence enclosing pasture land of John Llewelyn." Appearing as witnesses against them were John Llewelyn, Rees T. Rees and Joseph Beyer. Although the Taylor boys were minors, William twelve and John eleven, they were bound over for trial at the May term of the district court at Clay Center in 1885. Bail was set at $250 and they were released in their mother's custody.[2]

Shortly thereafter Rees noticed that old Ben Bethlemer, Mrs. Taylor's hired man, had disappeared. Without the slightest evidence, he started the whisper that maybe old Ben had been given a dose of the same "medicine" that had killed Jim Taylor.

Elizabeth Taylor must have been aware of the campaign of vilification being waged against her, for she bought a shotgun and ammunition on a visit to Clay Center for her protection. As she journeyed about Clay and Adams counties she asked livestock dealers and livery barn men to pass the word that any drifting cowboy headed for Texas could find grub, bed and tobacco at her ranch on the Little Blue if he was willing to work for his keep. Before long young Texans were bedding down from time to time at the Taylor ranch. Some remained only a few days, others several weeks. It gave Rees another opportunity to blacken her reputation. This time it was her virtue that was questioned. His scurrilous talk hinted that the reason the young Texans remained such a short time at the Taylor spread was because they refused to take the privilege of an hour in bed with Mrs. Taylor for wages instead of hard cash.

She owned a small tract of timber on the river. In an almost treeless country, timber was doubly valuable. When she discovered that some of her neighbors were cutting her trees, she demanded that they desist. No attention was paid to her complaints. The most persistent offender was a man named Edwin Roberts, a newcomer to Spring Ranch to whom she had leased the land he was occupying. She had also loaned him a team of horses. On January 8, 1885, she saw Roberts passing in his wagon and heading in the direction of her timber. Standing up in the wagon with him was Joseph Beyer, one of his neighbors. She ran out of the house and called to them to stop. They drove on, paying no attention to her.

At the time she had a young Texan, name unknown, working for her. She ordered him to hitch a team and go after the two men. Beyond question she gave him her shotgun, but whether her instructions were to use the gun to frighten Roberts and Beyer off her property, as she claimed, or to gun them down, as Rees charged, will always remain a question. It is not likely, however, that when the young Texan had a team hitched and was about to drive off that she would have permitted her two boys to accompany him if Roberts and Beyer were to be shot to death.

Some time later the Texan and the Taylor youngsters caught sight of the men returning from the direction of the river. Roberts held the reins. Both he and Beyer were standing up on the logs that filled the wagon, which obviously had been cut a day or two earlier. Roberts was driving. When he came abreast of the Taylor wagon, the shouting of the youngsters frightened his team and, as it bolted, Beyer was pitched off. The fall stunned him, but as he lay on the ground he heard a shot fired and saw the Taylor wagon racing off across the open field, with William Taylor holding the shotgun.

Beyer raised up. He couldn't see anything of Roberts. The team was galloping on, however. Getting to his feet, Beyer ran after the log wagon and overtook it as it approached the Rees house. By chance Rees, J. F. Eller, Grant Bozarth and a fourth man were standing in the yard when they saw the driverless wagon bearing down on them. They ran out and stopped it. The situation explained itself when they saw Roberts sprawled out dead on the logs, half of his face and head shot away. Rees had his opportunity now and he made the most of it. By midnight the two Taylor youngsters were behind bars in the county jail at Clay Center, charged with murder. There they remained, bail being denied them.

Why the young Texan who had been with the boys was not arrested at once defies explanation. When the law started looking for him, he had disappeared. Rees claimed he had seen him walking fence with Elizabeth's brother, with the latter carrying a shovel. When Tom Jones returned to the house, he was alone.

Rees inferred from the circumstances that the cowboy had been killed and put under the sod somewhere on the Taylor range. Deputy Sheriff Karnes, who was conducting the investigation, was aware of the hostility existing between Rees and Mrs. Taylor. Apparently he didn't think the tip had merit enough to warrant digging up the Taylor place.

Rees turned to more receptive ears and suggested that "it's time something was done about those Taylors." G. W. Vangilder, John Llewelyn, David Bennett and H. H. Hyde, all prominent in the Precinct, agreed with him. They called on the widow of the late Edwin Roberts and, after convincing her that she was in danger of bodily harm from Mrs. Taylor and Tom Jones, induced the woman to file a complaint against Mrs. Taylor and her brother Tom, demanding that they be put under bond to keep the peace. On January 31, they appeared before Justice of the Peace Louis N. Bryant, Spring Ranch Precinct, Clay County, and were ordered to put up a peace bond in the amount of $900 each and to swear under oath to "be of good behavior generally, and especially towards said Elizabeth Roberts."

This action had no purpose other than to continue the harassment of the defendants and further damage their reputation. Any doubt that Rees and his fellow conspirators were determined to drive them out of Clay County disappeared early in March, when Rees called for a secret meeting of the farmers of Clay County at the Mullen farm, two miles east of Spring Ranch. There is nothing in the evidence to say whether at that time they contemplated anything beyond the forced deportation of Elizabeth and Tom Jones, or had already decided that only their deaths would satisfy them.

Beyer's wife was a Bohemian and he learned to speak her language. Accordingly he took it on himself to contact her countrymen; Rees and Llewelyn canvassed the rest of the county. On the night of March 5, over half a hundred mounted farmers gathered in the Mullen field and were sworn to secrecy. Men who were present said afterward that through all the haranguing no reference was made to the elderly Mrs. John Jones and the child Maggie, toward whom no animosity was felt.

It was proposed by Rees that they ride to the frame house on the Taylor place, where Elizabeth and Tom were known to be living, call them out and escort them to the county line and forbid them to return under penalty of death.

Now for the first time the Bohemians understood why they were there. After talking it over among themselves and deciding that they wanted no part of what was to follow, they left in a body.

Rees and his fellow conspirators, accompanied by a score of wavering adherents, rode quickly to the Taylor house and, having it surrounded, called on the occupants to step out. They were answered by a blast of gunfire from every window, for by chance four (five if a lad by the name of Luther Wiggins is included), all, save one, Texans, happened to be temporarily "in residence." They were identified later as Texas Bill Foster, Nat Clark, Bud Ferrell, and Nelson Cellery, a Spring Ranch native. They were the ones who did the shooting. Tom Jones had no gun, and during the day, while Elizabeth Taylor was away, someone had entered the house and made off with her stock of ammunition.

No one was struck by the gunfire from the windows, for at the first blast Rees's followers had deserted him and only he and his ringleaders were left. They did not remain long.

The following night John Llewelyn's barn was burned. He promptly accused Mrs. Taylor of having had it destroyed. This time he was correct, for she had hired one of the Texans to set the barn afire. It was small satisfaction for all she had suffered at the hands of her neighbors. During the day, she, her brother and the others moved down to the old soddy, leaving her mother and little Maggie in the frame house on the hill. The soddy, with its thick walls, offered better protection against attack than the frame building. With growing horror she waited for the mob to return. Shortly after midnight on March 15, she heard men crossing her field. It was cold, still winter, with a skift of frozen snow on the ground. They had stopped at the corrals and seized a number of rope mule halters, which they had unraveled and knotted together.

Presently Rees's booming voice called on the occupants of the soddy to come out or dynamite would be dropped down the chimney and the place be blown to bits. A minute or two later the Texans, Cellery, and the boy Luther Wiggins came out, hands raised. Their hands were quickly tied behind their backs and they were led off up the road to the Rees house. Thomas Jones stepped out then, warmly clad. Behind him came Elizabeth, wearing only a nightgown. She asked for permission to get properly dressed. A man reached inside and got a shawl which he threw over her shoulders before her hands were strapped down to her sides. They had held a meeting and decided on what they had to do. They wasted no time now in carrying out their plans.

Elizabeth Taylor and her brother were marched down the Spring Ranch road to the iron and wooden bridge that spanned the shallow river. Nooses fashioned out of the mule halters were dropped over their heads and drawn tightly about their throats. They then were led down to the sand bar beneath the bridge, which at this time of year rose above the level of the water. Standing in their saddles, two men tied the loose ends of the ropes to a bridge stringer.

There was not more than ten feet of clearance between the bottom of the bridge and the river. It was room enough for the grisly business that was at hand. Elizabeth and Tom Jones were forced to mount two impatient horses. At a blast of gunfire the animals leaped away, leaving the victims strangling to death as they swung back and forth in the air.

The men held under guard at Rees's house were ordered to keep away from the bridge and to lose no time in getting out of Clay County. All save Nelson Cellery didn't have to be told twice. He went to his parents' farm and by daylight had recovered enough courage to send him scurrying across country to have a look at the bridge on the Spring Ranch road. He was horrified but he could hardly have been surprised at the sight of the two dangling bodies. A youth named Barker came along. Cellery enlisted him to spread word of what had happened and to bring witnesses. Soon Joseph Meehan of Pawnee Ranch, John Quinn, Edward Young and others reached the scene.

Cellery wanted to cut the bodies down. Meehan protested that they must be left where they were until the coroner viewed them, that otherwise the law wouldn't have evidence or proof of the crime. It was one o'clock in the afternoon before the coroner Jesse Eller and his jury of four men arrived at the bridge. After a cursory examination of the bodies, Eller ordered them cut down and removed to the Taylor frame house. While at the bridge one of the bystanders, a man named Clark, started to name the men who, in his opinion had lynched Elizabeth and her brother. Ellery cut him off and warned him to keep his mouth shut. The incident served notice in advance of what his verdict was to be, to wit: "That E. A. Taylor and Thomas Jones came to their death by hanging at the hands of persons unknown."

On the morning of March 16, Elizabeth Taylor and her brother were secretly buried in adjoining graves in Spring Ranch cemetery. Other than the undertaker who had brought the wooden coffins from nearby Fairfield, the only mourners were their mother, Mrs. Margaret Jones, Elizabeth's five-year-old-daughter Maggie, and her brothers William and John, who had come from their farms in Nuckhols County.

By then newspapers throughout the state were publishing the story of the double lynching in Spring Ranch Precinct and expressing shock and horror. That one of the victims was a woman in her early thirties made the crime doubly reprehensible. "The Shame of Nebraska" read an Omaha headline. "This State can now claim the terrible distinction of being the first in this country to lynch a woman."

It was an atrocious, bungled, needlessly cruel lynching, unjustified by any shred of evidence against the victims. But the campaign of vilification and malicious innuendoes had been accepted by many of the Spring Ranch people as fact. So while the Hastings *Gazette-Journal* said "the lynching of Mrs. Taylor and Tom Jones . . . is universally condemned in the most severe terms; people demand that the courts, the Governor and all other officers hunt up and punish the ringleaders," nothing was done, proving that the majority of those who were loudest in their denunciation of the lynchers did not want anything done. Hundreds of residents of Clay County could have named the ringleaders, but they did not come forward with any information. In fact if it had not been for the prodding of J. C. Kay, a lawyer and respected real estate dealer of Hastings, a staunch friend of Mrs. Taylor and the administrator of her estate, and the editor of the *Gazette-Journal*, it is not likely that any action would have been taken.

When Rees T. Rees and his lieutenants—G. W. Vangilder, John Llewelyn, David Bennett and H. H. Hyde—learned that warrants charging them with murder in the first degree had been issued, they armed themselves and forted up in the Metropolitan Hotel in Harvard. To avoid being taken by surprise, one man always remained awake while the others slept. This was five days after the lynching. When the sheriff and his deputies surrounded the hotel two days later, the former conferred privately with Rees, and some guarantee of safety having been given (it is assumed), the five men surrendered and were hurried off to the county jail at Clay Center. One week later they were brought before District Court Judge E. P. Burnett.

The defense presented no witnesses, the prosecution a great many, including the elderly mother of Mrs. Taylor and Tom Jones. The judge was brusque with her and the other prosecution witnesses. They might as well have stayed at home, for the predetermined purpose of the arraignment was to relieve the law of any future obligation to investigate the Taylor-Jones lynching.

According to a dispatch printed in the *Omaha Daily Bee*, March

31, "the applause in the courtroom was deafening when Judge Burnett declared the evidence against the five prisoners insufficient and ordered their release."

When Rees and the others walked out free men, it marked their last appearance in any court in connection with the lynching. It left the law with one embarrassment, however. After almost fifteen months the young Taylor boys were still in jail, charged with the murder of Edwin Roberts. They had been denied the privilege of attending their mother's funeral and had never been arraigned. Now, as the "good" people of Clay County examined their consciences, the long incarceration of the two youngsters without being brought to trial became a grievous miscarriage of justice. To quiet the rumblings, something had to be done. The district attorney notified defense counsel that he would be ready to go to trial on May 20. It was a very friendly confrontation, the lawyers for the boys asserting that the indictment had been faultily drawn and asking that it be set aside. The district attorney agreed, and the charge against the boys was dropped and they were released.

In the Spring Ranch cemetery five monuments, now slightly askew, stand on the Taylor-Jones family plot, marking the graves of Elizabeth Taylor, her parents, her brother, and her husband. Nothing disturbs their slumber today. But had Nebraska turned its back on violence and lawlessness with their death? Apparently not, for approximately ten years after the lynching of Elizabeth Taylor, another woman, Mrs. Thad Holton, was lynched in Keya Paha County.

Pearl Starr, Daughter of the Bandit Queen

BELLE STARR, the so-called "Bandit Queen," has been the subject of so many lengthy biographical accounts, articles and motion pictures that another telling seems unnecessary. Truth has long since been separated from fiction—no easy matter—and the only point that remains a matter of controversy is the identity of the man who killed her. On the other hand, very little is known about Baby Pearl, her daughter, born out of wedlock and fathered (beyond question) by the famous outlaw Cole Younger, head of the Younger clan of bandits—Cole, Bob, Jim and John—who rode to lasting immortality of a sort with Frank and Jesse James.

Belle mothered two children—her "Baby Pearl," born in Texas in 1867, to whom she gave the name of Pearl Younger, and Edwin (Eddie) Reed, fathered by Jim Reed, an outlaw of minor caliber, also born without the sanctity of legal marriage in 1868, in Rich Hill, Missouri. Reed was killed near Paris, Texas, in connection with the robbery of the San Antonio–Austin stage in 1874. After that a parade of "husbands" and lovers appeared and disappeared from Belle's life with mystifying frequency.

When she wed Sam Starr the son of the embattled Tom Starr, the Cherokee feudist—a legal marriage by Cherokee law—she acquired the property on the Canadian River which was to become famous as Younger's Bend, seventy-nine miles west of Fort Smith. With its two cabins, a "guest house" for visiting outlaws, and corrals and caves, no more secure stronghold for her activities outside the law could have been found. It was deep in wild country, where dim trails served as roads, and a stranger on horseback could be spotted and word of his coming "telegraphed" ahead by the "grapevine" in time for a wanted man to disappear.

Belle lived at Younger's Bend with her children, Pearl and Eddie, as they grew from childhood to adolescence. Although it may be true that the criminal tendency is not hereditary, it hardly can be denied that youthful environment usually dictates the direction in which the child will lean as he matures. Certainly its effect on Belle's children was inescapable, as time was to prove. In her deep and abiding love she foolishly believed that with money she could purchase respectability for them. In Texas, when Pearl was very young, she was the best-dressed child in Dallas. In addition to her schooling, there were piano, dancing and French lessons. No matter what befell, no matter what was necessary to provide the money, Belle was guided by one thought: "Pearl has to be a lady." It was the greatest wish of her life.

Belle had relatives in Carthage, Missouri, and Wichita. Eddie's grandparents and cousins lived in Bates County, Missouri. Occasionally Belle packed the children off to spend vacations with her relatives. But she was always unhappy until she had them back. It seems not to have occurred to her that they were growing old enough to understand perfectly what the new "papa" they invariably found waiting for them when they returned to Younger's Bend was doing there. Sometimes the new "papas" were white men; oftener they were mixed-blood Cherokees, Choctaws and in at least one instance a full-blood Creek. There were several reasons why none remained long. Belle either tired of a man and sent him packing, or, as frequently happened, the deputy marshals from Jude Parker's Fort Smith court caught up with him and he fell before their guns or was taken into custody and hustled off to prison.

Pearl Starr was so completely her mother's daughter, exhibiting the same deviltry, recklessness and disregard of the accepted laws of morality, that she best can be judged by cutting through the morass of myths, legend and fiction that have been woven about Belle Starr, the so-called Queen of the Bandits. Belle was acquitted

of the only robbery in which she was accused of participating—
the robbery of old Watt Grayson, a wealthy Creek Indian, on November 20, 1873. She faced Judge Parker, the famous Hanging
Judge, on only two occasions. The charge both times was the
larceny of a horse. She was acquitted in the first instance, and in
the second she was found guilty and sent to the House of Correc-
tion at Detroit, Michigan, along with her husband of the moment,
Sam Starr. She has often been accused of being the leader of an
organized horse-thief ring. Believably, she was its mastermind. But
horses were cheap, and she and her cohorts could not possibly
have stolen enough animals to provide her with the money she
always had on hand to engage the highest-priced lawyers, post
bail and spend thousands of dollars in winning commutation of
sentences for known outlaws.

There can be little doubt that she shared in the proceeds of
many robberies and holdups. It is also beyond doubt that she
planned many of these forays. She was educated, shrewd, cunning.
The men who gravitated around her were ignorant, uneducated
and incapable of doing for themselves what she could do for them.
Although she was openly suspected of consorting and conniving
with known outlaws, the infrequency with which she was charged
with participating in various crimes and brought to trial must be
regarded as proof of her audacity and cunning.

Of the husbands, legal and otherwise, who shared her bed at
Younger's Bend, only one escaped a violent demise.[1] That pattern
did not end with the killing of Sam Starr, who came to his death
in a shoot-out with Frank West at an all-night dance at "Aunt"
Lucy Suratt's cabin on the Briartown road. It was from Sam Starr
that she acquired the sixty-acre headright on the Canadian, to
which she added substantial acreage, leasing it out to farmers. Belle
did not remain a "widow" for long; Jim July, a handsome, well-
educated young Creek, twenty-four years old, moved in and provided Eddie and Pearl with still another new "stepfather." At
Belle's request Jim July added Starr to his name and became known
as Jim July Starr, afterward shortened to Jim Starr.

Things seemed to be going Belle's way again. A charge of grand
larceny against her had been dropped, and she had a vigorous

young "husband," nineteen years her junior, who made her forget that she was forty-one. Young Eddie was seventeen and showing traces of the wildness that ruled his father. But Belle told herself she could handle him. Although Pearl was now a very pretty young woman of nineteen, to Belle she was still a baby, her precious "Canadian Lily." All she asked was that they could go on as they were for another year or two, when she would have money enough to break away from her outlaw world and they could go far off and be happy among respectable people. It was an impossible dream. Pearl was her daughter and subject to the same passions that ruled her.

The inevitable happened; Pearl fell in love with a young man, part Creek, who lived below the Canadian. They came to Belle and asked her permission to marry. Her answer was a violent no. In a rage, she sent the boy packing and shipped Pearl off to visit friends in Chickalah, Arkansas. Pearl was back home two months later looking worried and depressed. She was five months pregnant.

Belle's world fell in ruins when she learned the truth. She raged and threatened to kill the man on sight who was responsible for Pearl's condition. But Pearl refused to name him. Very likely she couldn't with any accuracy, for she had been promiscuous for a year or more. She refused to accede to her mother's demand that an abortion be performed at once. Belle had promised that the best doctor in Fort Smith would perform the operation (which would have surprised the gentleman, for he had not been consulted) and that she would take care of all the expenses.

"Then leave my house," Belle screamed. "Take a team and get out. Leave it at Schroeder's barn."

Pearl left. She had some money, more than enough to get her to Rich Hill, Missouri, and Grandma Reed. Her brother was a Reed and she was sure they would take her in. They did, and when the old lady went to Siloam Springs, Arkansas, for her health, Pearl accompanied her. In Siloam Springs, in April, 1887, her baby was born, a girl whom she named Flossie.

Belle didn't want to see her grandchild, and never did. But she wanted Pearl back. Eddie, in the meantime, had got into trouble with some whisky peddlers and been shot during the fracas. He was in no danger of dying, but Belle wrote the Reeds at Rich Hill that if they knew how to reach Pearl by mail to tell her that if she wanted to see her brother alive, she must come home at once, but to come alone. Pearl was in Wichita. Taken in by the hoax, she left the baby with friends and hurried home to Younger's Bend.

Now that she had Pearl back, Belle was determined that her daughter should not leave her a second time. As Eddie recovered from his wound, she made new plans for a future that would spell happiness for all three. Her constant plea was that the aunt in Wichita, with whom Pearl had been living, be given authority to put Flossie up for adoption. This plan had some advantages for the child. For one, Flossie would grow up without a cloud of outlawry hanging over her. Pearl finally capitulated, and Belle managed the details.

On February 2, 1889, three days before her birthday, Belle rode as far as San Bois, in the Territory, with Jim July. He was going to Fort Smith to answer larceny charges against him. Belle turned back, visiting friends and stopping overnight with Mrs. Richard Nail on San Bois Creek.

She had had trouble with Eddie, and it weighed on her. The past July he had been sentenced to serve seven years in the Ohio State Penitentiary, which accepted federal prisoners from Indian Territory, on a charge of grand larceny. He had served only three months when he was paroled. This is alleged to have been the result of an arrangement made between Judge Parker and Belle in the hope that a taste of prison life would straighten the boy out. No proof of this exists, and it is likely just another of the fanciful tales that have been woven around Belle.

In any event Eddie had come home sullen and resentful. Shortly after his return, Belle had refused him permission to use her favorite horse, which she permitted no one but herself to ride, to go to a dance at Briartown. He had taken the animal nevertheless and, returning in the early hours of the morning, had put it in its stall without rubbing it down. She had gone out to the barn as soon as he was asleep and found the horse still hot from running, with flecks of foam on its mouth and flanks. In a rage, she had picked up a whip and, rushing into Eddie's room, had given him a terrible beating. He had finally managed to grab his clothes and bolt out of the house. Two weeks had passed since then, and he had not come home. Tales had reached her that Eddie was making threats against her. She had brushed them aside, confident that when he simmered down, he would come whimpering home to beg her forgiveness. It was the future of her handsome, incorrigible son that troubled Belle.

Contrary to the popular conception fostered by fiction and her screen impersonators, Belle was never a handsome woman. At forty-one her face was lean and bony, but she still possessed the fire and allure that made her desirable in the eyes of men. In the saddle, she was an incomparably graceful and daring rider. She never rode astride, holding it to be "unladylike." According to the record—and it has been researched beyond the possibility of error—she never robbed a bank or killed a man. As for the fortune she is supposed to have amassed—the tale of the $90,000 contained in a barrel in one of the caves at Younger's Bend—it is just folklore.

The trail Belle was using that Sunday afternoon, February 3, 1889, was pocked with puddles of water and mudholes left by the rain of the previous two days. In no hurry, she walked her horse. No more than a mile from home, she could see the buildings at Younger's Bend on the opposite bank of the Canadian. The trail circled around a field owned by Edgar Watson, with whom she had long been at odds. As she reached the corner of Watson's fence and the unused road that Milo Hoyt, her nearest neighbor, had fenced off, a shotgun roared from the fence corner. The charge, buckshot, struck her in the back. Her horse bolted and she fell face downward in a pool of muddy water. It was later determined that a second blast of smaller turkey shot, fired at closer range, tore into her arm, right shoulder and the side of her face.

Pearl rushed out as her mother's riderless horse trotted into the yard. Alarmed but not knowing what to do, she ran back and forth helplessly. In a minute or two, Milo Hoyt came dashing wildly across the ford to tell her that Belle had been murdered.[2]

Three men—Edgar Watson, Jim July and Eddie Reed—came under suspicion as the killer of Belle Starr. Watson was the prime suspect. Belle and Watson had been feuding for some time. On the afternoon of her slaying she had stopped at the cabin of Hyram Barnes to buy some of the freshly baked sour cornbread for which Mrs. Barnes was locally famous. As she turned in, Watson, carrying a shotgun, was out in the yard talking with Barnes. On seeing Belle, he left at once. It was surmised that he had hurried home and concealed himself in the brush at the corner of Milo Hoyt's fence and had killed her from his place of concealment. Watson was taken to Fort Smith. In a hearing before U.S. Commissioner Brizzolara no evidence against him could be produced, and the charge was dropped.

At Watson's hearing Eddie Reed was summoned as a witness, but he refused to testify against him. This added fuel to the feeling of many that he (Eddie) had killed his mother. Suspicion was then directed at Jim July. It was alleged that he hoped to get his hands on the eight to ten thousand dollars which John Middleton, an ex-lover of Belle's, had had in his possession when he was killed on the Poteau River by Sam Starr, her late husband. On February 25, three weeks after Belle's death, H. J. Vann, Clerk of the Canadian District, Cherokee Nation, made an entry in the official records that "witnesses had appeared before him and being sworn had deposed that they had heard Belle Starr say that if anything should happen or befall her, or that she should die, that the improvement on which she was living would be James J. (July) Starr's."

Unfortunately for Jim July, he had less than a year to go before he was mortally wounded while resisting arrest. In the meantime, being on the scout, he had never been in a position to establish his claim to Younger's Bend.

Since the publication of S. W. Harman's *Hell on the Border* in 1899, a score of historians have tried to fix the blame for Belle Starr's death where it belongs, this writer among them. While they do not agree on the individual who was responsible, the consensus has been that it was either Edgar Watson, Jim July or Eddie Reed. But in 1963 comes Edwin P. Hicks, who says it was none of these, but that it was Jim Middleton, the younger brother of the slain outlaw John Middleton, once the paramour of Belle Starr, and that Jim had killed her in retaliation for what he believed was her participation in the slaying of his brother.

Hicks puts up a strong argument for his case. He is one of the two best-informed writers who have tackled the Belle Starr–Judge Parker–Fort Smith segment of Western history. The late Homer Croy is the other. Croy says the killer was Edgar Watson, and with exhaustive documentation he pins Belle's murder on him. Hicks, on the other hand, bases his findings on years of personal interviews with a score of men and women who had some contact with Belle and the life that revolved around her at Younger's Bend. The weakness of such an approach is that the interviews took place forty, fifty, or even sixty years after the remembered events.

It has been the experience of this writer that such recollections, given after a long period of intervening years, are often, if unconsciously, a blend of fact and imagination. Croy says Edgar Watson killed Belle Starr, and I must believe him.[3]

A few months after their mother's death Pearl and Eddie found themselves in financial straits. This explodes the myth that Belle Starr was a rich woman and left her children a fortune. Actually her estate was limited to a few hundred dollars in cash and the property at Younger's Bend. Pearl and Eddie could remain there as long as they pleased, but they could not sell the land, that is, the original sixty acres, which was Sam Starr's headright and had become Belle's on his death. The improvements she had made— cabins, barns and livestock—passed to her children. They could either remove or sell them, but if they left the land, it reverted automatically to the Cherokee Tribal Council.

During the December preceding her death, Belle had brought an orphaned girl named Mabel Harrison to live at Younger's Bend so that Pearl might have some companionship. Will Harrison, a young man of twenty-four and Mabel's brother, also joined the household and did the work around the place that Eddie, who was seldom home, refused to do. Will was honest and capable and took charge of disposing of what was salable. In what appeared to be a love match, Pearl and he married and, with nothing more to hold them at Younger's Bend, they moved to Tamaha on the Arkansas River in Indian Territory. It soon became too tame an existence for Pearl. She deserted Harrison and he obtained a divorce.

For a time she lived in Van Buren, Arkansas, across the river from Fort Smith, with her brother Eddie. He was bootlegging whisky to the Indians, a federal offense, and although that was a "recognized" business, he managed to get picked up. In 1891, he was sentenced to the Ohio State Penitentiary for the second time to serve seven years. Shortly after he had been packed off to the East with other manacled prisoners, Madame Van's bordello in the shadow of the Iron Mountain Railroad overpass in Van Buren had a new "boarder," who chose to call herself Rosa Reed. Pearl had taken the step from which, for her, there was to be no turning back. She was on her own now.

It did not take her long to get what the profession called "broken in" to the nightly procession of men who paid for the privilege of possessing her body for a few minutes. She was young and far more attractive than her mother had ever been. Possessing that indefinable something that had always made Belle attractive to the opposite sex, she became Van Buren's most popular whore. But this was small-town stuff; the big money was across the river in Fort Smith. That became her goal, and she hoarded her considerable earnings against the day when she could establish her own house in the Border City's red-light district. If the life she was living, and the one she contemplated, caused her any pricks of conscience, and there is no evidence that it did, she could salve them by telling herself that what she was doing was to help Eddie. She had to have money so she could hire expensive lawyers to get him out of prison.

In November, 1891, Pearl leased the house at 25 Water Street (as it was then called) on the Row, where Fort Smith's bordellos were congregated. There, at various addresses, not for a few months or a year or two, as has often been stated, but for twenty-three years she was to hold forth in her dual roles of prostitute and madam.

The first thing she did was to drop the alias of Rosa Reed and boldly proclaim that she was Pearl Starr, Belle Starr's daughter.

Her mother had made the name famous. It had some commercial value, and she exploited it to the limit. Had she been anyone else, such long-established madams as Maud McGrath, Dot Parker and Laura Ziegler would have resented her as an intruder on their lucrative trade. Instead, they helped her to recruit "boarders" from Hot Springs and Memphis. Of course there was business for all, and to spare. Fort Smith, situated on the edge of the frontier, was enjoying its greatest boom. Being a wild, lawless town, it attracted hundreds of desperate men. Garrison Avenue, its principal street, was sprinkled with saloons and gambling rooms.

The notorious Row was located only three blocks from the courtroom of the famous Hanging Judge, beneath which was the prison known as the scourge of the Border. In one corner of the courtyard stood the gibbet on which eighty-six men were hanged.[4] To reach the Row from Garrison Avenue, the pedestrian had to cross a tangle of railroad tracks. The houses faced to the east, with the muddy Arkansas rolling along a few feet away. How many men were blackjacked, stabbed or shot and their bodies pitched into the river to be carried downstream will never be known.

Pearl made money so fast that early in 1892 she was financially able to keep the promise she made herself to do something for Eddie. She engaged the most expensive lawyers in Fort Smith to work for his release. They were successful, and in 1893 President Harrison pardoned him. He hurried back to Fort Smith, grateful to Pearl for what she had done for him until he learned how she had earned the money she had spent in his behalf. His masculine pride outraged, he turned on her and hired out as a deputy marshal for Judge Parker's court, operating in Indian Territory. This incident is used by the Judge's defenders to prove that he was a kindly man, befriending a twice-convicted felon. Actually Parker was having difficulty securing deputies in the number he wanted, from two to three hundred. The wages were poor, the danger great, and travel money payable only when a man brought in prisoners. Eddie moved down to Waggoner and dropped from sight in October, 1896, until he came to the aid of the town marshal and killed Zeke Crittenden and his brother Dick, themselves former Parker deputies, who were shooting up the town. The notoriety he received and whisky were his undoing. Several weeks later, in the little town of Claremore, he ran two saloonkeepers out of their place of business. The two men armed themselves, returned and killed him.

Eddie's death severed another old tie with the past for Pearl. In Fort Smith the rising demand that the Row be abolished and that the activities of its swarm of free-lance prostitutes be curtailed gave her something else to think about. Fort Smith had ordinances against bawdyhouses and streetwalkers that would have eliminated them had they been enforced. Instead, the madams and their "boarders" paid a weekly tax, and streetwalkers were fined five dollars whenever they were arrested for soliciting, which did not occur frequently enough to become burdensome. With great solemnity new ordinances were passed, one of them going so far as to make it a crime for prostitutes to "loiter in a city cemetery."

Pearl expressed her resentment against the current moral upheaval by having a garish star-shaped sign, outlined in red and white electric lights, put up on the front of her house. The reform element demanded that the police remove the sign. Pearl refused to capitulate. Even on nights when fog settled down over the river bottoms, it could be seen from blocks away, blazing its obscene welcome. If you knew nothing else about Fort Smith, you knew where "Pearl's Place" was located.

Although she was drinking heavily and spreading out until she tipped the scales at two hundred pounds, she was as determined as ever to accumulate a fortune. She had bought and sold pieces of property on Front Street and in the better section of Fort Smith as well. With one or two exceptions she had realized a profit from these transactions. When she bought the three-story frame apartment house on South Fourteenth Street, she put up $17,000 in cash and took out a mortgage for $8,000. It was called simply the "Flats." She told her intimates on the Row that when she retired from the business, she would make her home there. It was a dream that was never realized.

On June 29, 1894, Pearl gave birth to her second child, a girl, and named her Ruth Reed. On the birth certificate the space for the name of the father was left blank. Pearl claimed that he was her legal husband but was so prominent in Fort Smith that she refused to disclose his identity. Undoubtedly this fantastic tale was a fabrication, and yet throughout her childhood and young womanhood, Ruth was surrounded with luxury, given an education and kept in ignorance of her mother's profession.

Every Monday morning Pearl and the other madams from the Row appeared in city court to pay their weekly "tax" of fifteen dollars for operating a bawdyhouse, plus five dollars for every "boarder" in their employ. The callousness with which this evasion of the ordinance banning prostitution was conducted was somewhat softened by the fact that part of the money thus collected went to pay for the weekly medical inspection of the women on the Row. Without a "health card," no inmate of the houses could entertain visitors. The madams enforced the ruling for their own protection.

At St. John's Hospital in August, 1898, Pearl gave birth to a son, Arthur E. Erbach. The birth certificate named E. Erbach, a native of Germany, occupation musician, father of the child, and Rosa P. Reed, birthplace Missouri, as mother.

Pearl had fallen deeply in love with Erbach in what appears to have been the only real romance of her life, although she bore children by several other men. Erbach was younger than she, a handsome penniless adventurer who had only recently come to America. He was a talented, though not professional, musician, possessing a sophisticated manner that overwhelmed Pearl. She not only gave him a job at the piano in her house on the Row, but herself as well. She introduced him as her husband. There is no evidence, however, that they ever married.

It may or may not be true that Erbach was a titled personage, although Edwin Hicks, the knowledgeable Fort Smithian, says flatly, "Yes, Erbach was one of the 'Erbach' Counts." If so, it seems strange that Pearl Starr never referred to herself as the Countess Erbach—which, with her demonstrated audacity, she surely would have done on the slightest authority.

Just three weeks after the birth of his son, "Count" Arthur Erbach died of typhoid-malaria. Pearl erected an eight-foot-tall monument over his grave in Oak Cemetery. Within the year the child he had fathered passed away and was buried beside his father.

Pearl continued to prosper. It flattered her to be referred to as the "Queen of the Row." She had acquired a team of high-stepping trotters and fashionable buggy—the status symbol of the prosperous madam. She visited her daughter several times a week, making sure she was strictly sober. Ruth was six already and beginning to ask embarrassing questions.

On November 8, 1902, Pearl Starr became a mother for the fourth time. She named the baby, a girl, Jennette Andrews. The father was Dell Andrews, a well-known Fort Smith gambler. He and Pearl had been living together in common-law "marriage" for some time. He left town after the arrival of the baby and did not return for a year or more.

No fault can be found with the manner in which Pearl cared for the two little girls. When Jennette was old enough to begin school, Pearl took the two of them to St. Louis and placed them in a convent, where they would be beyond the slings and arrows of classmates that Ruth had suffered in Fort Smith.

In the next five years Pearl was in court so often and spent so much money for legal fees to keep herself out of jail that she began to rebel. She saw the temper of Fort Smith changing and realized that it was only a matter of time when the Row would be closed by the law and prostitution banned. In 1907, Indian Territory was abolished and became part of the new state of Oklahoma, with courts of its own. That change fed the fires of respectability that were changing the life of Fort Smith. Pearl had been warned against attempting to run the Flats for immoral purposes. She had given her pledged word that she wouldn't, but during the last week of February, 1916, she was caught red-handed and remanded to jail. She knew she was finished as a sportinghouse madam in Fort Smith. She called her attorneys and told them she was willing to leave town if the charge against her was dropped. That appears to have been exactly what the city wanted. There is a notation on Circuit Court Judge Little's docket, to wit: "By agreement of counsel it is by the court ordered that defendant be released from jail upon the condition that she leave the city and that she be re-arrested upon her return to the city."

Pearl was forty-nine years old when she was banished from Fort Smith. She lived in Hot Springs for a time and was later seen in Denver and San Francisco. She had been living at the old Savoy Hotel in Douglas, Arizona, down on the Mexican border, for a year when she died of a stroke on July 6, 1925. Her daughter Ruth had been living with her for some time. Jennette was sent for and between them they took care of the funeral arrangements To avoid publicity they buried their mother as Rosa Reed. It was only later that the citizens of Douglas realized that the woman they had known as Rosa Reed was Pearl Starr, Belle Starr's daughter. She was fifty-nine at the time of her death. Then, as now, Douglas was a sun-scorched copper mining town. Why Pearl elected to spend her last months there has never been explained.

Today she is largely unknown, but almost anyone can tell you something about Belle Starr.

The Myers Avenue Girls

ON THE NIGHTS WHEN SHE WAS "on the town," Grace Carlyle, an angel-faced, platinum blonde with the arrested mental equipment of a youthful adolescent—she was twenty-five—could always be found in Grant Crumley's Bennett Avenue saloon. And with good reason, for she was Crumley's favorite tart, which was a minor distinction, for he had many girls. As the head of the Crumley Gang, he was a man of some importance in the Cripple Creek Mining District. With his brothers Sherman and Newt and some others, he could do a neat job of blowing up a mine shaft or stopping a Wells, Fargo treasure coach.

When Grace was attending to business, it was at Pearl Sevan's popular bagnio, "Old Faithful," on Myers Avenue. The time she spent in Grant Crumley's Branch Saloon was all for fun. When the night grew late and she was giddy with alcoholic stimulation, she didn't mind being lifted to the top of the bar, where she disrobed and danced to the wild applause of the male patrons of the saloon. "Such hilarious antics were nothing more than an expression of the natural ebullience of the world's richest mining camp and the increased potency of good Bourbon at high altitudes," said the *Cripple Creek Crusher*, "and not to be taken as proof of the town's depravity."

No one could dispute the *Crusher's* claim that the Cripple Creek District (about six square miles embracing Victor, Independence, Altman and a dozen other camps) was the world's foremost gold camp. Since Bob Womack had made the original discovery in Poverty Gulch in 1890, its output to date surpassed the California Mother Lode and the Comstock. (In 1950, sixty years after discovery, it was still producing, and totaled at that time $412,294, 848.) As for the *Crusher's* charitable attitude toward Miss Carlyle and her kind, that, too, was characteristic of Cripple Creek.

Studying such evidence as is available leads the investigator to the conclusion that the town regarded its soiled doves in quite a different light than did other camps that were short on sophistication and long on money. Perhaps this was because Cripple Creek District was a "free" camp and not controlled by a syndicate. A poor man could make a strike, sell off shares in it to put his mine into production, and have enough left to make him rich. Winfield Scott (Old Man) Stratton, a three-dollar-and-a-half-a-day carpenter, was a case in point. After years of prospecting the Cripple Creek country, he got into pay dirt at Independence, and before he retired was many times a millionaire. So also were such friends as Jimmy Doyle and Jimmy Burns. In all, the Cripple Creek District produced at least thirty-five millionaires. With two exceptions they weren't kids when they struck it rich. With their advancing years and their fortunes secure, it would not have been surprising if they had turned their backs on the public women along Myers Avenue whom they had bedded in their grimy days. But they didn't. No doubt their example helped to create the feeling that such women as Hazel Vernon, Lola Livingston and a dozen other madams who had been in Cripple Creek a long time had made a place for themselves in the town.[1]

Two great fires swept over Cripple Creek. The first, on April 25, 1896, devastated the town. It began on the second floor of a tinder-dry shack at the corner of Third Street and Myers Avenue. During a quarrel between a man and his wife, a kerosene stove was kicked over. In a few minutes the flames were rushing down Third Street, where the dance halls and cheap variety theaters were located. The fire then burned up Myers Avenue, along one side of which were the parlor houses, and beyond them the cribs. Most of the block-long row of cribs were dynamited to check the fire, but the flames leaped the gap. The volunteer fire companies fought one another to get their hoses on the hydrants. If two hoses were attached, neither had water pressure enough to accomplish any good. The high wind dropped as the flames headed south, scorching the uncompleted National Hotel.

By late afternoon the fire was out. Johnny Nolon's big Manitou Saloon, the most popular resort in town, was completely destroyed. But by eight that evening Johnny was back in business, dispensing liquor at an impromptu bar arranged by laying a plank across two barrels. Next morning, H. B. Levie, the boss of the cribs, had carpenters on the job, throwing up one-room shacks in a hurry.

Three days later a second fire engulfed the Portland Hotel at the corner of Myers Avenue and Second Street. Several adjoining buildings began to burn. The fire was being contained when the Palace Hotel started to burn. Suddenly, the big boilers of the hotel blew up, injuring half a dozen firemen and scattering burning fragments right and left. A quantity of dynamite in a Myers Avenue grocery exploded. In all, ten saloons, several stores and harness shops were destroyed before the fire burned out. Thousands of people were homeless and hungry, but they were cheered by the news that a relief train from Colorado Springs was already on the way. This was manna from an unexpected source, for there was no love lost between Cripple Creek town and Colorado Springs.[2]

As the crow flies, it was only seventeen miles from the Springs to Cripple. But for the earthbound the distance was much greater, and they were long, rugged, uphill miles that led around Pikes Peak and over Ute Pass. Culturally, there was a gulf so wide between the two towns that the sophisticates of the Springs refused to waste their time measuring it. A man might make his fortune at Cripple Creek, but he had to come down the mountains to the Springs to learn his manners.

In its primal stage before man began "improving" it, Colorado Springs was one of the fairest spots on earth. In its back yard rose the imposing, snow-crested peak named for Zebulon Pike, who never ascended it. Farther to the west the majestic façade of the Front Range filled the horizon, and to the southwest the serrated peaks of the Sangre de Cristos towered to the sky. With such a scenic background, blessed with a salubrious climate and basking in the high, dry air of the plains, it followed that all that was needed to transform it into one of the country's famous spas and playgrounds was a convenient means of getting there. General William Jackson Palmer, the president of the Denver and Rio Grande Railroad, supplied it. Colorado Springs fitted nicely into his dream of building a transcontinental railroad connecting Denver with the West Coast. He drove the D. and R. G. rails southward from Denver to the Springs and on to Pueblo, where, after some trouble with the rival Santa Fe Railroad, he turned west up the Arkansas River and eventually surmounted the Continental Divide at Tennessee Pass and went on to Salt Lake City.

If the Springs was to develop into the great health resort and national vacation capital that he visualized, it needed hotels. When the spacious and magnificent Antlers was opened to the public, it was acclaimed the finest resort hotel in the United States. General Palmer was about to get some help that he didn't want. To the Springs had come Count James Pourtales, a German with estates in Silesia. His main purpose in coming to Colorado was to marry his French cousin Berthe Pourtales, who was living temporarily in the nearby town of Florisant with her brother Otto. In fact, she had brought Otto to that faraway place to save him from drinking himself to death. Of somewhat less importance to Pourtales than marrying the beautiful Berthe, which he did, was his ambition to acquire some of the wealth with which most Americans were so bountifully supplied. His first venture was in the dairy business with a man named Willcox who had established the Broadmoor Dairy Farm and was rapidly going bankrupt. Pourtales had a knowledge of scientific dairying and under his skillful management the good ladies of the Springs were soon buying the Count's Broadmoor milk and butter.

Bitten with success, he launched what he called "Broadmoor Estates, a select community for ladies and gentlemen, replete with an artificial lake and gambling casino to be conducted in the European manner." General Palmer put his foot down; Pourtales could dig his lake and sell all the lots he cared to, but there would be no gambling casino. The Count persisted and his casino opened in June, 1891. Unfortunately it was in the face of the growing financial depression that was sweeping the country. It soon became obvious that the promotion was a failure. The Count turned his attention to Cripple Creek, and with his friend Tom Parrish, an amateur prospector, began tramping the hills and gulches looking for pay dirt. The blind luck that sometimes seems to take care of the innocent and the helpless led them to Steve Blair's hole in the ground on the north slope of Bull Mountain, which he called the Buena Vista. On borrowed money Pourtales and Parrish bought an option on the property for the unheard-of sum of $80,000. Confidence in the Cripple Creek District snowballed and helped everyone, and Pourtales and his partner sold off enough shares in the Buena Vista to raise the money for its development. It proved to be the best investment their stockholders ever made.

Staying at the Antlers, in Colorado Springs, were a group of young sophisticates from the East. Most of them owned a sheepskin from an Ivy League college, and some of them were scions of rich and influential families, like the Penrose brothers, Spec and Dick, and Horace Devereaux. They were hell-raisers and toss-pots. To the naked eye they were typical tenderfeet who could be trimmed and sent back to papa sadder and wiser. That proved to be an embarrassing miscalculation; Spec and his friends were only part-time playboys. Beneath their gaiety and nonsense was a serious intention to rip out a fortune in the quickest and easiest way possible within the limits of the law. Spec was the first to go up to Cripple Creek to engage in the real estate business with his old Philadelphia friend Charlie Tutt, another improbable millionaire in the making. His brother Dick and most of the others followed, and they made merry and raised a lot of hell in the parlor houses on Myers Avenue.

The fires of 1896 were the best thing that could have happened to Cripple Creek; the shack town disappeared and in its place rose a substantial brick and stone city with a population of over 35,000. (The number was to rise to 50,000 in 1900, Cripple's biggest year.) The "fireproof" National Hotel opened its doors a few months later: four stories, topped with the swank penthouse of W. K. Gillett, the railroad promoter; private baths; telephones on every floor and an elevator, the first in the District. The grand opening was by invitation. Late in the evening the festivities were temporarily disrupted when Spec Penrose and a new girl from the "Homestead," Hazel Vernon's luxurious Myers Avenue bagnio, rode into the National barroom on horseback and had to be served champagne cocktails before they agreed to leave.

Hazel Vernon was Cripple's most popular madam. Her new establishment, built of pressed pink brick according to her specifications, got the "carriage trade"—in other words, the big spenders. She conducted the Old Homestead with a degree of decorum not found at Pearl Sevan's Old Faithful or Ella Holden's The Library, her most important competitors. She was strict with her girls, and because the money they earned in her house was so good, she had no difficulty keeping herself supplied with the prettiest "boarders" in town. Because it was her way to avoid publicity and scandal, she was enraged by the conduct of the recent addition to her staff who had disrupted the festivities at the National Hotel that she ordered her to pack her belongings and leave.

A man who sought diversion at cheaper places like the Mikado, the Golden Peacock, or a dozen other such houses, ran the risk of being rolled for his money, if he was well along in his liquor. Gentlemen who patronized the "Homestead" could be sure they were safe no matter what condition they were in.

Of course the new appearance Myers Avenue now presented did not cause the wives and mothers of Cripple to regard the women who dwelt there in a kindlier light. Many of them suspected, both rich and poor, that their lords and masters were, or had been, intimately acquainted with Hazel Vernon and her kind. When they encountered Hazel while shopping on Bennett Avenue, they looked away, but only after making sure they saw what she was wearing.

By common agreement Hazel Vernon was the handsomest, best-dressed woman in Cripple Creek. It was well-known that popular Johnny Nolon, the gambler and saloonkeeper, was her man. She was from Ohio and had reached Cripple Creek by way of Denver, where she had spent two years in Mattie Silks' first Market Street house. The town was taken by surprise when she sold the Old Homestead in 1897 and left Cripple for California. The new madam was a young, willowy blonde named Pearl De Vere, which proved to be only her professional name. She was from Denver, and a wealthy young Denverite had supplied the money for the purchase of the Myers Avenue place.

In new hands, the Old Homestead lost money from the start. Things became desperate when the new madam's Denver backer refused to put up more money. It produced tragedy. The Cripple Creek *Times*, which had succeeded the *Crusher*, handled the matter as discreetly as it could:

> Pearl De Vere, madam of the "Old Homestead," died early today from an overdose of morphine. According to a denizen of the house, a gay party was in full swing when Pearl excused herself, saying that she felt indisposed. She refused to let anyone go with her to her room. She was in high spirits all evening, a woman said, and never seemed happier or more carefree. No one could offer any reason why the madam should want to end her life. The body was discovered . . . lying across the bed fully clothed.

This was not the first Myers Avenue suicide. Very likely it would not have aroused city-wide attention if it had not been disclosed that money for the burial of Pearl De Vere would have to be raised by public subscription. That provided Cripple Creek with an opportunity to show its open-handedness that was not to be overlooked. Money rolled in, more than enough "to give," as a Bennett Avenue bartender put it, "the little girl a real sendoff."

On a cold, blustery January afternoon Pearl De Vere was buried in Pisgah graveyard. The funeral procession was headed by the Elks band, contingents from the fire companies and Union Hall followed and a miscellaneous group from the dance halls and the brothels, riding in rented carriages, brought up the rear. At the graveside the Reverend Franklin spoke briefly, using for his text the familiar "Let him who is without sin cast the first stone." The shivering mourners appreciated his brevity and hurried back to town, feeling better and in need of a drink.

The Florence and Cripple Creek railway, a narrow-gauge, had reached Cripple in 1894. In the meantime the M-T (short for Midland Terminal Railroad) was building an eighteen-mile, stan-

dard-gauge spur from the Colorado Midland's whistle stop at Hay-
den Divide to Cripple. Its builders were Harry Colibran, general
manager of the Colorado Midland Railroad, and W. K. Gillett,
passenger auditor of the Santa Fe. Building an eighteen-mile spur
at a cost of $70,000 a mile required money. They didn't have it,
but with guts, gall and some financial shenanigans, they put their
rails into Cripple Creek in December, 1895. The Midland Terminal
circled in on the eastern slopes of the District, past the Buena
Vista, Victor, Vindicator and on around Battle Mountain to the
Independence, Strong and Portland—the biggest producers. Naturally it got their ore to ship. In two years it was out of debt and
making a fortune. By then, it was facing the competition of the
Short Line, which ran directly from the Springs to Cripple Creek.

These were golden years for the District. Stratton, the "Midas
of the Rockies," had died and several other faces were missing,
but mine owners were getting richer by the minute and Cripple
was booming. Only the working stiffs who were producing the
wealth and toiling in the tunnels, reduction mills and chlorination
plants were being denied their piece of the pie. Organizers for
the Western Federation of Miners had moved in and were unioniz-
ing the men. The powerful Mine Owners' Association derided the
effort and did nothing about it. But a storm was in the making
that, before it was over, was to inflict a wound from which Cripple
Creek was never fully to recover.

In 1894 the Western Federation of Miners had won the first
skirmish when it forced the owners to agree to pay a minimum
wage of three dollars for an eight-hour shift. Now, in 1904, it was
back for more. In the interim it had become the most powerful
industrial union in the United States, led by Big Bill Haywood, its
executive secretary, an implacable, radical specialist. From Union
offices in Denver, he called out the workers of the Standard Mill
at Colorado City. The following day, 3,500 Cripple Creek miners
laid down their tools in half a hundred mines. It was the beginning
of the longest and bloodiest strike in Colorado history.

State troops were brought in on several occasions and the Mine
Owners' Association hired an army of Denver mercenaries to
guard their property. Violence flared in many directions. Both

sides were equally at fault. Stores in which food and clothing were gathered for doling out to union men and their families were broken into and the merchandise scattered or burned. Without any vestige of law, the Mine Owners' Association began deporting union men, rounding them up like felons, shipping them out of the country by train, and dumping them several hundred miles away on the Kansas prairies. Haywood retaliated by sending two of his accomplished dynamiters, Harry Orchard and Steve Adams, into the District.

At 2 A.M. on the morning of June 6, 1904, half a hundred non-union miners who had just come off the night shift at the Findley Mine were gathered on the Florence and Cripple Creek Railroad platform at Independence. While they were waiting for the down train that was bringing the graveyard shift to work, two terrific explosions shattered the station platform, hurling the dead and maimed skyward. Thirteen men were killed; a score more critically injured, some of whom were saved by the amputation of arms and legs.

Harry Orchard and Steve Adams had triggered the blasts with homemade mines. In the shock and horror of what had happened, the strike reached its gory end. It had lasted eleven months. The grip of the Western Federation of Miners of Colorado was broken for all time. In Cripple Creek town business had been at a standstill for almost a year. The National Hotel was in bankruptcy, and a dozen Bennett Avenue stores had "for rent" signs in their windows. Myers Avenue was half deserted; most of the cribs had lost their inmates and the two or three parlor houses that remained open had dropped their rates to a dollar. The girls who had once made them attractive had fled to Denver and been replaced by overage tarts.

And yet in its shabby days Myers Avenue was to receive its greatest notoriety. You may be acquainted with the incident. In October, 1914, the highly esteemed magazine writer, Julian Street, came up on the Short Line Railroad from the Springs and spent an hour in Cripple Creek. He took a look at Myers Avenue and what he had to say about it in an article in the November 21 issue of *Collier's Weekly* was so offensive to Cripple Creek that Mayor

Hanley demanded a retraction, which he did not get. Refusing to let the matter drop, he called a meeting of the board of aldermen that evening. Without a dissenting vote, they approved a motion changing the name of Myers Avenue to Julian Street.

Undoubtedly it salved some raw feelings and caused Julian Street some embarrassment. But there was no point in raking up dead ashes; Cripple Creek was a dying camp with a population of fewer than 5,000. As for Myers Avenue, it had written its own obituary long before Mr. Julian Street saw it.

Baby Doe—from Riches to Rags

BY THE TIME SHE WAS SEVENTEEN, Bessie McCourt, with her wealth of golden hair, seductive smile, inquiring eyes and rounded figure, was recognized as the prettiest girl in Oshkosh, Wisconsin, her home town. She was one of a family of fourteen children. Her father, Peter McCourt, a bubbling Irishman from County Armagh, was a tailor by trade and owner of a small clothing store. Although he was from the north of Ireland, he was a staunch Roman Catholic and reared his numerous progeny in the faith.

No one has bothered to learn why Elizabeth's parents and brothers and sisters fastened the family pet name of "Baby" on her. Of course "Baby" McCourt was as unknown to the world as Elizabeth McCourt. But a young man named Harvey Doe, the son of a prosperous lumberman, came along and he and "Baby" fell in love. Despite family objections, they were married. To get away from the bickering at home and in the hope of bettering themselves, the young couple migrated to Central City, Colorado. But Harvey Doe did not prosper. Perhaps this was because his beautiful young wife had caught the lecherous eye of Horace A. Tabor, the richest of the bonanza kings, on his frequent business trips to Central City.

According to Bill Hamill, mine owner and political boss of Clear Creek County, which included the towns of Central City, Blackhawk and Georgetown, he was sitting in the spacious lobby of the palatial Windsor Hotel in Denver one morning, chatting with

Tabor, when Harvey Doe and his wife walked past. " 'There goes the most beautiful woman in Colorado,' I remarked to Tabor. 'I know it,' he agreed. 'I've offered Harvey Doe a thousand dollars for an introduction.' "

This incident, if true, is proof enough of Tabor's previous interest in her. Did this have anything to do with the fact that, for no known reason, Harvey Doe lost his job as bookkeeper at the Ajax Mine and could not find another? Was this part of a scheme to break up his marriage? It raises another question. Was Baby Doe acting on her own initiative when, on the night of March 1, 1890, in an effort to gain evidence for a divorce, she, accompanied by Policeman Edward Newman, "forced" her way into Lizzie Preston's sporting house and found her husband there, or was she carrying out the instructions of an unknown party?

Following the raid, she filed for a divorce on the grounds of adultery and nonsupport, alleging that she was "penniless and destitute." Judge Amos Steck heard her appeal and granted the divorce. A few days later Baby Doe took up her residence in the Windsor Hotel, occupying a suite on the same floor with Tabor. Presently, with some "unknown" person footing the bills, she became the best-dressed woman in Denver.

Forbes Parkhill, the former Denver newspaperman and author of the authoritative *The Wildest of the West*, excuses the fact that no Denver newspaper printed a line about the Doe divorce case "because the name of the lovely Baby Doe had not yet been linked publicly with that of Colorado's bonanza king and was not therefore newsworthy." A more believable reason would be that Tabor's various enterprises were big users of newspaper advertising space. In any event, the record of the action disappeared for years and was not found until Baby Doe, about to become the mother of a child by Tabor, needed evidence of her divorce to make the baby legitimate. To quote Parkhill: "There is no shred of evidence to indicate that Tabor paid for Baby Doe's divorce, nor that he paid Harvey Doe $5,000 to give up his wife." Documentation may be missing, but the circumstantial evidence is abundant that Tabor was guilty on both counts.

In the days before radio and television, newspapers exercised an almost complete monopoly of the news. When they came under the domination of political satraps or men of great wealth, they played down, ignored or slanted what they printed in such manner as best to serve the interests of the men or institutions that controlled them. Nowhere was that truer than in Denver in the heyday of H. A. W. Tabor, a crude, semi-illiterate, raised almost overnight from his humble role of mining camp storekeeper to overpowering wealth. No word unfavorable to him appeared in the Denver press. Even unmentioned was the fact that he was living apart from Augusta Tabor, his wife of many years. She remained at the hundred-thousand-dollar Tabor mansion on Lincoln Avenue, while he divided his time between the two most expensive hotels in Colorado, the Windsor in Denver and the Clarendon in Leadville, both of which he owned, enjoying the companionship of the recently divorced Baby Doe. No Denver newspaper wondered out loud how the self-declared "penniless and destitute" beauty could afford such luxurious surroundings.

"That he [Tabor] was reckless, foolish, idled away much of his youth, squandered a great fortune as if he were an imbecile, fought, gambled, swore, chewed tobacco, drank red liquor, consorted with loose women, divorced an old and quarrelsome wife and married a young and attractive colleen of less than half his age, used his wealth to further his political ambitions, and raised hell generally, all this merely proves that he belonged in his environment," says Lewis Cass Gandy, his most lenient biographer.

Tabor was fifty-two when he met Baby Doe. She was twenty. Augusta was forty-eight, a once handsome woman grown lean and dour from years of penury and hard work and with a tongue that had grown sharper with constant use. The only illusion she had left was that she was still in love with Tabor. She closed her eyes to what she didn't want to see and her mind to what she didn't want to know. Although she had borne him a son, a boy named Maxcy, who was now approaching twenty, it must be assumed that Tabor had had no sexual interest in her for years. In Leadville, where his meteoric rise to great riches began and he could afford to indulge his lusts, he became a frequenter of the parlor houses clustered around State Street and the lower end of Harrison

Avenue, the most popular of which were the establishments of
Mollie May, Sallie Purple and Frankie Page. The town's most
celebrated courtesan was Josie Mansfield.[1]

Tabor was then in his middle forties and obviously determined
to make up for some of the pleasures he had been missing. When
business trips to the East became necessary, he did not travel
alone. The woman who accompanied him was a luscious young
prostitute by the name of Willie Deville, a former inmate of Lizzie
Allen's famous Chicago bordello. He gave her several thousand
dollars and dropped her on discovering that she was planning to
blackmail him.

Long before they moved to Denver, Augusta Tabor was aware
of the philandering of her faithless husband. Few women could
lay better claim to a man's loyalty and gratitude. Although she had
never laid eyes on beautiful Baby Doe, too many tales had reached
her ears for her not to know that Tabor was infatuated with the
woman. She must have realized that the years of succeeding
failures, when she had "kept the wolf from the door" with the
money she earned by baking bread and serving meals in one mining camp after another, were meaningless now that her husband
was lost to her.

It was not until 1877 that the town of Leadville was established.
For years, hundreds of placer miners had been swarming over
California Gulch, washing out millions in gold. They had only
curses for the heavy black boulders that got in their way. When
the placer claims had been exhausted, they were ready to move on.
A. R. Meyer, who was something of a metallurgist, was curious
about the "black stuff" the prospectors had so roundly damned.
He built a small smelter at the foot of the gulch and quickly discovered that what he was "cooking" were rich carbonates of lead
and silver. Lead was cheap and almost valueless, but silver was
selling at $1.11 an ounce. News like that couldn't be held back.
The stampede to Leadville began. Tabor, who had a store at Oro
and another at Buckskin Joe (Alma), moved his stock of merchandise to the new camp and got there in time to be named the first
mayor of Leadville.

The story of how Horace Tabor, the Leadville storekeeper,

grubstaked two Germans, August Rische and George Hook, in return for which he was to receive a one-third interest in whatever they found, and how after digging a shaft only twenty-six feet deep they drove into a rich body of carbonates and named their prospect the Little Pittsburg, which was to produce upward of twenty million dollars, and how Tabor invested his first hundred thousand in the Matchless mine, which was to return an even greater reward, has been told too often to need repeating. To better understand this man of many millions, who was to become lieutenant governor of Colorado and briefly a U.S. senator from that state, it is necessary to turn back the years to the time when he was a young journeyman stonecutter traveling all over New England in his quest for work. Tabor was farm-bred from Holland Pond, Vermont, up near the Canadian border. According to all accounts, he was a rugged, broad-shouldered, handsome young man. He must have been ambitious, for in two years at Quincy, Massachusetts, he put his apprenticeship behind him and struck out as a full-fledged stonecutter. In Boston, he met Adam Pierce, who had taken a contract for the stonework on the new state insane asylum at Augusta, Maine. He needed stonecutters, and he hired young Tabor and took him home to Augusta. There he met and fell in love with Augusta Pierce, his employer's spirited and attractive daughter.

The young couple became engaged, but Tabor's meager savings did not warrant his becoming the head of a household. With more prudence than he usually showed in later years, he proposed that he join one of the parties of settlers that the anti-slavery New England Emigrant Aid Company was sending out to Kansas to insure its coming into the Union as a "free" state. Once in Kansas, he would file on a homestead, build a cabin and find work for a few months at Fort Riley, the new cavalry post the government was building. He took up land on Deep Creek, some twenty miles from Fort Riley, and managed to get involved in the bitter partisan war that was to win the name of "Bloody Kansas" for what was then Kansas Territory.

After an absence of almost two years Tabor returned to Maine and married Augusta. He had saved his money, and with the help they got from her father, they were well provided for when they set out for their new home in Kansas. Because of the drouth that killed the crops they planted and the dark clouds of the approaching war between the North and the South, Kansas was a disaster for them. There, on Deep Creek, their first and only child was born. In February, 1859, a man who was returning from prospecting in Colorado stopped at the cabin and raised their spirits with the news that gold in paying quantities had been found on Clear Creek and neighboring streams. He had the evidence to prove it in a buckskin bag filled with dust and nuggets.

For several months the Tabors had been living largely on ground corn. They reasoned that they had little to lose by pulling up stakes and moving on to Colorado. In April they yoked their oxen, packed their belongings in the wagon, and set out on what was becoming known as the Republican River Route, which took them to the Platte west of Fort Kearney and up the South Platte to Julesburg and on to Denver. They located on what was then called Payne's Bar, and later Idaho Springs. All around them, at Blackhawk, Central City, and later at Buckskin Joe, Fairplay and California Gulch, men were getting rich. But fortune continued to elude the Tabors. That they survived was due to the money Augusta's baking and cooking brought in. Whether it was at Augusta's urging or an acknowledgment of defeat on his part, Tabor turned from prospector to storekeeper. It was to prove to be the luckiest decision he ever made, climaxing on that never-to-be-forgotten day in Leadville, in May, 1878, when he and his grubstake partners gazed in disbelief at the exposed riches of the Little Pittsburg.[2]

It has often been said that his great wealth destroyed Horace Tabor and put any real happiness beyond his reach. It was to spell only unhappiness for Augusta; and for Baby Doe, both unhappiness and misery.

Whether from vanity or from a genuine affection for the town, in the two years that followed his rise to great wealth, Tabor made Leadville over to his liking. It was the beneficiary of his largesse. Almost singlehanded he bought, tore down and altered buildings along Harrison Avenue until it became an imposing main thoroughfare. He built the Clarendon Hotel, which although somewhat smaller than Denver's Brown Palace was every bit as elegant. Adjoining it he erected the Tabor Opera House, cited by the leading actors who played there to be the finest theater west of Chicago. He built the Bank of Leadville, of which he was the president. He is said to have supplied the money for building the big Roman Catholic Church of the Annunciation, and he was a heavy contributor to other church building funds.

It followed that in Leadville he was regarded as the man of the hour, destined for high political office. When the nomination for lieutenant governor was thrust on him, he accepted, regarding it as a steppingstone to higher office. How much money he poured into the coffers of the Republican party of Colorado will never be known, but it may have totaled as much as half a million dollars.

Leadville had been transformed from a mining camp to a town of 5,000 by the end of 1879. A year later the population had soared to 15,000. The Denver and Rio Grande had been the first railroad to reach it. Soon after, the narrow gauge Denver and South Park got there, running the last thirty-five miles over D. and R. G. tracks. By 1881, sixteen trains daily were operating between Leadville and Denver.

City records show that while more than nine hundred dollars a month was collected in license fees from houses of prostitution, gambling rooms and saloons in 1879, a year later the figure had climbed to over seventeen hundred dollars a month. The number of stabbings and shootings and other crimes of violence had increased proportionately. Tabor was powerful enough to have done something about it, but he did nothing. Leadville was a wide-open town, and he wanted it kept that way. He liked to gamble. Pop Wyman's notorious resort at the corner of State and Harrison, where all forms of vice were for sale under one roof, was his favorite spot.

If he ever entertained the idea that Leadville would overtake Denver and become the capital city of Colorado, which is doubtful, he certainly discarded it when he purchased the finest private residence in Denver, the site of which covered an entire city block. Determined not to be outshone by other bonanza millionaires, he spent $100,000 on the mansion and grounds before he and Augusta took possession in 1880. They would have been more at home in a two-room cabin. In fact, Tabor spent as little time there as he could manage. He was spending money at a dizzy pace, investing in so many enterprises that a true accounting was not arrived at until years after his death. They included a score of gold and silver mines, hotels, office buildings, banks, gasworks, canals, railroads, newspapers, toll roads, smelters and lumber companies. His greatest achievement, and the one for which he is remembered, was the huge, five-story Tabor Grand Opera House in Denver, with its complex of theaters, stores and offices.[3]

Denver had matured socially to the point where it recognized that there were two kinds of women; Augusta Tabor represented respectability; Baby Doe, her husband's lovely mistress, the other side of the coin. If the "good" women of Denver rallied around Augusta, no one, it appears, took up the cudgels for Baby Doe. No one had the temerity to advance the absurd argument that it wasn't for money but out of love for the aging, uncouth, personally slovenly Tabor that she had given herself to him. He had taken her in lust but, to his surprise and hers, he fell in love with her and was determined to make her his wife. Instead of using an attorney, he sent Billy Bush, the manager of the Tabor Grand, for whom Augusta had shown a warm regard in the past, to induce her to agree to a divorce, promising not to contest any settlement the court decreed. Augusta informed Bush that under no circumstances would she institute divorce proceedings. Tabor was to find that he had a tartar on his hands in Augusta. Foolishly, he filed a divorce action against her in secret in Durango, in southwestern Colorado, alleging desertion. His plea was granted, without (at the time) any notice of the action appearing in court records. Eventually this bit of nonsense was to ruin his political ambitions.

Mrs. Tabor had not been served and knew nothing about what had occurred at Durango. But eleven days later, her lawyer, ex-Judge Amos Steck, who had granted Baby Doe her divorce, filed a separate maintenance suit in Augusta's behalf. In it she petitioned the court to direct that the Tabor mansion be placed in her name and that Tabor be directed to pay her $50,000 a year support money. She listed a partial list of his holdings totaling $9,076,100, and set forth that his income amounted to $100,000 a month.

She charged that Tabor had repeatedly asked her to divorce him, offering her a part of his huge fortune, but that she had refused and was now asking only for separate maintenance. She stated that he had deserted her and had not contributed to her support in months. There were other charges of a personal nature. The Denver press printed none of them and gave the suit only a few lines.

Down at Durango a new set of town officials had been elected. A deputy in the district clerk's office was thumbing through the docket book when he discovered two pages glued together. Curious, he split them and discovered the record of the secret Tabor divorce. He knew he had discovered a political bombshell. He made a copy of the record and mailed it to Mrs. Tabor. She was shocked, but Steck, her lawyer, assured her it was completely meaningless, since she had never been served. What his answer would have been had he known that, on September 30, Tabor and Baby Doe had been secretly married at the Southern Hotel in St. Louis remains a matter of speculation. If the secret divorce was invalid, then the St. Louis marriage was bigamous.

Tabor returned to Denver ten days before the legislature was to meet to elect two senators, one for six years and the other for thirty days to finish out the unexpired term of Senator Teller, who had been elevated to President Arthur's cabinet. Tabor knew he was sitting on a keg of dynamite. If word of the secret divorce and secret marriage leaked out, he was a ruined man. In a panic, he instructed his lawyers to offer Augusta a quarter of a million dollars to drop her maintenance suit and divorce him. She refused. But a week before the legislature was to meet, she dropped her suit and filed for divorce. Amos Steck, her lawyer, explained her strange behavior better than anyone. "This doesn't mean that she has forgiven her unfaithful, philandering husband. But she loves him. She has always loved him, and always will. Someday this creature, Tabor, will lose his fortune and will come whining to Augusta to help him, and she will help him." [4]

Tabor was denied the six-year term, but to keep him in line, he was elected to the thirty-day unexpired term. He and Baby Doe left for Washington at once and were legally married in the Willard Hotel on March 1, 1883. President Chester A. Arthur was present; so were members of the bride's family. Tabor's son Maxcy was not there, and the wives of the Colorado delegation were also conspicuous by their absence. But Tabor's marital difficulties were far from over. When he and his bride got back to Denver and settled down at the Windsor, they were ignored by local society, which gathered in a solid phalanx to greet Augusta on her return from California, where she was to make her new home.

The storm that was hanging over the heads of the new Mrs. Tabor and her wealthy husband broke into the open early in March, when a clerk in County Judge Harrington's court, in making a routine check of the docket, discovered that there was no record of any disposition having been made of the divorce action Baby Doe had instituted against her husband Harvey Doe. When several days of earnest searching failed to turn up the decree in her favor, which Judge Amos Steck had granted at the time, Judge Harrington ordered Baby Doe to appear before him and show cause why her divorce action should not be dismissed because of her failure to prosecute.

Harrington's order was issued on March 4, 1884, but it was not served until January 20, 1885, almost a year later. Judges and juries were not sacred to Tabor. He had bribed them before. If his money was not at work in this instance, how can the long delay be explained? Or how else can the fact be accounted for that Judge Amos Steck's decree, written in longhand, granting the divorce, suddenly turned up in the jacket covering the case? Its effect was to render the Washington marriage valid and legitimize the child born to Baby Doe Tabor on July 13, 1884.

Her first child by Tabor, a girl, was named Elizabeth Bonduel Lillie Tabor. This girl Lillie resembled her mother and was to become a beautiful young woman. Tabor was far too busy to be cast in the role of a doting father. He was at the peak of his financial success, and although his marital difficulties were behind him, his political enemies unearthed the facts concerning his secret divorce from Augusta and his secret marriage in St. Louis and used them against him so effectively that he went down to defeat every time he ran for office.

In 1886 he bought the Watson estate on Sherman Avenue, then regarded as the finest residence in Denver, and made it over as his young wife wished. Nothing she could ask for was beyond his generosity—diamonds, Paris gowns, fine carriages, and a retinue of servants. Seated in her silk-lined box at the Tabor Grand, she attracted as much attention as the famous actors on the stage. But, as the old song has it, "she was only a bird in a gilded cage." No one ever heard her complain at the price she had paid for the luxury in which she lived. Her second child by Tabor, a boy named Horace Joseph Tabor, was born October 17, 1888, and died a day later.

Her brother Peter had come out to Denver, and Tabor had made him his secretary. He proved to be a capable young man. Through him she perhaps realized before Tabor did that he was heading into financial difficulties. His multiple investments were largely sound, but they were so closely related that trouble in one direction was quickly reflected in another. The weakness in Tabor's thinking was his refusal to believe that such big producers as the Matchless and a score of other mines would ever get into borasco. But the cold hard fact was that returns from the Henriette, Maid of Erin, Tam O'Shanter and Bull Domingo were diminishing week after week. A new strike in the Matchless relieved the situation temporarily and he ceased to worry. On December 17, 1889, his wife presented him with a second daughter, the much publicized Silver Dollar.

Baptized Rose Mary Echo Silver Dollar Tabor, she was to become in her time as widely known as her mother. Her hair was as black as Baby Doe's was golden, but she was no less beautiful. She spoke with a slight lisp which seemed to give her added charm. Unlike her sister Lillie, who had inherited her father's stubbornness, Silver Dollar was a laughing, merry-hearted child. She was not yet four, too young to realize what it meant, when the Tabor empire collapsed.

In the fall of 1892 the most disastrous financial panic the United States had suffered (up to that time) was spreading throughout the country. In the East, thousands of men were out of work;

business was at a standstill; banks failed; the national debt rose from day to day. Grim as the situation was, Colorado was less affected, at first, than other parts of the country. But shortly after President Cleveland's inauguration on March 4, 1893, disaster struck. Under terms of the Sherman Act of 1878, authorizing the coinage of silver, the U.S. Treasury was buying 4,500,000 ounces of silver a month. It gave silver a false value, the silver dollar being worth approximately only seventy cents in gold. Powerful "sound money" forces demanded the demonetization of silver and repeal of the silver purchase act as a prerequisite to ending the panic. President Cleveland, a Democrat, coerced his own party against its will into voting the repeal, and the Bland-Allison Act, demonetizing silver, became the law of the land. It dealt the silver mining industry of Colorado a blow from which it was never fully to recover.

None of the bonanza kings was as vulnerable as Tabor. He had borrowed heavily on his real estate holdings. When the loans were called, he could not meet them. Everything went, including the Sherman Avenue home. In the Leadville district mines that had been producing on a limited scale were forced to shut down, being no longer able to operate at a profit. It was the same story with the smelters and reduction mills. His old friend Stratton, over at Cripple Creek, voluntarily loaned him $30,000. The hole Tabor had dug for himself was too wide and too deep to be plugged by such a sum. He went to Leadville and found it a stricken town. As he walked the length of Harrison Avenue, he encountered a hundred men whom he had befriended in the past, but not one offered to help him in his extremity.

Augusta Tabor had died at Pasadena, California, in 1895. Her son Maxcy had brought her body back to Denver and buried her in Evergreen Cemetery. Her friends had always predicted that Baby Doe would desert Tabor if misfortune ever overtook him. They were confident she would leave him now. She was only thirty-three and still beautiful. Their expectations were not fulfilled. She left Denver with her two daughters and moved into a cabin with Tabor near the hoisting works of the Matchless at Leadville.

Hoping against hope that a stroke of fortune would extricate him from poverty, Tabor struggled on. But there was no rift in the clouds. By 1897 he was reduced to wheeling slag at the Globe Smelter for three dollars a day to feed his family, an impossible job for a man nearing seventy. When all hope seemed lost, his old political enemy, Senator Wolcott, induced President McKinley to appoint him postmaster at Denver. The bitter irony of it was that he had given to the government the land on which the post office stood when it was valued at $60,000.

Tabor died peacefully in 1899 and was buried in Mount Calvary Cemetery, which was abandoned years ago. His death left Baby Doe with two teen-age daughters in a friendless town. Somehow she managed to hold the family together, spending the summers at the Matchless Mine and the winters in Denver. She had never shown any marked reverence for her Catholic religion, but when her daughter Lillie insisted on marrying a first cousin, which was forbidden by the Church, Baby Doe quarreled violently with her. Lillie and her husband moved to Milwaukee, and if Baby Doe ever saw her again, it was not more than once. The other daughter, beautiful Silver Dollar, remained with her mother for years and was her principal support. She was thirty-six when, on a visit to Chicago, she was accidentally scalded to death, in March, 1925.

After that Baby Doe never left the Matchless. At first she managed to get a small mortgage on the mine and put several men to work trying to find a new deposit. It came to nothing, and the mortgage holder got title to the Matchless. But again Stratton came to the rescue, satisfied the mortgage and gave the looted Matchless to Baby Doe. There she remained for the rest of her life, living alone and in dire poverty.

Many reasons have been advanced to explain the frightful and self-imposed austerity in which she lived, when various avenues of charity were open to her. The explanation advanced the oftenest is that Tabor's dying words to her were, "Never give up the Matchless." Heard less often but probably as true was that she was expiating the wrong she had done Augusta Tabor. Whatever the reason, it was her secret, and she died without divulging it. She was seventy-five when she was found frozen to death one morning in March, 1935.

Calamity Jane in Fact and Fiction

CALAMITY JANE, the legendary frontierswoman, would be largely unknown today were it not for what the fictioneers and the romanticists, bent on presenting her as a tragic, misunderstood soap-opera heroine, have done with her, mindless of the facts. In her lifetime they had her cooperation, for she not only never denied the tales that were written about her, but invented countless shockers of her own.

By the time she was twenty-four, she was a confirmed alcoholic. She could outcurse, outshout and outdrink most of the men with whom she consorted. She was also fearless; she could drive a bull-team as expertly as any male bullwhacker. She was loyal to her friends and could ride anything a man could ride. In Deadwood, where she lived most of her turbulent years, she enjoyed filling newspapermen from the East with tales of her prowess with pistols and rifle and of the number of Indians and road agents she had killed in her time. Actually there is no record of her having killed anyone.

Several writers of consequence have wondered if her fondness for wearing male attire and the aversion with which she regarded other women were not signs of sexual deviation. That need not be taken seriously. The Black Hills was wild, lonely country in the years in which she was supporting herself by freighting to the different camps with her bull train. They were far apart. It meant bedding down on the ground where night overtook her. Certainly

dressing like a man was the practical thing to do. As for her ab-
horrence of other females, the only ones to whom she might have
turned, rough and tough as she was, were the girls in the red lights.

Although early photographs show her never to have been a
pretty girl, she was attractive, with a rounded, rather stocky figure.
She had appealed to men and, having no inhibitions, had spent the
night under the blankets with many. It was only after steady drinking and advancing years had put their mark on her that her face
became hard and masculine.[1]

However much one chips away at the myths and legends that
surround Calamity Jane, she occupies an authentic niche in Western
history that will survive the ravages of time, and largely because
she is always coupled with James Butler (Wild Bill) Hickok. At
least a million words about her alleged romance with Hickok have
been published. During the twenty-seven years that elapsed between his death and hers, she missed no opportunity to couple
their names. As she was dying in Deadwood, she capped her long
and persistent campaign by saying—and her last words are treasured
by her admirers—"Bury me next to Wild Bill." (That was done,
or almost, only a distance of twenty feet separating their graves
in Mount Moriah Cemetery.)

Following Calamity's death in 1903, multiple versions of her
"romance" with Wild Bill reached the newsstands and bookstores.
"Colorado Charley" Utter, his brother Steve, California Joe,
"White-Eye" Jack Anderson and Hickok's other old friends
writhed as they faced this flood of melodramatic trash, some of it
masquerading as history, with pages of "dialogue." Charley Utter
asserted angrily that "Wild Bill would have died rather than share
a bed with Jane." In corroboration, Joseph G. Rosa, Hickok's
most authentic biographer, says in his *They Called Him Wild Bill:*
"Of all the women associated in any way with Wild Bill, she
[Calamity] had the least to do with him."

The Mary J. Holmes–Laura Jean Libbey school of "literature"
had long been finished with Calamity Jane and her contemporaries,
most of whom had passed away, when a woman identifying herself
as Jean Hickok McCormick appeared in Billings, Montana, in
1941. She claimed to be the daughter of Wild Bill Hickok and

Calamity Jane, announcing that she had the evidence to prove it. She said she had been born on September 25, 1870, at Benson's Landing (Livingston), Montana. If so, she would have been sixty-eight when she came forth with her story. Photographs of her do not show her to have been that old.

The Billings, Montana, *Gazette* was the first newspaper to interview her. Other newspapers were quick to take up the tale. Feature writers from all over the country arrived in Billings, and in a few weeks a nation-wide audience was reading about Jean Hickok McCormick. "White-Eye" Jack Anderson was in Cheyenne. He went up to Billings to see for himself what was in her "papers." He studied them carefully before shaking his head skeptically. "I don't believe it. I think these things are fakes. . . . There were several years in which I did not know about Bill's doings, nor those of Jane. But I do know that when she came into our train at Fort Laramie (1876) there was no friendship between Bill and her. She slept with Steve Utter, ate her meals with us, and helped drink up Bill's whisky."

In addition to an old scrapbook, in which were inscribed many letters written in diary form, allegedly by her mother, this woman who had appeared out of the past had a page torn from a Bible on which had been written in ink what purported to be a marriage license, uniting in holy wedlock Jane Cannary and J. B. Hickok. It was dated "Enroute to Abilene, Kansas, Sept. 1, 1870, and read:

> I, W. F. Warren, Pastor, not having available a proper marriage certificate find it necessary to use as a substitute this page from the Holy Bible and unite in Holy Matrimony—Jane Cannary, age 18, J. B. Hickock—31.
> ### Witnesses
> Carl Cosgrove, Abilene, Kansas
> Rev. W. K. Sipes, Sarasville, Ohio
> Tom P. Connel, Hays City, Kansas

The authenticity of these documents now came into question. The diary had to be accepted as genuine, since no other examples of Calamity's handwriting could be found. The Reverend Mr. Warren was dead, but he had married Wild Bill and Agnes

Thatcher Lake in Cheyenne in 1876, and the handwriting on the two certificates could be compared. Rosa says this was done and they proved to be dissimilar. Glenn Clairmonte in her *Calamity Was the Name for Jane* says: "The samples of handwriting of the Rev. W. F. Warren were examined by the government handwriting expert, Rowland K. Goddard, and he certified: 'It is my opinion that they were written by the same person.' "

Miss Clairmonte infers that this decision hastened the granting of an old-age pension to Jean Hickok, for which she had applied. It is difficult to understand the connection. More likely it was her appearance on the Columbia Broadcasting Company's show "We the People" which gave her nation-wide publicity and won the pension for her.

Included in this album containing Calamity's alleged "diary" was a loose leaf on which was written what has become accepted as a "confession." It is only the last two lines that are important: "I was legally married to Hickok and [Clinton] Burke. I dare anyone to deny these facts."

It is a matter of record that she married Clinton (called Charley) Burke on September 25, 1891, in Deadwood, where he was employed driving a hack. He had lost a leg in the Civil War and was a widower with a daughter of ten. Before coming to Deadwood, he and Calamity had conducted a small restaurant in Boulder, Colorado, where they had lived together for several years. Although physically handicapped, he was a sober, industrious man who put up with her tantrums and long absences for seventeen years. According to her, they first met at Yuma, Arizona, in 1884, where "I served as an army scout in 1870." It is one of her more preposterous lies. In the spring of 1901 she had gone East to appear as an attraction at the Pan-American Exposition in Buffalo, New York. When she was intoxicated, which was most of the time, she became the terror of the midway. The management fired her, and she was stranded in Buffalo until Buffalo Bill Cody, looking for talent for his Wild West Show, arrived there and staked her to a railroad ticket to Montana. When she got back to Deadwood, she found that patient Charley Burke had finally decided that he had had enough of her and had left for parts unknown.

It has never been Calamity's marriage to Charley Burke over which the irreconcilable pro-Hickok and anti-Hickok factions have contended. It is her alleged marriage to Wild Bill that so sharply divides them, one side contending that enough evidence has been presented to confirm its authenticity, and the other side protesting vehemently that the documents presented by Jean Hickok McCormick, thirty-eight years after Calamity's death, were a cleverly conceived hoax. They base their argument on the fact that a change occurred in the "confession" after it was first published in the Billings *Gazette*. In the original presentation Calamity said she had been married twice, the first time to James Butler Hickok, a cousin of James Butler "Wild Bill" Hickok, and the second time to Clinton (Charley) Burke, and further stating that the cousin was the father of her child. In photostats of the diary in its altered version, Calamity states that the man she married was *the* Wild Bill. It must be remembered that Martha Jane (Calamity) Cannary was an uneducated woman; that her schooling had stopped when she was a child of ten and that the men with whom she consorted during her mature years did not possess any "book learning" that could rub off on her.

Brushing aside the incredible nonsense that has been written about her, Martha Jane Cannary, up to the time that she was one of the half dozen "sporting women" employed by E. Coffey and Cuny at their "hog ranch" five miles west of Fort Laramie on the north side of the Laramie River, was a widely traveled, coarse, slovenly frontier whore. That was in 1875. She was twenty-three years old.

Born on her paternal grandfather's farm near Princeton, Missouri, in May, 1852, the eldest of the six children of Robert and Charlotte Cannary, she had just begun her primitive schooling when the family removed to Kirkwood, Missouri, a few miles from St. Louis, where her father had bought an unimproved forty-acre farm. The principal reason for settling at Kirkwood appears to have been because the community had asked Cannary to be its lay minister. Between 1838-39, fifteen thousand Mormons had been driven out of Missouri. Thousands of others of that persuasion, although not avowed Mormons, remained. That Robert

Cannary was one of the latter seems inescapable. In 1865, at the close of the War Between the States, he had bundled his family into a covered wagon and had joined a train of converts bound for Salt Lake City.

Being under some compulsion to get out of Missouri as quickly as possible, it must be assumed that the caravan headed north, crossed the Missouri River into Iowa, and on striking the old Mormon Road that the Saints had carved deep in the prairie soil in their exodus from Nauvoo, Illinois, in 1847, followed it across the state to Council Bluffs. After crossing the Missouri for the second time, they went up the Platte River to Fort Laramie and the valley of the Sweetwater. They had been five months on the road. It was late October now, well beyond the season for safe travel, and their difficulties increased as the freezing rains and drifting snows of those high altitudes struck them. Mrs. Cannary died and was buried in an unmarked grave beside the trail.

"We made it to Virginia City, Montana, and then headed south to Blackfoot, Idaho, where we wintered," Calamity told an interviewer years later in recalling that tragic journey across the plains. She had her facts muddled, which was not uncommon with her. It is true that when the Cannary and the other wagons reached the turnoff to Salt Lake City and found it blocked with snow, they continued on over the Lander Road to Blackfoot, Idaho, and spent the winter there, not going on to Salt Lake until the following spring. Her acquaintance with Virginia City, and Last Chance Gulch as well, after it became Helena, did not occur until she was working the honky-tonks.

The dreams Robert Cannary had entertained of finding a new and successful life in the Mormon capital did not materialize. He acquired land, but long before it became productive, he was forced to accept public charity. Ill and discouraged, he took to his bed and in a few days was dead. It meant the breaking up of the family. The younger children were put out for adoption. The two who were old enough to do some work in return for their keep found a home with a Mormon couple from Missouri. It left the future Calamity Jane to face the world alone, a girl of fifteen. Her story really begins here. She was strong, self-reliant, sharp-tongued but confused even at that early age by the conflicting emotions of absurd sentimentality and stark realism that were to plague her for the rest of her life.

Nothing is known of how she spent the following year in Salt Lake, but when gold was discovered near South Pass City in 1868 and the rush to the new diggings began, she joined it and went to work as a cook in a South Pass City restaurant. She promptly fell in love with a young army officer and shared his bed, only to have him desert her a few weeks later. The Union Pacific Railroad was building westward across Wyoming. She says she donned man's clothing and worked with a track-laying gang for several months. This must be put down as one of her fanciful lies, for late in 1868 she is known to have been in Virginia City as a dance-hall girl, which is synonymous with saying she was earning her living as a tart. In 1868 she was in Cheyenne. She could not have remained there long, for in 1870 she went down the Texas trail to Ogallala, Nebraska, and from there to Hays City, Kansas, where, taking her story at its face value, she met Wild Bill.

Hickok was there, serving as sheriff of Ellis County and town marshal ex-officio. There is no evidence—none whatsoever—that Calamity Jane was there. Its proximity to Fort Hays, its trail business and remaining buffalo hunters' trade, made the town a lucrative spot for a limited number of madams and their bawds. They seldom got their names in the paper if they behaved themselves. But that rules out Calamity, for she was becoming notorious for her drunken brawls. If she had never been in Hays, why did she pin her story on having become acquainted with Hickok there? Certainly for the obvious reason that it was a widely known historic fact that Wild Bill's name was associated with Hays City.

It is obvious on many counts that whoever concocted the so-called Calamity Jane "diary" was unacquainted with the country covered. This is also true of her adoring female biographers. We are told, for instance, that "the difficulties in the Apache country diminished by 1870, and the scouts [of whom she was one] were dismissed. Jane meant to go back to South Pass to have a visit with Lena and Lije [her brother and sister] before she looked around for another job, but on her way there she stopped off at Hays

City, Kansas. . . . She rode constantly on the tireless Bess. That four-footed symbol of freedom swept Jane over the face of the earth like a meteor." [2]

It was over a thousand miles from Fort Yuma to Fort Hays, across savage, mountainous country. The good mare Bess would have needed wings for such a journey. It is only one of many absurdities projected by Calamity's adherents leading up to her alleged "marriage" to Hickok. According to them, she and Wild Bill were making a hasty exit from Hays City, following a fracas in which he killed three unnamed toughs, and were riding eastward across the prairie when they encountered four horsemen riding west, two of whom were dressed in ministerial garb. They are supposed to have asked Hickok if he could direct them to Abilene. Why they should have asked to be directed to Abilene, through which they had already passed and which was now a hundred miles behind them, must be attributed to the geographic ignorance of the compiler of the "diary."

Allegedly Jane and Hickok asked the preachers to marry them, and the Rev. W. F. Warren obliged—in proof of which we have the improvised marriage certificate. (Warren was later pastor of a Cheyenne church and in 1876 married Wild Bill to Agnes Thatcher Lake, the owner of Lake's Circus.) The witnesses to the ceremony on the open plains, the Rev. W. K. Sipes, Carl Cosgrove and Tom Connel, were never heard of again except in Calamity's alcoholic maunderings in Deadwood. It tests one's credulity to believe that Hickok would have gone to the Reverend Warren, in Cheyenne, to officiate at his marriage to Mrs. Lake if Warren had previously married him to Calamity Jane, from whom he had not been divorced. It does explain how the author of the "diary" was familiar with the Reverend Warren's name, for the Cheyenne papers had publicized the Hickok-Lake marriage.

In Calamity's account she and Hickok arrived in Abilene (no mention is made of Ellsworth, through which they would have had to pass) and, after spending a few months there, they headed north together for Benson's Landing, Montana—another little journey of eight hundred and fifty miles (the faithful Bess must have been getting used to these ramblings), where, the narrative states, she gave birth to a baby, fathered by Wild Bill, the event taking place in a hillside cave on September 25, 1870. This was the child who was to appear out of nowhere sixty-eight years later as Jean Hickok McCormick.

There is such wide divergence between the Calamity Jane version of the so-called "Hickok episode" and the provable facts that to take it seriously is impossible. The circumstances under which Wild Bill left Hays City are a matter of record. It wasn't to escape the vengeance of a gang of town toughs that he made a hasty departure in July, 1870. The previous winter, in his dual role of sheriff and town marshal, he had had numerous difficulties with the troopers of the Seventh U.S. Cavalry, two companies of which were stationed at Fort Hays, and with Captain Tom Custer, the General's brother. In January, having failed in his bid for re-election, he had taken a train east to Topeka, where he spent the winter gambling for a living. In July, as a private citizen, he was back in Hays City on a visit. It was then that the often disputed showdown with the Seventh Cavalry occurred. In Tommy Drumm's saloon he was jumped by five troopers, two of whom he killed. A third died later. Friends smuggled him aboard the next train east to Ellsworth, where he hid out in the home of his friend Harry Pestana until the hunt for him died down.

It is only with James Butler Hickok's connection with Martha Jane Cannary, real or fancied, that this brief narrative is concerned. Suffice it to say that she did not accompany him when he left Hays City and that he did not leave on horseback. She was not with him in Ellsworth and was unknown in Abilene, the first of the wild Kansas cow towns, where he was appointed town marshal on April 15, 1871, and served until December 13 of that year. It was there that he met Agnes Thatcher Lake when she brought her circus to Abilene.

In 1872 Hickok took his first plunge into the unknown, to him —the world of show business. Colonel Sidney Barnett of Buffalo, New York, the promoter, came West and after Hickok had engaged a number of frontiersmen, the party set out up the Republican River to capture a number of live buffalo and engage Indians and cowboys for the exhibition which was to be staged on the

Canadian side at Niagara Falls. With great difficulty six buffalo were captured and shipped East, along with some Longhorns and the Indians. The animals and performers arrived at Niagara Falls on July 20. A month was lost while an arena was built, and it was not until August 28 and 30, according to the Niagara Falls *Gazette*, that performances were given. They were well attended, but Barnett's expenses had been so heavy that the venture was a financial failure. But the Grand Buffalo Hunt could lay claim to being the first Wild West show presented in the East—outdoors, that is, for Buffalo Bill Cody and "Texas Jack" Omohundro had previously offered a Wild West entertainment in theaters.

Barnett attempted to take the Grand Buffalo Hunt on the road, but the returns did not warrant continuing. He shipped the Indians and cowboys back to Omaha and called it a day. Mrs. Lake was performing in nearby Rochester. Wild Bill visited her. Renewing his acquaintance with the attractive and talented Agnes provided him with an opportunity to advance his cause with her. In view of their subsequent marriage, he must have been successful.

On returning to Kansas, he took a job as house gambler in a Topeka saloon. He was broke, a condition in which he often found himself, and one common enough among gamblers. When he had won himself a stake, he went on to Georgetown, Colorado, where his old friend "Colorado Charley" Utter was running a profitable miners' boarding house. Several of Utter's boarders recalled later that Wild Bill had spent the early part of the winter there, playing poker most of the time. He had received letters from "Texas Jack" Omohundro and Buffalo Bill Cody urging him to join them in the stage show Ned Buntline, the popular Dime Novel author, was readying for them. He had put off answering, but in response to their urgent request to meet "White-Eye" Jack Anderson at Fort McPherson, Nebraska, and talk things over, he left Georgetown for the meeting with Anderson, who had agreed to take part in the confection labeled *The Scouts of the Prairie*. Wild Bill was won over, and on December 16, 1872, he was on stage in Chicago.

Establishing James Butler Hickok's whereabouts in 1872-73 may be a roundabout and possibly tedious way of proving that he could not possibly have been the father of the child to whom Martha

Jane Cannary claims she gave birth on September 25, 1873. In fact the gruesome circumstances surrounding the alleged birth— the earthen cave, its only furnishing a blanket spread on the floor, food gone and the expectant mother lying there attended only by the badly frightened Wild Bill—strongly suggest that what we are asked to believe never happened.

Instead of stopping there, Calamity adds a development to the birth of her "baby" that stretches credulity beyond the breaking point. After Bill had deserted her, as she tells it, a shadow fell across the mouth of the cave, and she looked up, thinking Hickok had returned. To her amazement (and the reader's) a man in "store clothes" stood there and he said, "Can I be of any assistance?" Thus she introduces the incredible and kindly salt-water sailor, Captain James O'Neil, master of the Cunard steamship *Madagascar*,[3] plying between American ports and Liverpool. O'Neil and his wife were to adopt the baby who was to become Jean Hickok McCormick and take her to England. The McCormick part of her name de- rived from her marriage in France during World War I to a Lieutenant Edward McCormick, a young airman who was killed just prior to the Armistice.

In a little pamphlet published in Deadwood in 1896 entitled *Life and Adventures of Calamity Jane, by Herself* (which it surely wasn't), she contradicts and confuses much that she had given out in previous interviews. She was not only a congenital liar but seemed to find a ribald amusement in constantly changing her story. She had at least four versions of how she came to be called Calamity. The one most believed is that a Captain Egan, in com- mand of troops on Goose Creek in 1873, was wounded in a skirmish with the Indians and that she carried him to safety and cared for him, and he called her "Calamity Jane, heroine of the Plains." No verification of this exists, but it is as valid as her saying that it was Wild Bill who first dubbed her "Calamity Jane."

In the "papers" Jean Hickok presented as having been written by her mother, Calamity says that when she journeyed to Omaha to turn her "baby" over to the O'Neils, who were leaving for England, she was stricken with smallpox. This would account for her pitted face, and very likely for the fact that, with her looks gone, she was reduced to finding employment in the various "hog ranches," the cheapest houses of frontier prostitution. The military permitted these to operate at a distance of five miles from an army post. Her scarred face may have been another reason why she turned to alcohol for escape.

It could hardly have been by accident that Agnes Thatcher Lake came to Cheyenne to visit her old friend Mrs. S. L. Moyer, who had once been a member of her troupe. Hickok was in town, and they were married on Sunday, March 5, 1876, in the home of the Moyers, by the often-mentioned Reverend W. F. Warren. Gold had been discovered in the Black Hills and the rush there was on, but apparently Wild Bill was not caught up in it, for he and his wife left for the East and spent their honeymoon in Cincinnati with her relatives. But the news from the Black Hills grew more exciting, and he left his bride in the Ohio town and returned to Cheyenne determined to get to the new town of Deadwood at once.

He found his old friends, "Colorado Charley" and Steve Utter, "White-Eye" Jack Anderson, young Charley Anderson and a fifth man called Pie, a friend of the Utter brothers, preparing to leave for the Black Hills. Wild Bill was invited to join their mess, making six in all. The Utters had a good four-horse outfit. Hickok's contribution to the well-being of himself and his fellow travelers was a five-gallon barrel of whisky.

With their spirits properly fortified, they reached Fort Laramie without incident. Here they found some thirty wagons, including the previously mentioned "load of whores," rendezvoused for the dangerous journey to Deadwood.

It was there—and there is no evidence to the contrary—that Calamity Jane and Wild Bill came face to face for the first time. When he was asked to assume the responsibility of wagon master, he refused. Reluctantly, Charley Utter accepted the job. As the wagons were about to pull out for their first stop at Government Farm, Utter was requested by the officer of the day to take another woman with them, who "had had a high time the night before and had been thrown into the guardhouse. It was Calamity Jane." [4]

"She was nearly naked," according to "White-Eye" Jack Anderson. "Charley and Steve Utter outfitted her with a buckskin shirt, buckskin pants and a wide-brimmed hat. When she spoke to Wild Bill, she addressed him as Mr. Hickok."

What Calamity did on reaching Deadwood is not known. But it is a certainty she was not living with Wild Bill. Reams of nonsense have been written about her activities. If repetition is any indication of truth, she changed professions and became a bullwhacker, freighting merchandise and machinery to the outlying camps and for a time tooling the Spearfish stage across the hills. She was still young, only twenty-four, but coarse, crude, unfeminine and too ignorant to have written the often mentioned "diary."

It is a largely overlooked fact that Hickok had spent very little time locating any claims, and that he had been in Deadwood only twenty days when he was killed by Jack McCall in Carl Mann's Number Ten Saloon, the details of which are so well-known they need not be repeated. Calamity may have been in Deadwood on the afternoon of the shooting, but there is no proof of it. However, one of her more romantic biographers, who boldly proclaims that "all the material in this book is authentic," insists that she was and pictures her elbowing her way through the crowd that had gathered in Mann's saloon, only to turn back when she realized that "she had no rights over the long-adored body." But that evening she has Calamity confronting McCall in the hut where he was being held awaiting trial, and forcing from him the details of the plot to assassinate Wild Bill, none of which were produced in McCall's second trial at Yankton that resulted in his being found guilty and hanged. Further, she accounts for Calamity's absence from Wild Bill's funeral by saying: "She didn't dare to attend the funeral because her emotions were far from under control."

In the fall of 1878, when smallpox swept through Deadwood and men were dying like flies, Calamity, immune to the disease herself, was tireless in administering to the sick and the dying. It was perhaps her finest hour. The Deadwood *Black Hills Pioneer* called her "An Angel of Mercy." That gave the magazine feature writers a new image to play with, and they made the most of it. Calamity complained about "the damned lies they're printin' about me." They were lies certainly, but they got them direct from her in many cases. She was freighting between Deadwood and Fort Pierre by way of Rapid City, about one hundred and fifty miles of what had become reasonably safe trail. But she fed the innocents who interviewed her some tall stories of hairbreadth escapes from Indians and road agents. Deadwood read with amusement what they wrote, but for the first time in her life Calamity became a celebrity.

Her story of how on a small borrowed stake she had run her winnings up to $25,000 in the gambling tents of Deadwood received such wide publicity that Buffalo Bill Cody decided he needed her for his Wild West show. Her recent good fortune and the publicity she was receiving had given her an inflated idea of her importance, and she scorned Cody's offer.

The amount of money she claimed to have won at poker was more than a tenfold exaggeration of the truth. She claimed, many years later, that she had borrowed her original stake from Teddy Blue Abbott, who was then a young, unknown cowpuncher. In his *We Pointed Them North*, which made him famous, he says only that he saw Calamity in Deadwood, and his description of how she was dressed indicates that he was confusing her with Madame Vestal, the lady gambler from Denver.[5]

In 1884 she made her celebrated and much-disputed trip to California, stopping off in Ogden for a belated and futile search for the two young sisters and brother who had been put out for adoption at the time of the death of their father. Supposedly it was while returning from the Coast by way of the Southwest that in Yuma she met Charley Burke, whom she married in Deadwood in 1891, after living with him for seven years.

As related, she made a brief and disastrous appearance at the Pan-American Exposition in Buffalo, in 1901, from which she returned to Deadwood to sink into obscurity. She was forty-nine and becoming increasingly aware that her eyesight was failing. Hickok had suffered from the same affliction for some time before his death and kept it secret, realizing that his life depended on keeping the world from knowing. Medical authorities have expressed the opinion that in both instances the loss of sight could have been due to some long-forgotten exposure to venereal infection that had settled in the eyes. Whisky was her only means of escape from reality. She turned to it, and in her last years was seldom sober.

On July 31, 1903, she rode to the nearby camp of Terry on an ore train. She was so ill when she arrived that she was carried over to the Callaway Hotel, across from the tracks. There, the following afternoon, August 1, she died. The body was taken to Deadwood, and after funeral services that filled the Methodist Church, the mourners followed the horse-drawn hearse to Mount Moriah Cemetery in which Wild Bill's remains had been re-interred after their removal from the abandoned Ingleside Cemetery in 1879.

When, in 1941, the woman calling herself Jean Hickok McCormick made her disclosures and published her *The Real Calamity Jane*, she gave the world a Calamity who bore little resemblance to the woman history had known. Whether Jean Hickok McCormick was just a personable adventuress presenting a series of alleged documents which she had devised over the years and which she hoped to use for her own profit, the reader must decide for himself. She received wide publicity, but the financial returns appear to have been slight. She was seventy-eight when she died in 1951. By that time the world had lost interest in her. It is not likely ever to lose interest in Martha (Calamity) Jane Cannary.

Ella Watson and Mythical Cattle Kate

ELLA WATSON WAS just another one of the countless girls who had
"gone wrong" as the easiest escape from poverty. If she had lived
out her life and died a normal death, she would never have been
heard of. As it happened, however, she became the most widely
known woman in Wyoming when a lynch mob jerked her to
death on the Sweetwater in 1889.

Long before Wyoming was sheared off from Dakota Territory
and gained territorial status of its own in 1863, tens of thousands
of emigrants had crossed it from east to west, beginning with the
pioneers bound for the Pacific Northwest on what was to become
famous as the Oregon Trail, followed by the exodus of the Latter-
day Saints over the Mormon Road to their new Zion in Utah,
and concurrently the mass of stampeding gold seekers bound for
California on what was to be the great Overland Trail. Very few
of those migrating thousands remained in Wyoming. It was the
hunting ground of the Brulé and Ogalalla Sioux, the Northern
Cheyennes and Arapahos, and they fought desperately to retain
possession of it.

Even after the Indian wars were over and the white man could
claim possession of the country, there appeared to be little in-
centive for the settling of Wyoming. The buffalo herds had been
thinned out; the fur trade was a thing of the past; and its ranges,
second to none, were empty. The situation changed drastically in
1870, when thousands of Longhorns were driven north from the

Kansas cattle market over what came to be known as the Texas Trail. The advent of Texas cattle was followed by the great influx of Oregon cattle that were trailed eastward across the Snake River Plains of Idaho and put on grass in the Big Horn Basin.

Presently the size and value of the Wyoming range cattle business rated second only to that of Texas. Settlers moved in to take up land, homesteaders, "nesters" and farmers, although the farming seldom amounted to little more than raising hay with which to winter-feed livestock. And with the others came cattle thieves, rustlers and maverickers. The latter practice, which was universal, can be described simply as slapping your brand on any unbranded calf or yearling you might find.

Naturally the big owners had to do something to stop this nefarious business which, they claimed, was costing them thousands of dollars annually, no doubt a pardonable exaggeration. Out of their deliberations came the Wyoming Stock Growers' Association—and there never was another stockmen's association anywhere to compare with it. It arrogated to itself the triple powers of judge, jury and executioner. It controlled the press and not only controlled the Territorial government, it *was* the government. It put its own brand inspectors in the field, hired range detectives (who could double as gunmen whenever required), and made life miserable for those honest dissenters who criticized the high-handedness of the cattle barons who ruled their empire from their posh headquarters in the Cheyenne Club.

It was under such circumstances that Jim Averell brought down on himself the ire of the Association. He ran a grocery and saloon on the Sweetwater, in the vernacular of the country a "road ranch," three miles east of Independence Rock, the landmark so frequently called "the register of the desert," on which thousands of emigrants had scratched their names.[1] He was an educated man and foolishly reckless in his condemnation of Tom Sun, Albert J. Bothwell, John Durbin, Ernest McLain, R. B. Conners and R. M. Gailbraith, who controlled sixty miles of range along the Sweetwater. He wrote letters to the *Casper Weekly Mail*, which had the intestinal fortitude to print them, condemning the "range hogs who by threats of bodily harm and other forms of intimidation are preventing settlers from locating along the Sweetwater."

All of the aforementioned cattlemen were members in good standing of the Wyoming Stock Growers' Association. One of them, Tom Sun, a Frenchman by birth, was a Wyoming pioneer, dating back to the fur trade days. He was the first man to import Oregon horses and cattle into the Territory. His sprawling Hub-and-Spoke ranch at Devil's Gate on the Sweetwater was known throughout Wyoming. But he was a hard man, as ruthless as his neighbors along the Sweetwater, when his interests were threatened.

It was not Tom Sun but Albert Bothwell who did most of the huffing and puffing about driving Jim Averell out of the Sweetwater valley, a big slice of which he regarded as belonging to him, although it was in the public domain. He had title only to the quarter-section on which his ranch buildings stood. He didn't own the rest, nor did he want to own it. All he wanted was the exclusive right to use it for ranging his cattle. That was the position taken by all the big cow outfits. What made Averell's intrusion particularly offensive was the fact that he had homesteaded at the foot of the hills along the Sweetwater upon land that Bothwell claimed as his range.

No phase of the range cattle business has been more distorted by overexaggeration than the losses suffered by the big companies from various kinds of theft of livestock. Cattlemen's associations always stressed the amount of range losses, and it was from them that we first learned about 'organized rustling rings." Fiction writers took it up from there. In Owen Wister's time it was thought sufficient for Trampas and his gang to run off a handful of steers. Today we see on the screen and read about whole herds of steers being hazed across the plains to some secret corral where they can be held and rebranded at leisure, and presumably with some degree of security.

Undoubtedly some of the yearlings belonging to Bothwell and his neighbors were disappearing. There is no evidence that Averell was buying them from the cowboys who made his road ranch their hangout. But Bothwell was convinced of it. Several times in 1887, he warned Averell to get out of the country while he still had his health. The warnings went unheeded. If Averell wasn't popular with the owners, he was popular with the men they hired and fired. In two years' time he had built up a profitable business, and he didn't propose to be run out.

In December, he rode down to Rawlins on the Union Pacific Railroad, the shipping point for the Sweetwater country, fifty miles to the south. Rawlins may have had a winter population of thirteen hundred, not more. But it was wild, lively and wide-open. In one of its half-dozen brothels Averell renewed his acquaintance with a high-spirited, adventurous young strumpet by the name of Ella Watson. Only twenty-seven, she had already put in a long apprenticeship at her trade in Dodge City, Ogallala and Cheyenne. A corn-bred farm girl from Lebanon, Kansas, she was a bit on the stout side but very attractive. Dismissing love as a possible explanation, one wonders what inducement Averell offered to persuade her to return to the Sweetwater with him. Helena Huntington Smith, in *The War on Powder River*, conjectures that he "brought her out to the Sweetwater to boost business for his road ranch and brighten his personal life besides."

Whatever the cause, the arrangement did not last for long. On March 24, 1888, she took up a homestead a mile west of Averell's on a rill of running water called Horse Creek, where she built a one-room cabin and fenced off a small pasture. Witnesses subsequently testified that in the enclosure they sometimes saw from two to six head of cattle, never more, branded EW, which was not a recorded brand, the Carbon County brand committee having rejected her application. Likewise, Averell had applied five years running to have his brand recorded, only to be turned down on every occasion. No explanation for this highhanded treatment was ever given, but it shows clearly enough that the Wyoming Stock Growers' Association and its agents were in complete control of the range cattle business.

Usually it takes an unexpected act of violence to whip into sudden flame a long-smoldering situation such as prevailed on the Sweetwater. But there is nothing in the record that such was the case in this instance, unless it was a continuation of growing conflict in the eastern part of the Territory that was to culminate in the Johnson County War several years later. There was a meeting at Bothwell's ranch at which his five neighbors were present. As a further guarantee of unanimity, George B. Henderson, manager of John Clay's big 71 Quarter Circle ranch with headquarters at the Three Crossings of the Sweetwater, was also present. A decision was reached to present Jim Averell and Ella Watson with an ultimatum: Get out of the country or be forcibly ejected.

That left the couple a choice. But overnight that choice disappeared, and when Bothwell and the others set out the following afternoon to vent their wrath, it was with the bloodthirsty determination to string up Jim and Ella and get the business over with as quickly as possible.

It was July 20, 1889, a hot, sunny Saturday. Bothwell, grim and sadistic, led the way in a buckboard. Tom Sun, John Durbin and Rob Conners rode with him. Ernest McLain and R. M. Gailbraith followed behind in the saddle. All were armed with rifles. Henderson, who may have been the co-author, along with Bothwell, of the grim business about to take place, presumably had returned to the Three Crossings.

Fortunately for history there were some witnesses to what followed. Although they must be regarded as prejudiced, it is largely from their testimony given under oath and their signed letters, which were published in the *Casper Weekly Mail* and the *Carbon County Journal*, that the events of that July afternoon on the Sweetwater can be put together. The first writer of consequence to publish the facts was Alfred J. Mokler of Casper, for seventeen years editor and publisher of the *Natrona County Tribune* (1897 to 1914), in his *History of Natrona County, Wyoming*, published in 1923. Although he is silent about the trickery with which the puppet press of the Wyoming Stock Growers' Association metamorphosed Ella Watson almost overnight into Cattle Kate, the notorious woman bandit who had killed one of her husbands and an unknown number of other men, and who "had stolen more cattle than any man in the West," he must have known Cattle Kate Maxwell was a myth, a creature who never existed, and who was created in the editorial room of the Cheyenne *Leader*.[2]

The barrage of misinformation spewed out by the Association's controlled press for the purpose of turning public opinion against the woman who had been lynched on the Sweetwater almost succeeded, the general opinion being that "she got only what she deserved."

Ella and John DeCorey, described as a cowboy in her employ (which damaging admission indicates that she had work for such a man to do), were returning from the river about two o'clock in the afternoon. She had gone to buy some beaded moccasins from some Indians who were camped there, when Bothwell and his companions drove past them. No words were exchanged, but when Ella and her hired man reached her cabin, they found Bothwell and the others waiting.

"I was at Ella's trying to catch up a pony when they [the lynch party] rode up," testified fourteen-year-old Gene Crowder, a range waif who had attached himself to Jim Averell. "John Durbin took down the wire fence and drove the cattle out [he doesn't say how many head], while McLain and Conners kept Ella from going to the house. After a while they told her to get into the wagon and she asked them where they were going. They told her to Rawlins. She wanted to go to the house and change her clothes, but they would not let her and made her get into the wagon. Bothwell told her he would rope and drag her if she did not get in.

"She got in then and we all started toward Jim's. I tried to ride around the cattle and get ahead, but Bothwell took hold of my pony's bridle and made me stay with them."

They caught up with Averell at his second gate, some three hundred yards from the house, where he was hitching a team, preparing to drive to Casper for supplies. They told him to throw up his hands and said something about having a warrant for him. When he asked to see it, they patted their rifles and told him that was warrant enough. They made him get in the buckboard with Ella and then drove off in the direction of Independence Rock.

"I started to follow them," John DeCorey testified at the inquest, "but Bothwell pointed his rifle at me and told me to go to the house and stay there."

DeCorey and young Crowder spurred quickly to the store.

With the windows and doors open, it was cool in the big room and four or five men were sprawled out on the chairs and counter enjoying the breeze from the river. With one exception their reputations were not of the best, and when they were told what had happened, they were too concerned for their own safety to do anything. The exception was Frank Buchanan. He had ridden for John Clay and Tom Sun, among others, and was rated a reliable man. But he was reckless and foolishly brave. He proved it by leaping into the saddle and taking off after the lynch mob armed with only a pistol.

From a distance he saw them swing around the western end of Independence Rock, cross at the ford and continue up the bed of the river for a mile or more. When they turned up Spring Creek Canyon, he lost sight of them.

It took Buchanan some time to reach the gulch up which the lynching party had disappeared. When he did, he proceeded carefully, following the fresh tracks on the canyon floor. He got down from the saddle, tethered his horse and continued on foot, hearing angry voices somewhere ahead of him. At this time of the year there was no flowing water in Spring Creek Canyon, but it was clogged with high brush and gigantic boulders, which afforded him cover enough to get within sight of the mob and its victims and close enough to overhear what they were saying.

Ropes, ordinary lariats, had been thrown over a limb of a scrub pine that projected out over the floor of the canyon from a limestone ledge a few feet above the rocky, boulder-strewn floor.

"Bothwell had the rope around Jim's neck," Buchanan testified at the inquest, "and had it tied to a limb. He told him [Averell] to be game and jump off. McLain was trying to put the rope around Ella's neck, but she was jerking her head so that he did not succeed at that time.

"I opened fire on them, but do not know whether I hit anyone or not. They turned and began shooting at me. I unloaded my revolver twice but had to run, as they were shooting at me with Winchesters. I ran to my horse and rode to the ranch [Averell's place] and told them Jim and Ella had been hanged, and then I started for Casper to get the sheriff."

It was a good fifty miles to Casper. No one volunteered to accompany Buchanan, so he set out alone. In his excitement he lost
the trail during the night, and it was three o'clock in the morning
when he pounded on the door of Tex Healy's homestead shack,
still twenty-five miles from Casper. Healy pulled on his breeches
and volunteered to go for the sheriff. After giving his horse several
hours in which to recuperate, Buchanan turned back to Averell's
road ranch on the Sweetwater.

Healy was in Casper by noon Sunday. The little town had been
showing some signs of growth and now claimed a population of
three hundred. It was shocked by news of the double hanging and
that one of the victims was a woman. Only a few Casperites had
ever heard of Ella Watson, but no matter what she was, the fact
that she was a woman was enough to unleash an outpouring of
outrage.

Undersheriff Phil Watson, who made his headquarters in Casper,
began organizing a posse, deputizing a number of men, including
Dr. Joe Benson, the acting coroner, who swore in his own coroner's
jury. It took time, and the party did not leave Casper until daylight Monday morning. As a consequence, it was some time after
midnight when Sheriff Watson and his men reached Averell's
roadranch, where they found Frank Buchanan and Ralph Cole,
a friend of Averell, waiting for them. While awaiting their arrival,
Buchanan and Cole had built a rough pine box in which to inter
one of the bodies and had a second box partly completed. Buchanan
suggested that he and Cole be given time to finish it before the posse
started for the river. Sheriff Watson said no; they would start for
the scene of the lynching at once.

With several men armed with lanterns to light the way, the
posse set out for Spring Creek Gulch. By then the telegraph wires
from Rawlins to Cheyenne were sizzling with the first tales of the
execution of the "cattle thieves who had terrorized the Sweetwater valley for years and were guilty of numerous murders."
They were on their way to the Cheyenne *Leader*. This is believed
to have been the work of George Henderson, Clay's superinten-
dent, who just "happened to be in the capital" the following day.

That he was in some way connected with the lynchings was admitted by the taciturn Clay thirty years later.

Dawn was not far away when the posse, directed by Frank Buchanan, reached the scene of the lynching. Suspended by their necks were Jim Averell and Ella, swaying lifelessly in the dawn breeze. It was now July 23. For almost three days, under a blazing summer sun, the bodies had been hanging there, and their bloated, blackened faces were almost unrecognizable. The ledge from which they were pushed off had allowed them only a two-foot drop, insufficient to break their necks, which meant that they had slowly strangled to death.[3]

The bodies were cut down and taken to Averell's place, where the coroner held an inquest. On the evidence given by Frank Buchanan, Ralph Cole, Gene Crowder and John DeCorey, it returned a verdict to the effect that "the deceased man and woman, James Averell and Ella Watson, came to their deaths by being hanged by the neck at the hands of A. J. Bothwell, Tom Sun, John Durbin, R. M. Gailbraith, Bob Conners, E. McLain and an unknown man."

"The next morning two graves were dug a short distance east from the Averell building," says Mokler. "Although the graves were quite shallow, it is said there was at least twelve inches of water in them when the bodies were interred, the water having seeped through from the river, which was about on a level with the burial spot."

Warrants were served on the accused and they were given a preliminary arraignment in Rawlins a week later. By all the rules of legal procedure the hearing was a travesty on justice. It was held in a hotel room, not in court; no witnesses were called; and although first-degree murder, the charge, was not subject to bail, the defendants were admitted to bail in the trifling sum (considering their wealth) of $5,000 each; furthermore, they were permitted to sign one another's bonds.

Only the Wyoming Stock Growers' Association could have thwarted justice in that highhanded fashion. It had wheeled its big legal guns, attorneys Corlett, Lacey, Riner and J. R. Dixon, into action. Tom Sun, Bothwell and their fellow conspirators were in no danger of being found guilty. In the controlled press of the Territory the stream of defamation against Averell and the Watson woman continued. By now Averell was firmly established as the King of the Cattle Thieves and Ella as Cattle Kate Maxwell, the Bandit Queen. Reading this trash today, one can only have contempt for the pitiful hack who produced it.

Friends of Averell took up a subscription to see that he got justice. They might better have saved their money, for the issue at stake was not to find the accused men innocent of unwarranted murder, but to prove to all dissidents that the Wyoming Stock Growers' Association was not to be trifled with.[4]

Ella Watson had no one to come forward in her behalf, other than her father.[5] Not that it would have made any difference. She had led an immoral life and undoubtedly had used her sex to purchase the cattle that appeared in her pasture. But she had been brutally murdered and given a character that justified the deed. The judgment was about to be made permanent.

The grand jury of Carbon County convened in Rawlins on October 14. First on the docket was the case of the Territory of Wyoming vs. Albert J. Bothwell, Ernest McLain, Robert B. Conners, Tom Sun, Robert M. Gailbraith and John Durbin, with Judge Samuel T. Corn presiding. The state was represented by David H. Craig, the prosecuting attorney for Carbon County, and the assistant prosecutor, D. A. Preston.

An air of expectancy hung over the crowded courtroom as the proceedings began. More than half of the spectators could be classified as cowboys. The fall shipping season was about over, and they had remained in town to attend the trial, many of them aware, no doubt, that it concerned them. Solemnly Judge Corn charged the jury:

"It is not ordinarily necessary to charge a grand jury with reference to special crimes, but it has come to my ears and is the subject of much conversation in this community and has been widely published in the newspapers that certain persons are charged with the hanging of a certain man and woman by lynch law in this county, and it is evident that there is great feeling and excitement in the community in regard to it. In such matters you are pre-eminently the guardians of the safety of the people and the good order of society. You have sworn to present none through malice or ill, and to leave none unrepresented through fear, favor or affection. It becomes you in connection with this matter to be especially regardful of this oath. Some of the ancients portrayed Justice as a goddess blindfolded. Her eyes were hood-winked [sic], that she might not even know the persons upon whom she was called to pass judgment. In one hand she held the balances to weigh the evidence with impartiality, and in the other a sword with which to execute her decrees. This idea of 'Justice blind' should be your guide in this matter. Weigh the evidence with absolute impartiality and without regard to persons, and then strike, no matter where the blow may fall."

This pious twaddle was a subterfuge to persuade the populace that dispensing justice was uppermost in the minds of judge and jury. Actually there was not a member of the sixteen-man jury who did not know before he entered the courtroom what the verdict would be. That became apparent to even the meanest intelligence when the prosecutor began calling his witnesses and found that his key witnesses had either died or disappeared.

The jury retired briefly and "after due deliberation" returned to the jury box and informed the court that it had not found a true bill against the accused, whereupon Judge Corn ruled:

"The grand jury at the present term of this court, having failed to find a true bill indictment against the defendants, or either of them, it is ordered by the court that the above named defendants [Bothwell and the other five] and each of them, and their bonds be discharged."

The Cheyenne *Leader* and its satellites chortled with glee over the acquittal of Bothwell and the other big owners. They said nothing about the missing witnesses, but others did. Says Mokler: "Buchanan, the material witness for the prosecution, who was under a five hundred dollar bond to appear, was 'induced' to leave the country. He came to Casper in September and slept in a livery stable for two nights, then mysteriously disappeared and has never again been seen by anyone here. His bonds were forfeited and suit ordered against his bondsmen to recover the amount. John De-Corey and Ralph Cole also mysteriously disappeared, and Gene Crowder, the fourteen-year-old boy, died of Bright's disease, before the case came to a hearing." According to Asa Mercer, the embattled editor and author of *The Banditti of the Plains*, "He [Crowder] was taken in charge by the cattlemen. He lingered some weeks and died—rumor strongly insisting at the hands of his protectors by the administration of a slow poison."

Regarding the disappearance of Ralph Cole, Mokler says: "Cole left the Averell ranch the night after the hanging, and he was followed by George Henderson. Cole reached a surveyor's camp late at night and remained there until morning. The next day, while trying to make his way to a station on the Union Pacific Railroad, he was overtaken by Henderson, who shot him, and the body was burned to ashes." Mercer says, writing in 1894, "he [Cole] was hunted like a wild beast, and the supposition is that he sleeps in some lonely mountain gorge."

John DeCorey, the fourth witness who had so conveniently disappeared, was seen in Steamboat Springs, Colorado, two weeks after the lynching. No trace of him was found after that. If the law had not been under the complete domination of the rich, vested interests, some legal effort would have been made to determine the fate and whereabouts of the missing witnesses. But nothing was done.

It will be recalled that the boy Gene Crowder testified at the inquest following the lynching that John Durbin, one of the six conspirators, opened the gate to Ella's pasture and "drove out the cattle." A few days later the Cheyenne *Tribune* reported that Durbin had repossessed forty head of maverick cattle at a sale conducted by the Territorial Livestock Commission. The *Tribune* didn't say that they were the cattle found in Ella Watson's pasture, but the reader was left to infer that they were. This tale may have been partly true, but there is no evidence that she ever had as many as forty head of stock in her possession at any time. The only cattle found at Averell's place on the afternoon that he was seized were two milch cows.

Of the seven men involved in the lynching of Jim Averell and Ella Watson, George Henderson was the first to die. He was shot and killed several months later in a dispute with a cowboy over wages. As proof of the bitterness that remained over the lynching, his killing was regarded as a salutary act of retributive justice.

Time has erased the landmarks connected with the tragedy on the Sweetwater. The buildings of Averell's road ranch were soon torn down and carted away for lumber. Bothwell put skids under Ella's cabin and had it dragged acrosscountry to his ranch, where it was used as an icehouse for many years. Gone with the other landmarks are the graves in which Averell and Ella were buried. The sickly pines in Spring Creek Gulch have disappeared. All that remain are the boulders and limestone ledges. Even the ghostly figure of the beautiful and mythical Cattle Kate who never was, with her diamonds and band of range desperadoes, has largely eroded the memory of plain Ella Waston, in her sunbonnet and calico skirts.

Pegleg Annie Morrow,
the Heroine of Bald Mountain

NO ONE CAN SAY WITH CERTAINTY who gave the beautiful but unwarranted name of Mountain Home to the cluster of cabins that became the tough, brawling mining camp in southern Idaho in Civil War days. Gold was being discovered in so many different places that for a time it was erroneously believed that you could find "color" wherever you drove a pick into Idaho's auriferous rock. A score of camps sprang into existence, but Mountain Home was there first and it became the hub of the district and the jumping-off place for such camps as Featherville, Rocky Bar and Atlanta.

A so-called "miners' road," which was nothing more than an unimproved trail, ran north along the South Fork of the Boise River, fifty-three miles to Rocky Bar and over 9,000-foot Bald Mountain for another fourteen miles to Atlanta, which was backed up against the lower ranges of the Sawtooth Mountains.

On July 4, 1864, Steve McIntyre trudged into Rocky Bar with his four-year-old daughter Annie in a pack on his back. He had carried her almost all of the way from Mountain Home. Having recently lost his wife, he was determined to keep his daughter near him.

McIntyre was not penniless, as some grass-roots historians have stated. He bought a cabin in Rocky Bar and managed to find an

Indian woman to keep house for him and take care of Annie. His old friend George Jackson was in Rocky Bar, which may explain why McIntyre had come up from Mountain Home. They struck up a partnership. Their first venture was the Golden Star Mine. It soon became a profitable operation. McIntyre was able to provide Annie with the best that money could buy, which wasn't much in a wild, roaring camp where there were few children, no schools and where four-fifths of the women were prostitutes.

Annie was twelve when McIntyre's luck ran out and he was killed in a street brawl. It can be imagined what her life was like, growing up an orphan, dependent on charity, in a town, where, as Lamont Johnson so nicely put it, "no angel could keep her wings unruffled and which any priest would think was the founding home of Satan." But despite the odds against her, she developed into a beautiful young woman, and because she was beautiful, she became the target of every lecherous male in Rocky Bar. To escape them, she married a man named Bill Morrow before she was eighteen.

By the time Annie was thirty-five, she was a widow. Morrow was dead and so were three of the five children she had had by him. Despondent, she began drinking so heavily that Morrow's relatives took the two remaining boys away from her. Rocky Bar had grown. Her old friends had moved away. What followed was predictable. Nearly destitute, she took the only course left to her. She crossed Bald Mountain to Atlanta and took her place in a bordello in its Red Light Alley. To add to her bitterness, the company that now owned the Golden Star Mine had struck a bonanza and it was being hailed as one of the richest properties in Idaho.

Up until now Annie Morrow had done little to make her anybody's heroine; she had suffered some hard knocks and was a pathetic figure—nothing more. But late in March, 1898, she willfully set out on snowshoes to cross Bald Mountain to Rocky Bar for the sole purpose of attending a big spring dance and thumbing her nose at the camp. She was accompanied by another strumpet by the name of Emma Von Losch, a big German, known on the line as Dutch Em.

Both women had often used snowshoes. Indeed it was about the only means of travel in that country during the winter, where a fall of three to six feet of snow overnight was not unusual. The trail to the cabin at the summit of Bald Mountain was well-packed and well-defined. Bill Tate, the mailman, made the trip every other day, meeting Bob Jackson, the carrier from Rocky Bar, at the summit, where they exchanged mail sacks and returned to their respective destinations. Warm chinook winds from the northwest had been expected for several days, but they had failed to come, and on the morning that Annie and Dutch Em set out, the sky looked cold and ominous. They fortified themselves with a hearty slug or two of whisky and were off.

A blizzard was beginning to lash through the pines when Mailman Tate passed them five miles out of Atlanta. When he met the Rocky Bar carrier at the summit, he told him he had seen the two women.

"You better tell them to turn back with you," Bob Jackson advised. "We're in for a real storm."

Tate looked for them on his return trip but failed to find any sign of them. His hope was that they had sought shelter among the pines. To spread word that the two women were lost, he hurried on to Atlanta in a storm that was to last three days.

When it was over and a searching party was being organized, Tate volunteered to cross Bald Mountain and get another searching party started from Rocky Bar. He reached the cabin at the summit but found no one. He reasoned that if Annie and her companion had got that far, they would have remained there. Consequently they must be lost somewhere on the northern (Atlanta) slope. But he went on to Rocky Bar with his news of the disaster.

Although it seemed impossible that the two women, lost in the Arctic cold of the past three days, would have survived, a dozen men set out with Bill Tate to find them. By that time the rescue party from Atlanta was spread out across the northern slope and nearing the crest, dragging several sleds loaded with blankets and stimulants.

It was almost noon when a posseman exploring a side canyon

half a mile east of the mail route beheld a sight that rendered him speechless for a moment or two. Down below him in a hollow where the fresh snow had been beaten down to the old crust, Annie was crawling around on her hands and feet, muttering unintelligible sounds that might have come from a stricken wild animal. The warm, fur-trimmed coat she was wearing when she had left Atlanta was gone, so were her woolen underskirts. A thin dress was all she wore to protect herself against the icy blast that swept the mountain.

A cry to the other possemen alerted them and they were soon gathered about Annie, staring in disbelief as she continued to babble without any sign of recognition. They roped her down on a sled after dosing her with whisky and bundling her up in blankets. While several men started for Atlanta with her at once, others searched in vain for Dutch Em.

It was no sooner suggested that a messenger be dispatched for Dr. Newkirk in Mountain Home than it was realized that he could not get there in time to save Annie's life. To give her a chance of surviving, her feet would have to be amputated.

The miners who gathered about her as she regained consciousness the day after she was brought in were not notable for their gentleness, but they listened anxiously as she began to speak.

Her first question was about Dutch Em. They had to tell her they were still searching for the German woman.

"She had no fight in her," said Annie. "She was so cold I gave her my coat and underskirts. I remember we saw a big black rock that for a minute we thought was the cabin the mail carriers use. We got in close, trying to get out of the wind. Em lay down in the snow and refused to move. If I had gone on, I might have made it. But I couldn't leave her.

"I don't know how long I stayed there. When I saw that she was dead, I went on. But I'd waited too long."

The listeners turned away with a catch in their throats, knowing that if Annie's life hung in the balance, it was because she had sacrificed herself for her friend. Courage and loyalty were matters they could appreciate. Annie's moral lapses were forgotten.

Dutch Em's lifeless body was found the following day and

brought in and buried in Atlanta's growing cemetery. But a matter of far greater urgency possessed Tug Wilson and the five men who sat at a table in Henry Longheme's saloon that afternoon. They knew that the operation that might save Annie's life could not be postponed any longer. They looked around the table for a volunteer. Tug Wilson must have been a stouthearted man. He said quietly:

"I'll do it. You fellows give her a couple shots of whisky and hold her down on the table. It shouldn't take too long."

With a hunting knife and a meat saw he amputated Annie's feet above the ankles. Instances of so-called "buckshot surgery" are common enough. None was ever more urgent or more successful. In a few weeks Annie was crawling about and could hop into a chair with the agility of a cat. In time the fund began by her friend Henry Longheme, the Italian saloonkeeper, provided her with a set of artificial limbs, which she mastered in due course. With his assistance she opened a combination rooming house and restaurant.

Annie and Longheme never married, but they lived together for twenty-two years. In that time she managed to save between eleven and twelve thousand dollars. When he left Idaho in 1924 on a visit to his relatives in Italy, she gave him her savings to deposit in her name in a San Francisco bank. No record of the deposit having been made was ever found. He wrote her once from New York, but she never heard from him again. Though it appears rather obvious that he had made off with her savings, she refused to believe it and insisted until her death that he had either been murdered or accidentally killed without leaving a clue to his identity.

She was sixty-four at the time. When she was no longer able to take care of herself, friends in Mountain Home made a home for her and she died there in 1935. The Idaho she had known for so long was gone, but the old-timers came down out of the hills to pay their last respects to Pegleg Annie Morrow. The newcomers, who had never heard of her, wondered why.

—◃{ X X I I I }▹—

Diamond Lil—the Original

BACK IN THE 1920's when Mae West, the well-known actress, starred in a play of her own authoring entitled *Diamond Lil,* and in which she appeared on the screen with Cary Grant playing opposite her as a young Salvation Army captain, it was widely believed that the play and motion picture were based on the real life of the fabulous sporting world woman of that name. But the stage Diamond Lil bore no relation to the real Diamond Lil. Actually when honky-tonk singer and yodeler Evelyn Hildegard had a small diamond set in one of her front teeth, she became known not as Diamond Lil but as Diamond-tooth Lil. It was her trademark. When she died, it was found that she had willed the stone to an orphanage.

She was a hearty, robust and beautiful brunette, with raven black hair. Despite the hectic life she led, she retained her good looks until she was well over forty-five. As a young woman of twenty, already twice married and divorced, she first attracted nation-wide attention as a song-plugger at the St. Louis Exposition in 1904, belting out and making popular the ditty, "Meet Me in St. Louis—Louie." She had a big, untrained voice, and was a natural yodeler, a gift from her childhood. In the days before microphones, volume was as important as tone in a singer. Coupled with the fact that she was a self-taught piano player, she never had any difficulty finding employment. In the course of an interview in her old age she recalled the amount of money she had been paid as an entertainer. "The most I was ever paid was in Goldfield, Nevada, in Tex Rickard's Northern Saloon. I was pulling down two hundred and seventy-five a week—you better make that three hundred. It'll sound better."

Undoubtedly it was the same sort of arithmetic she used in recalling that she had been married and divorced thirteen times. She well may have lived with thirteen different men in her lifetime without bothering about such details as a marriage license, for she was always a freewheeler, making the rules as she went along. Her story of her childhood cannot be questioned.

"I was born in Vienna in 1882," she told a reporter for a Boise, Idaho, newspaper. "My mother was a Bohemian, my father an Austrian. He was a puddler in an iron foundry. We were very poor—sometimes not enough to eat. I had two brothers who were older than me. My name was Katie Prado."

When asked why the family had come to America, she said:

"My uncle Franz, my father's brother, was here. He was working in the steel mill at Youngstown, Ohio. He sent my father the money to come and promised there would be a job for him in the mill."

She didn't remember much about Vienna; she was too young. But she recalled the long steerage passage across the Atlantic, the stench, the poor food.

"Mama was sick all the time. But we finally got to Youngstown and Papa went to work in the mill. There were a lot of Hungarians and Bohemians in Youngstown. They could speak some English; we didn't know a word. We had to go to school. The kids made fun of us and called us bohunks. After school and on Saturdays the three of us had to go on the railroad tracks and pick up coal that had fallen off the cars. When no one was watching, my brothers used to get up on the cars and throw off some big lumps. But we had enough to eat—and beer; we had to have beer with supper."

By the time Katie was twelve, she was big and strong and able to speak English, and Americanized enough to be ashamed of her shabby clothes and her poverty. In her words:

"I looked older than I was and could pass myself off for fifteen with the boys I met at the dances in the foreign-speaking section of town. There was a lot of drinking and fighting, especially between the Hungarians and the Austrians. One night a Hungarian was stabbed and seriously wounded. The story got into the papers and caused a lot of talk. My folks didn't know I was sneaking off to dances. The fight in Potock's saloon got me into trouble at home. Papa found out that I had been present. He gave me a beating with a strap that raised blisters on my behind.

"It didn't stop me from trying to have a good time. Many kids in the neighborhood picked up coal along the tracks. I didn't stop there; I began picking up anything I could carry off that the junkman would buy. Of course it was stealing. I got caught and was put in jail. I was locked up for a week. My folks didn't do anything, didn't come to see me. They were poor, ignorant and didn't know what to do. There were no juvenile courts in those days. After I had been locked up for a week, I was turned loose. I went back to stealing and saved up enough money to buy a dress and a decent pair of shoes. They must have been cheap and god-awful. I thought they were wonderful. I didn't know any better. They were the first halfway decent things I ever owned. I've worn some expensive clothes since then, but they never meant to me what the first pink dress did. I guess Mama knew how I got the money to buy them. She just shook her head and said nothing. I guess she was getting ready to wash her hands of me. As for me, I knew I wanted something better out of life than what I was getting.

"My mother was taking in washing to make ends meet. Among her customers were the Eichelbaums. They had four boys. They were Russian immigrants. Later, after the boys—Sam, Albert, Harry and Jack—grew up and changed their name to Warner, they became famous as Warner Brothers, the theater and motion-picture magnates."

Katie Prado was fourteen when she met a flashy, well-dressed young man named Percy Hildegard, who was in the process of squandering the small inheritance his father had left him. He was nineteen. Full-bosomed Katie, with her pretty face and milk-white skin, must have appealed strongly to him, even though she was an ignorant bohunk from the wrong side of the tracks.

With his money and the airs he gave himself, he bowled her over. Naturally he seduced her. It was an easy conquest, for he spelled escape to her from a life that was hateful. It became a reality several weeks later when he asked her to marry him. To get a license, she had to lie about her age, giving it as sixteen. A few hours later they were on a train bound for Chicago.

"At first I was the happiest girl in the world," Lil recalled. "Percy gave me money to buy clothes. I got myself some nice things so he didn't have to be ashamed of me. We took in some shows. I'd never been in a theater. Before I knew what was happening, I was stage-struck. I wanted to be up there singing and dancing. But it was too good to last long; Percy's aunt tracked us down and took us into court and proved I wasn't of legal age when we got married. To save him trouble, I agreed to a divorce. There I was, a kid alone in a strange city, but I swore I wasn't going back to Youngstown. A few days later I got a job singing in the chorus at the Apollo Theater on Clark Street. It was rough, tough, but I loved it."

The Apollo was more a saloon and dance hall than a theater. It catered to streetwalkers, pimps and small-time gamblers and strong-arm men. Although the majority of the nightly crowds that patronized the place were often in and out of jail, they were (in the vernacular) "suckers" for a sentimental song, especially about Ireland. Whether Lil discovered that fact for herself or had it pointed out to her by the management, she took credit for it and nightly pulled a tear or two out of some of the most hardened women on the Chicago streets with her ballads about "mother" and the Emerald Isle.

Among the sporting crowd that patronized the Apollo was a young boxer, a welterweight by the name of Ma Hoy, who had won some renown and had changed his professional name to Kid McCoy. He was soon to be recognized as the welterweight champion of the world. He fell in love with Lil and they were married. When he left Chicago for a bout in San Francisco, she accompanied him.

The city that sits beside the Golden Gate made a lasting impression on Lil, especially the roaring, boisterous Barbary Coast. Between 1898 and 1906, the year of the great fire, she returned to it many times. After eighteen months of following her husband around the country, living with him in his training camps, she wearied of that routine. He had the limelight to himself and she was ignored. They were divorced in 1902—in Los Angeles, she claimed—and she returned to San Francisco and resumed her career as a singer and dancer on the Barbary Coast, appearing at Ned Foster's Bella Union at Washington and Kearney streets.

Although in her last years she talked freely about the ups and downs she had known, she never had much to say about the period between 1902 and 1904 that she spent in San Francisco, perhaps because her tales of her numerous marriages and divorces, some of which must have occurred in those years, would not stand inspection. There is no doubt, however, that she left California in the spring of 1904 for St. Louis and the Louisiana Purchase Exposition, still calling herself professionally Evelyn Hildegard, to which she had no legal right.

She was only twenty, but she already had put a considerable amount of living behind her. She was promiscuous; but seemingly, variety did not make her romantic experiences less enjoyable. Perhaps it was the freedom of choice she exercised that enabled her to keep any man from getting his fingers on the snug nest egg she was stashing away.

She has been called the Toast of the Barbary Coast and the Belle of New York. She was neither, but as the featured singer in the Anheuser-Busch Pavilion, she was the Voice of the St. Louis Fair. It was a time when every middle-income family in the United States had a piano in the parlor and sheet music sold into the millions. Her photograph on the title page became familiar from coast to coast. It is the best picture of Diamond Lil we have.

In St. Louis she became intimately acquainted with flamboyant Diamondfield Jack Davis, a get-rich-quick operator and mining stock swindler who had spent some time in jail. He was "in the chips," as Lil put it, when she met him. In addition to his diamond rings and studs he carried about with him a pocketful of uncut stones. Once when asked where he got his diamonds, he said he had "a field of them near Florence, Colorado." Naturally he was dubbed Diamondfield Jack.[1]

Perhaps influenced by his sparkling display, Lil took a step she had been considering for some time and had a small diamond set in one of her front teeth. He may have given her the stone. Neither then nor thereafter for the rest of her life was she conscious of the vulgarity of such garish adornment.

"That diamond made me rich," she often said. "I had more engagements offered me than I could fill. Wherever money was rolling in, men wanted to see Diamond-tooth Lil."

She was back in San Francisco, singing at the Saratoga, when the great fire destroyed the city in 1906. It had just become possible to go by overnight Pullman from San Francisco to booming Goldfield, the bonanza mining camp in the southern Nevada desert. Thirty-five miles to the north, Tonopah, where the original strike had been made, was producing millions. Rhyolite, Bull Frog, and half a dozen other camps were all in production. For the mining West, all roads led across the sagebrush wastes of the lower Nevada desert. The Mizpah and the Mohawk mines had just produced a record $5,000,000 in one hundred and six days. The owners complained that their miners highgraded a hundred thousand more by walking off the property with rich ore concealed in their clothes. Millionaires from the East, men like Barney Baruch, Charlie Schwab, John Reynolds of the Pullman Company, Ex-Governor Lowden of Illinois, and such Nevada nabobs as George Nixon and George Wingfield, were gathering in Goldfield, arriving in their private cars or risking the desert roads in their shiny Packards, Stanley Steamers and sleek Stevens Duryeas. Goldfield was the place to be. Julius Goldsmith, the leader of the five-piece orchestra in the posh Palm Grill, where formal dress was a requisite and oysters and quail under glass were a commonplace, it was said, never received less than a hundred dollars in tips each night. That was heady news for Lil. She couldn't get to Goldfield fast enough.

"Tex Rickard remembered me from the time when I was the Kid's (McCoy's) wife. Of course he knew I'd been a big hit at the Exposition." Lil smiled at the recollection. "He was promoting his first fight. The purse was thirty thousand dollars, the biggest ever offered up to that time. Tex had put up a third of it himself. He had an eye for business; he knew he would get it back and more, too. He told me to run over my music and be ready to go to work that evening."

The purse in minted double eagles was placed on display in a window of George Wingfield's bank, with two armed Wells Fargo messengers to guard it. The first Joe Gans–Battling Nelson fight proved to be a promoter's dream. It put the town on the map as nothing else could have done. It brought thousands of people to Goldfield. Special trains rolled in, running so close to one another that they appeared to be one train. The town had no accommodations for the visitors. The fight mob lined up for blocks on Crook Avenue and Main Street, waiting for a turn to get into a restaurant and wolf down a bite to eat. In the twenty-four hours before the fight, the Northern Saloon sold twenty barrels of whisky. The Palace, Mohawk and Hermitage did nearly as well.

The first Joe Gans–Battling Nelson fight was the kind of contest fight fans dream about but never expect to witness. For forty-one rounds the two men fought, with Gans, the faster and better boxer, cutting and slashing. But the sturdy Nelson refused to go down. In the forty-second round Nelson delivered a low blow and Gans was declared the winner, retaining his title of light-weight champion of the world.[2]

Arrangements had been made to film the fight, but the company entrusted with that operation ran out of film during the thirty-eighth round, and the last four rounds were not recorded. Rickard's part in arranging the battle changed the course of his life and started him on the way to becoming the country's premier boxing promoter.

The mining district of southern Nevada, with its three standard gauge railroads where before there had been none, a depot at Rhyolite costing $60,000, and three- and four-story bank buildings on such thoroughfares as Crook and Golden avenues, appeared permanent enough to attract a wide assortment of purveyors of vice and crime. With a population 85 per cent male, that meant whores. In Goldfield alone, down in Pickhandle Gulch (the name undoubtedly having some phallic significance in the mind of the man who bestowed it), upward of five hundred prostitutes plied their trade. There were numerous parlor houses uptown, but they were so second-rate that Lil seriously considered opening one of her own that would compare favorably with the best in San Francisco.

To her discerning eye Rickard and his pals, Nat Goodwin, the famous actor, and Riley Grannan, the "honest gambler," had skimmed the cream off Goldfield and were casting about for a new source of revenue. It happened in 1908 when they decamped with their entourage for Rawhide, a barren valley a hundred and ten miles to the north. Lil wasn't there to see them leave. She had left a few months earlier for New York City. Whether she left alone or with a paying male companion is debatable. In any event she was, in her words, "working a few weeks later in a cabaret on Broadway for Tom Sharkey, the prizefighter."

Lil is slightly mistaken in saying she was working on Broadway. Tom Sharkey's establishment was an uproarious saloon, offering dancing and some entertainment, on Fourteenth Street. It was the scene of incessant brawls, knifings and occasional shootings. In response to demands that the joint be closed, the police were often in attendance. But Sharkey had the protection of Tammany Hall and continued to operate until night life moved uptown and Fourteenth Street became a street of cheap movies, penny arcades and hot dog stands.

Instead of moving uptown, Lil went in the other direction and appeared at Sam Mintz's Bowery Theater, billed as others before her had been, The Queen of the Bowery. It appears to have been her last connection with the theatrical world of New York. The East was not for her, and she knew it. She went to Denver and then on to Reno, Nevada, where she was living quietly when news of a big strike at Silver City, Idaho, became a front-page story. She didn't need money, but she couldn't resist the urge to join the stampede.

Silver City, in southern Idaho, was inaccessible by rail. It was a hundred and seventy-five miles north of Winnemucca by an unimproved road that looped over the sagebrush plains by way of old Fort McDermitt and the Jordan Valley. It could also be reached by going to Ogden and doubling back across Idaho on the Oregon Short Line to within forty miles of Silver City. Lil chose the latter route, and with her she took four girls from Reno's Red Light [3] district. Whether or not the mines produced, she knew the girls would.

The Silver City excitement lasted long enough to make her first venture as a madam profitable. But those were years when as one camp began to fade another took its place in the headlines, and the game of boom and bust continued. Murray, Clearwater, Salmon River, Idaho City, the Coeur d'Alenes—Lil didn't miss any of them. She was past forty-five when she called it a day and settled down in Boise, where, known simply as Miss Lil, she built and ran a select "rooming house" for years. When the State Legislature was in session, she imported a girl or two for the convenience of the members. There was no secret about the nature of her "house," but she conducted it so discreetly that the police never bothered her.

It may have been some latent desire or just plain boredom that led her to break away from her rooming house in the middle 1940's. The country was prosperous again and World War II was drawing to a close. Roads had been improved. America was on the move in its Fords and Chevys. It was getting so that every improved highway had its motor courts and tourist cabins. The first generation of such roadside camps, usually a row of five or six tiny peak-roofed hutches, uncomfortable and an offense to the eye, were disappearing and being replaced by cottages that were equipped with heat and showers. Where possible, they were being set far enough back from the road to escape the traffic noise, and preferably among trees or on the bank of a running stream.

Lil was astute enough to realize that what was occurring was the beginning of an industry with a fantastic future. She started looking for a spot. She found one that satisfied her on the outskirts of Boise. It must have been the right place, for ten years later she was still there, aging but hale and happy. Business tapered off with the coming of winter, but when the days turned warm again and the skies were blue, the No Vacancy sign usually had to be put up by six o'clock. She spent most of her time seated in a rocking chair beneath the giant cottonwood that shaded the office.

"I like to gas (her word for it) with the folks who stay with me," she told an interviewer. "They don't know who I am. To them I'm just an old woman now with store-bought teeth and a nice little business. But once in a blue moon some old-timer out of the past comes along and we sit up all night, having a drink or two and cutting up old touches."

"Lil, if you had it all to live over again, what would you change?"

"Nothing," was the spirited answer. "I know I've outlived my time—so many of the people I knew have passed away. The Coast is no more. I understand the old Mizpah Hotel and a filling station are about all that's left of Goldfield. Silver City is a ghost town. But I have my memories to keep me going, and they're all happy ones."

When her health began to fail, she left Boise and went to California, where she died in 1957.

Notes

CHAPTER I

1. Of the dozen or more performers who appeared on its stage and went on to stardom, the Bella Union could claim Ned Harrigan as its own, for his career began there. He was a rank amateur, recently come down from Vallejo, where he had been employed in a shipyard. He was popular at once, but it was not until he met Tony Hart and they formed the team of Harrigan and Hart that he rose to nationwide fame.

CHAPTER II

1. The cowyard was a U-shaped building several stories high. Around its central opening were as many as two hundred cribs, from the doors of which the inmates could do their hustling.

CHAPTER III

1. This "little girl" was Sarah Althea Hill of Cape Giradeu, Missouri, who arrived in San Francisco in 1870 and became entangled with William Sharon.

CHAPTER IV

1. For a lively and informative account of Ben Holladay's disastrous endeavors to make himself the railroad overlord of the Pacific Northwest, see Ellis Lucia's *The Saga of Ben Holladay*.

2. Hoey had married Teresa, but she had soon left him. To escape from his threats to kill her, she had come to San Francisco. He had followed her, and one night at Bell's Bush Street home Hoey had brushed past the butler and fired several shots at the group gathered in the living room. Teresa drew a pistol and killed him. Hoey's death was not reported to the police. Mammy took charge and had him buried under an alias.

3. This was several years after the Big Four, the so-called railroad kings, Huntington, Crocker, Hopkins and Stanford, built their pseudo-palaces on Nob Hill.

4. Mammy's preposterous explanation of how her fringed blanket was found on the stairwell was that she had loaned the blanket to Bell.

CHAPTER V

1. Originally the word courtesan was ascribed to the female members of a royal court, but by the end of the eighteenth century it had taken on a quite different meaning and was used to designate the mistresses of a king and his courtiers. In Europe, wantonness in such lofty circles was regarded as being far removed from the lower forms of commercialized harlotry. That spirit was echoed in San Francisco in the gold rush days, when it turned out to welcome the Countess Landsfeld, née Lola Montez.

2. Many of the fantastic tales about Lola and her alleged escapades have been preserved in the files of various California historical societies. In recent years several writers of note have, inexcusably, accepted them as valid source material.

3. No San Francisco landmark is more famous than Lotta's Fountain in the small triangle at the intersection of Market, Geary and Kearney streets. Originally a watering place for animals, it was replaced by an ornate bronze fountain for human beings that Lotta gave to the city in 1875. There, on Christmas Eve, 1910, Luisa Tetrazzini, the world-famous Italian soprano, sang Christmas carols to an estimated assemblage of thirty thousand.

CHAPTER VI

1. Lola had been out of the cottage only a day or two when souvenir hunters and looters began carrying off what she had been unable to sell. The garden was uprooted and her rosebushes dug up. Articles that had little value aside from once having belonged to Lola Montez were spread across the valley. As late as 1910, in the parlor of a Marysville dentist, one of her gold leaf chairs occupied a place of honor as an ornament, which no one was permitted to sit on.

2. In later years Miriam Follin distinguished herself by becoming Mrs. Frank Leslie, wife of the publisher of *Leslie's Weekly.*

CHAPTER VII

1. Although it bears his name, Pancake Comstock was not the discoverer of the Comstock Lode, nor is he known to have profited from his fancied connection with it beyond a paltry three to four thousand dollars.

2. This was the so-called "Mormon War" of 1857, when President Buchanan sent 1,500 troops under Colonel Albert Sidney Johnston to Utah to force compliance with Federal laws. The troops got no further than Black's Forks (Fort Bridger). In the spring of 1858 a peace was negotiated and the matter ended.

3. A second child, a girl, was born to Eilley aboard ship on their tour of Europe, but it died in infancy. A third child, adopted, died in Reno at an early age.

CHAPTER VIII

1. The incident of a mourner on horseback plunging through the rotten planking to a mine tunnel beneath occurred in the course of the Sandy Bowers funeral, not during the Julia Bulette procession.

2. See Swift Paine's *Eilley Orrum, Queen of the Comstock,* page 161.

CHAPTER IX

1. Describing himself as a "country banker," it was in Columbia that Darius Ogden Mills, a forty-niner from North Salem, Westchester County, New York, began putting together his millions. He was shrewd, tightfisted and lucky. His building of the Carson and Colorado Railroad, which took off from nowhere and got nowhere until Tonopah and Goldfield startled the world with their treasure and made a railroad indispensable, transformed his embarrassing C. and C. "orphan" into a golden link with the Southern Pacific.

2. Austin was not a Johnny-come-lately. It could claim with honor that it was from Austin that the fabled sack of flour that was sold at auction in camp after camp began its journey around Nevada in Civil War days, raising a reputed $300,000 for the Sanitary Fund, the forerunner of the Red Cross.

CHAPTER X

1. Thomas J. Smith was not unknown when he was named marshal of Abilene. As a construction worker during the building of the Union Pacific Railroad, he had taken part in the Bear River riots and had won the sobriquet of Bear River Tom Smith. He is believed to have been a member of the New York police department, but no documentation has ever been discovered to prove it.

2. James Butler Hickok married Alice Thatcher Lake in Cheyenne on March 5, 1876. After a brief honeymoon in Cincinnati, he left her there and returned to Cheyenne. She never saw him again, as he went on to Deadwood, where he was murdered.

3. In his *Historic Sketches of the Cattle Trade,* published in 1874, Joseph McCoy states that "237,000 head of cattle were received at Kansas City alone in 1871." Not all of them had been shipped from Abilene. But if 60 per cent were and are added to the hundred thousand or more head that were trailed north to stock the ranges of Wyoming and Montana, the number reaches the almost incredible total of 250,000.

CHAPTER XI

1. It was this fracas that caused Bat to hobble around with the aid of a cane. When he returned to Dodge City, his friends presented him with a gold-headed cane, the use of which was for practical purposes, not due to his alleged foppery.

2. This incident followed by five days the slaying of Sheriff Cap Whitney by Billy Thompson, Ben's brother. See this writer's *Wild, Woolly and Wicked,* Chapter 13.

3. Joseph McCoy, who had moved down from Abilene, superintended the building of the Wichita stockyards, the largest in Kansas, with seven chutes and equipped to load 2,500 Longhorns daily.

4. Sheriff John Meagher was the younger brother of Mike Meagher, four times marshal of Wichita and one-time marshal of Caldwell.

5. Skiddy Street was named for Francis Skiddy, the head of the Katy's Land Grant Railway and Trust Company, a suave Eastern financier and socialite, who shuddered every time the street was mentioned. It is now Chestnut Street.

CHAPTER XII

1. Quotation from the *Trail Drivers of Texas,* edited by J. Marvin Hunter.

2. When living in Hays City, before coming to Dodge, Kelley owned a pack of hounds, some of them the gift of Lieutenant Colonel George Armstrong Custer, the post commander at Fort Hays, which explains the origin of the sobriquet Hound Dog, which in Dodge was shortened to Dog.

3. Contrary to the claims he makes for himself in his alleged autobiography, *Wyatt Earp, Frontier Marshal,* Earp was twice assistant town marshal, never marshal.

CHAPTER XIII

1. It was not in Springfield, Missouri, as has been stated, that Mattie Silks first attracted attention as a young madam. During the last years of the War Between the States, thousands of Union soldiers were gathered at Springfield, Illinois, and it was infested with prostitutes and petty criminals.

2. The underworld was of two opinions about it, the skeptics suggesting that Mattie had finally wearied of Cort and had deliberately fed him enough laudanum (opium) to kill him.

3. The premises at 1942 Market Street were purchased by the Japanese colony and maintained as a Buddhist temple until it became too small for the colony's needs and a new temple was built at Twentieth and Lawrence streets, following World War II.

CHAPTER XIV

1. The yellow omnibus, restored to its original form, became a familiar sight on Deadwood streets for years.

2. The cards Hickok was holding when he was shot were to become famous as the "dead man's hand." They were the ace of spades, the ace of clubs, the eight of spades, the eight of clubs and the jack of diamonds. "Aces and eights" are a part of the language of the poker table.

CHAPTER XVI

1. The name spelled Ogallala is a corruption on the Sioux tribal name Oglala.

2. This was long before juvenile courts to try youthful offenders were established, largely due to the pioneer work of Judge Ben Lindsey of Denver.

CHAPTER XVII

1. Paul I. Wellman in his *A Dynasty of Western Outlaws* errs in saying that "Blue Duck, a white man, masquerading under that fantastic alias, was killed in July, 1886, by 'an unknown party' . . . in all probability the jealous and murderous Sam Starr." Blue Duck was a Cherokee, and after Belle had succeeded in getting his life sentence for murder commuted, he returned to Indian Territory to die of tuberculosis in 1896.

2. Detailed accounts of the killing of Belle Starr will be found in *Last of the Great Outlaws* by Homer Croy, *Belle Starr and Her Pearl* by Edwin P. Hicks, and *Outlaws on Horseback* by Harry Sinclair Drago.

3. Croy's on-the-spot investigation of Edgar Watson took him from Oklahoma (Indian Territory) to Florida, where he uncovered Watson's bloody past and his violent demise.

4. Annually thousands of visitors come to Fort Smith to visit the Fort Smith Restoration of Judge Parker's day and the Old Commissary Museum. The Row is gone, long ago destroyed by fire, but one house still stands to remind the stranger of its lurid past.

CHAPTER XVIII

1. Marshall Sprague in *Money Mountain,* the standard work on Cripple Creek, relates an amusing incident concerning Mrs. Bert Carleton, wife of the banker and mining tycoon, and her Negro cook, John Gee. She was discarding some Paris frocks, when Gee asked if he could donate them to the Salvation Army. Mrs. Carleton praised him for his thoughtfulness and gave him the gowns. A few days later she was surprised to see Hazel Vernon and two of her "boarders" driving up Bennett Avenue wearing the dresses she had given her cook. She mentioned the matter to Bert and he discovered that Hazel and her girls had paid John $100 apiece for the dresses they were wearing.

2. It was typical of the eccentric Stratton that when a hastily formed "relief committee" met at Colorado Springs to do something about the plight of Cripple, he told his fellow members: "We've got to move and move fast! No time to get money pledges. Charge everything to me. We'll divide the bills afterwards."

CHAPTER XIX

1. America had largely forgotten Josie Mansfield, the famous courtesan, for whose favor Edward S. Stokes had shot and killed Jim Fisk, Jr., Jay Gould's partner, in the Grand Central Hotel in New York on January 6, 1872, when she arrived in Leadville in the spring of 1884. According to the Leadville *Herald,* she did not remain long.

2. The generally accepted story is that the riches of the Little Pittsburg lifted the Tabors from grinding poverty to unbelievable wealth. Augusta always denied it, claiming that by saving every dollar the store produced they had accumulated $35,000 by the day the great strike was made.

3. The Tabor Grand survives as a motion-picture theater, the last traces of its former elegance gone.

4. Quoted from Forbes Parkhill's *The Wildest of the West.*

CHAPTER XX

1. In 1874 she survived a siege of smallpox, which left her face pitted.
2. A quote from *Calamity Was the Name for Jane* by Glenn Clairmonte.
3. Hickok historian Joseph G. Rosa, in checking with the Cunard Steamship Company, was told—"No ship of the name of *Madagascar* was in our service at any time, nor has there been a Captain O'Neil among Cunard captains."
4. Quoted by Rosa in a letter from "White-Eye" Jack Anderson to Raymond W. Thorp.
5. The usually reliable Teddy Blue says that "I saw Calamity Jane for the last time in Gilt Edge, Montana, in 1907. We had some drinks together." Of course he is mistaken, Calamity having been dead for four years.

CHAPTER XXI

1. To be exact, Averell's ranch was located on the Sweetwater where the Rawlins-Lander stage line crossed the old Oregon Trail.
2. Ed Towse of the Cheyenne *Leader* is identified by Helena Huntington Smith as the creator of the Cattle Kate fiction.
3. At the time Ella was hanged, she was wearing beaded moccasins, probably the ones she had purchased that afternoon. Several days after the tragedy Mr. and Mrs. E. C. Jameson went to the scene to take photographs. They picked up the moccasins and carried them away to exhibit as grim souvenirs of the lynching.
4. "A brother of Averell from Tacoma, Washington, succeeded in working up a very strong feeling against the accused . . . it became so intense that no one in the Sweetwater country ventured from his premises without being well armed." (See Mokler, page 269.)
5. "Ella Watson's father, a poor man, came from his home near Lebanon, Kansas, for the 'trial.' He made his headquarters at Rock Springs, where he remained until after the case was disposed of by the grand jury." (See Mokler, page 270.)

CHAPTER XXIII

1. Diamondfield Jack Davis spent his last years as a gunman in the employ of the big cattle outfits in Nevada and Idaho. Although Diamond-tooth Lil often claimed to have been married to him, no mention was made of such a connection when he was killed in a taxicab accident in Reno in 1941.
2. In the rematch in 1908, Nelson won the title from an ailing Gans but held it for only two years.
3. The origin of the term "red light" for houses of prostitution has erroneously been attributed to the practice of railroad men leaving their red lanterns on the doorstep of such dives while they were busy within. The first authentic use of the red light by prostitutes to denote their calling can be traced back to the days in Chicago when such women "worked" the hundreds of parked wagons of the produce farmers who had arrived for the opening of the market the following morning. The rustics soon learned that any woman carrying a red lantern was a whore.

Bibliography

Abbott, E. C. (Teddy Blue) and Smith, Helena Huntington, *We Pointed Them North*, Farrar and Rinehart, New York, 1939.

Aikman, Duncan, editor, *The Taming of the Frontier*. By ten authors, Prospect Press, New York, 1925.

———, *Calamity Jane and the Lady Wildcats*, Holt, New York, 1933.

Annals of San Francisco, Soule, Frank; Gihon, Johnn H.; Nisbet, James. Western Press, New York, 1855.

Asbury, Herbert, *The Barbary Coast*, Knopf, New York, 1933.

Askew, Garrett L., *The Pageant of the Packets*, Appleton, New York, 1929.

Athearn, Robert G., *High Country Empire*, McGraw-Hill, New York, 1953.

Beebe, Lucius, and Clegg, Charles, *U.S. West, the Saga of Wells Fargo*, Dutton, New York, 1949.

Bennett, Estelline, *Old Deadwood Days*, Sears, New York, 1928.

Brandt, Fred, *Fascinating San Francisco*. Privately printed, San Francisco, 1924.

Clairmonte, Glenn, *Calamity Was the Name for Jane*, Sage Books, Denver, 1959.

Clay, John, *My Life on the Range*, University of Oklahoma Press, Norman, 1962.

Connelley, William Elsey, *Wild Bill and His Era*, Press of the Pioneers, New York, 1933.

Croy, Homer, *He Hanged Them High*, Duell, Sloan and Pearce, New York, 1952.

———, *Last of the Great Outlaws*, Duell, Sloan and Pearce, New York, 1961.

———, *Jesse James Was My Neighbor*, Duell, Sloan and Pearce, New York, 1949.

Dayton, Frederick E., *Steamboat Days*, Stokes, New York, 1947.

Dee, D. (Dora Duffran), *Lowdown on Calamity Jane*, Gate City Guide, Rapid City, South Dakota, 1932.

DeQuille, Dan, *The Big Bonanza*, Knopf, New York, 1947.

Drago, Harry Sinclair, *Wild, Woolly and Wicked*, Potter, New York, 1961.

——, *Outlaws on Horseback*, Dodd, Mead, New York, 1963.

——, *The Steamboaters*, Dodd, Mead, New York, 1967.

Drury, Wells, *An Editor on the Comstock Lode*, Farrar and Rinehart, New York, 1936.

Dunn, Allan, *Carefree San Francisco*, Elder, San Francisco, 1913.

Frink, Maurice, *Cow Country Cavalcade: Eighty Years of the Wyoming Stock Growers' Association*, Old West Publishing Company, Denver, 1954.

Gandy, Lewis Cass, *The Tabors, a Footnote of Western History*. Press of the Pioneers, New York, 1934.

Hafen, LeRoy and Ann, *Handcrafts for Zion*, Clark, Glendale, 1860.

Harman, Samuel W., *Hell on the Border*. Fort Smith Publishing Company, Fort Smith, Arkansas, 1899.

Harolds Club, *Pioneer Nevada*. Harolds Club Publisher, Reno, 1951.

Harrington, Fred Harvey, *Hanging Judge*. Caxton Publishers, Caldwell, 1951.

Hicks, Edwin P., *Belle Starr and Her Pearl*, Pioneer Press, Little Rock, Arkansas, 1963.

Holdredge, Helen, *The Woman in Black*. Putnam, New York, 1960.

——, *Mammy Pleasant*, Putnam, New York, 1953.

Horan, James D., *Desperate Women*. Putnam, New York, 1949.

Hunton, John, *John Hunton's Diary*, edited by L. G. "Pat" Flannery. Flannery publisher, Lingle, Wyoming, 1956-60.

Irwin, Will, *The City That Was*. Huebsch, New York, 1906.

Lee, Mabel Barbee, *Cripple Creek Days*. Doubleday, New York, 1958.

Lewis, Oscar, *Silver Kings*. Knopf, New York, 1947.

Lloyd, Benjamin Estelle, *Lights and Shadows in San Francisco*. Published by author, San Francisco, 1876.

Lloyd, Benjamin Estelle, *Lights and Shadows of Chinatown*. Published by author, San Francisco, 1896.

Lyman, George D., *The Saga of the Comstock Lode*. Scribner, New York, 1947.

Masterson, V. V., *The Katy Railroad and the Last Frontier*. Oklahoma University Press, Norman, 1952.

Mazzula, Fred and Jo, *Brass Checks and Red Lights*. Published by the authors, Denver, 1966.

McMullen, Jerry, *Paddle Wheel Days in California*, Stanford University Press, Palo Alto, 1944.

Miller, Max, *Holladay Street*, No imprint, Denver, 1960.

Mercer, Asa Shinn, *The Banditti of the Plains*. Privately printed, Cheyenne, 1894.

Mokler, Alfred James, *History of Natrona County, Wyoming*. Lakeside Press, Chicago, 1923.

Monaghan, Jay, *The Overland Trail*. Bobbs-Merrill, New York, 1947.

Mumey, Nolie, *Calamity Jane, 1852-1903, A History of Her Life and Adventure in the West*. Range Press, Denver, 1950.
——, *Poker Alice*. Artcraft, Denver, 1951.
O'Conner, Richard, *Wild Bill Hickok*. Doubleday, New York, 1959.
Paine, Swift, *Eilley Orrum, Queen of the Comstock*. Bobbs-Merrill, New York, 1929.
Parkhill, Forbes, *The Wildest of the West*. Holt, New York, 1951.
Quinn, John Philip, *Fools of Fortune, Gambling and Gamblers*. Donahue, Chicago, 1892.
Rascoe, Burton, *Belle Starr, "the Bandit Queen."* Random House, New York, 1941.
Rollinson, John K., *Wyoming Cattle Trails*. Caxton Printers, Caldwell, Idaho, 1948.
Rosa, Joseph G., *They Called Him Wild Bill*. Oklahoma University Press, Norman, 1964.
Smith, Helena Huntington, *The War on Powder River*. McGraw-Hill, New York, 1966.
Sollid, Roberta Beed, *Calamity Jane, a Study in Historical Criticism*. Western Press, Helena, Montana, 1958.
Sprague, Marshall, *Money Mountain*. Little, Brown, Boston, 1953.
Spring, Agnes Wright, *Seventy Years: A Panoramic History of the Wyoming Stock Growers' Association*. Privately printed, Cheyenne, 1942.
——, *Cheyenne and Black Hills Stage and Express Routes*. Clark, Glendale, 1949.
Stegner, Wallace, *Gathering of Zion*. McGraw-Hill, New York, 1964.
Streeter, Floyd Ben, *Prairie Trails and Cowtowns*. Chapman and Grimes, Boston, 1936.
Vestal, Stanley, *Dodge City: Queen of the Cowtowns*. Nevill, London, 1955.
Wells, Evelyn, *Champagne Days of San Francisco*. Appleton-Century. New York, 1939.
Williams, Jean, *The Lynching of Elizabeth Taylor*. Press of the Territorians, Sante Fe, 1967.
Willison, George Findlay, *Here They Dug For Gold*. Reynal, New York, 1946.
Wilson, C. C., *Chinatown Quest: the Life of Donaldina Cameron*. Press of the Pioneers, New York, 1931.

Newspaper files consulted: San Francisco *Call, Call-Bulletin, Alta California, Examiner, Sacramento Bee, Sacramento Union, Nevada State Journal, Territorial Enterprise,* Denver *Post, Rocky Mountain News,* Cheyenne *Leader, Wichita Eagle,* the *Omaha Daily Bee,* Laramie *Daily Boomerang,* and the Hastings, Nebraska, *Gazette-Journal*.
Magazine files: *Sunset, Overland Monthly, Harper's Weekly, Touring Topics*.

Index

Index

268 *Index*